THE WAGES
OF SIN

TRINITY OF SIN

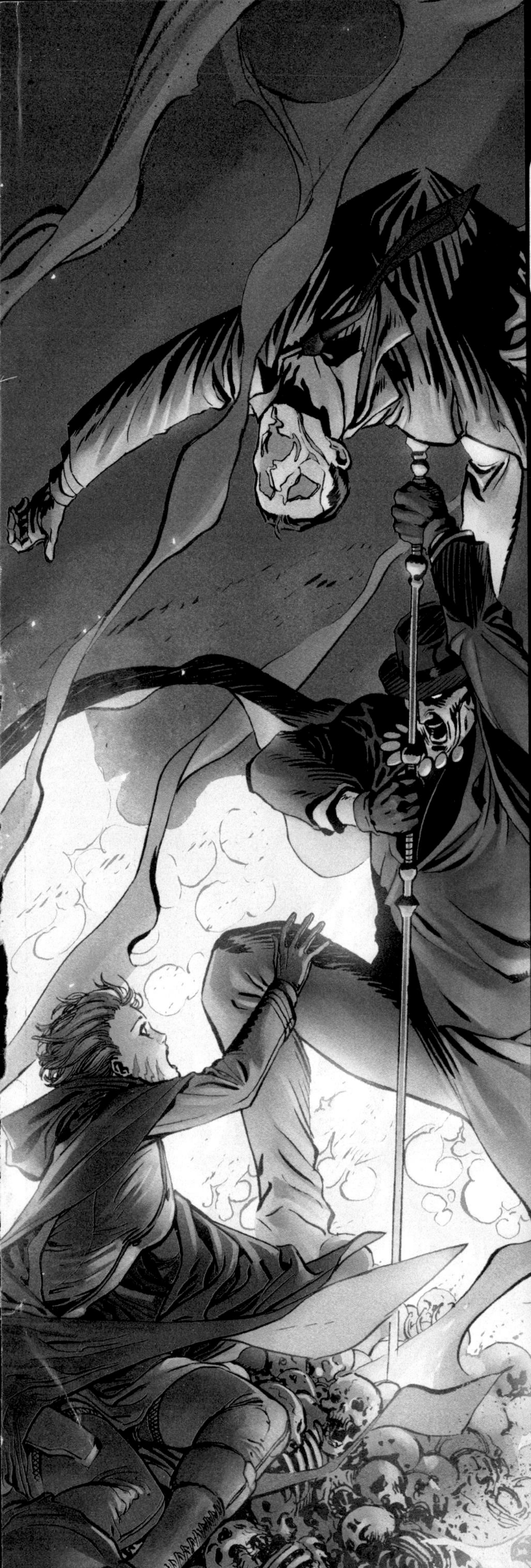

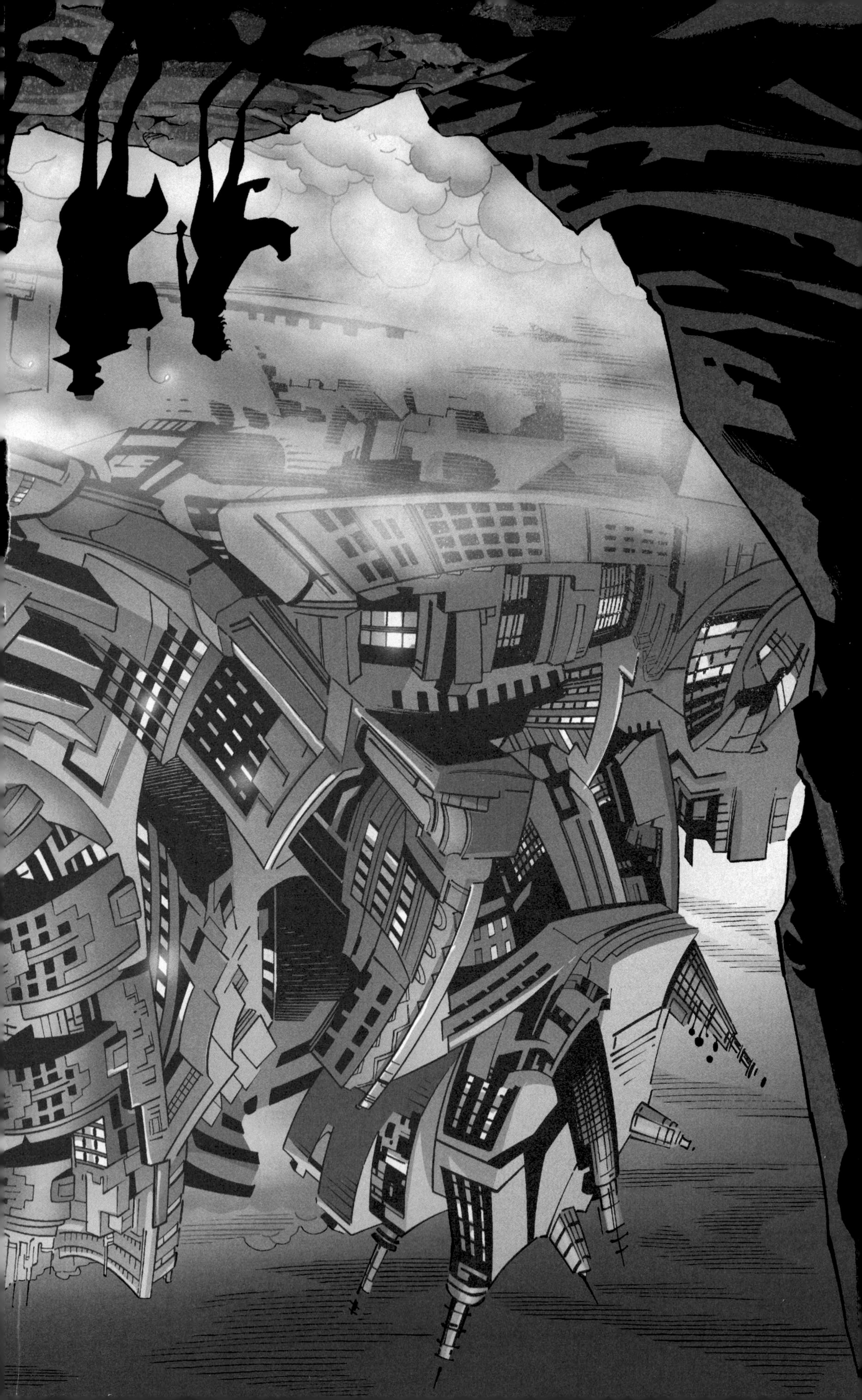

TRINITY OF SIN

THE WAGES OF SIN

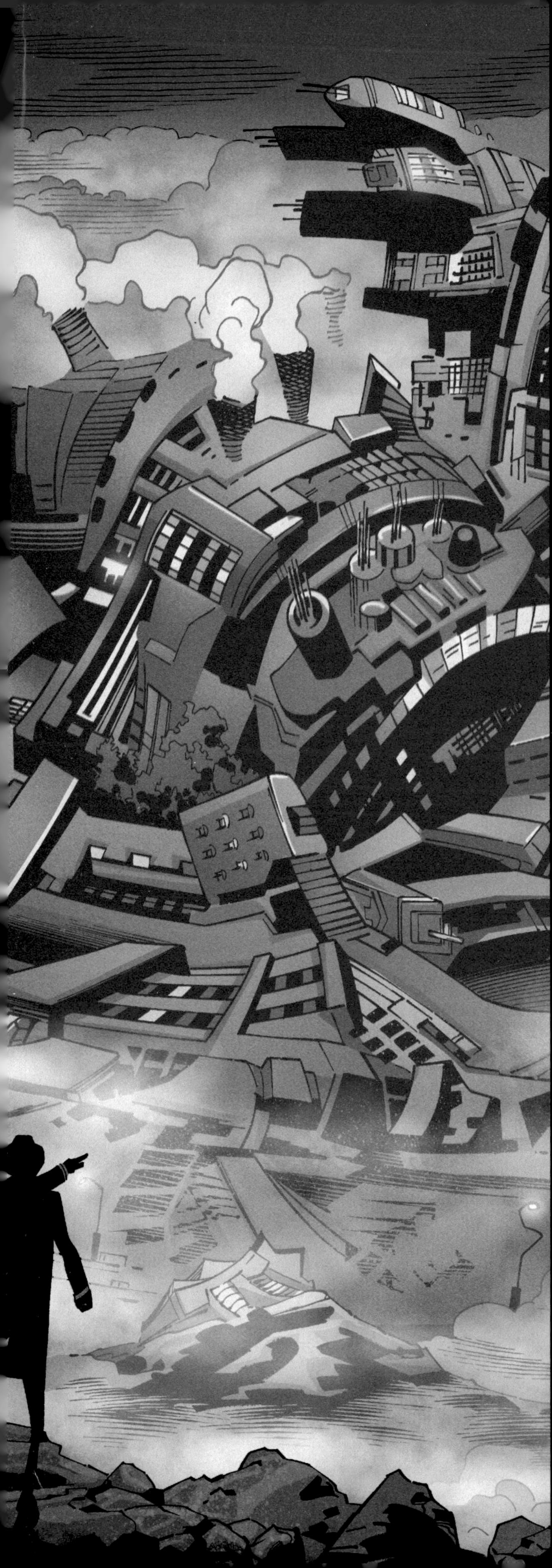

WRITTEN BY
J.M. DEMATTEIS

PENCILS BY
YVEL GUICHET

INKS BY
JASON GORDER

COLOR BY
GABE ELTAEB

LETTERS BY
CARLOS M. MANGUAL
TAYLOR ESPOSITO
TRAVIS LANHAM
DEZI SIENTY

SERIES & COLLECTION COVER ART BY
GUILLEM MARCH
& TOMEU MOREY

FRANK PITTARESE DARREN SHAN Editors - Original Series
HARVEY RICHARDS Associate Editor – Original Series
LIZ ERICKSON Editor
ROBBIN BROSTERMAN Design Director – Books
DAMIAN RYLAND Publication Design

BOB HARRAS Senior VP – Editor-in-Chief, DC Comics

DIANE NELSON President
DAN DIDIO and JIM LEE Co-Publishers
GEOFF JOHNS Chief Creative Officer
AMIT DESAI Senior VP – Marketing & Franchise Management
AMY GENKINS Senior VP – Business & Legal Affairs
NAIRI GARDINER Senior VP – Finance
JEFF BOISON VP – Publishing Planning
MARK CHIARELLO VP – Art Direction & Design
JOHN CUNNINGHAM VP – Marketing
TERRI CUNNINGHAM VP – Editorial Administration
LARRY GANEM VP – Talent Relations & Services
ALISON GILL Senior VP – Manufacturing & Operations
HANK KANALZ Senior VP – Vertigo & Integrated Publishing
JAY KOGAN VP – Business & Legal Affairs, Publishing
JACK MAHAN VP – Business Affairs, Talent
NICK NAPOLITANO VP – Manufacturing Administration
SUE POHJA VP – Book Sales
FRED RUIZ VP – Manufacturing Operations
COURTNEY SIMMONS Senior VP – Publicity
BOB WAYNE Senior VP – Sales

TRINITY OF SIN: THE WAGES OF SIN

Published by DC Comics. Compilation Copyright © 2015 DC Comics. All Rights Reserved.

Originally published in single magazine form as TRINITY OF SIN 1-6 © 2014, 2015 DC Comics. All Rights Reserved.
All characters, their distinctive likenesses and related elements featured in this publication are trademarks of DC Comics.
The stories, characters and incidents featured in this publication are entirely fictional. DC Comics does not read or accept
unsolicited ideas, stories or artwork.

DC Comics, 4000 Warner Blvd., Burbank, CA 91522
A Warner Bros. Entertainment Company.
Printed by RR Donnelley, Owensville, MO USA. 6/19/15. First Printing.
ISBN: 978-1-4012-5494-0

Library of Congress Cataloging-in-Publication Data

DeMatteis, J. M., author.
Trinity of sin. Vol. 1, The wages of sin / J.M. Dematteis, Yvel
Guichet, Jason Gorder, Gabe Eltaeb.
pages cm. — (The New 52!)
ISBN 978-1-4012-5494-0 (paperback)
1. Graphic novels. I. Guichet, Yvel, illustrator. II. Gorder, Jason,
illustrator. III. Eltaeb, Gabe, illustrator. IV. Title. V. Title: Wages of sin.
PN6728.T77D44 2015
741.5'973—dc23
                                        2015020226

SUSTAINABLE Certified Chain of Custody
FORESTRY   20% Certified Forest Content,
INITIATIVE 80% Certified Sourcing
www.sfiprogram.org
SFI-01042
APPLIES TO TEXT STOCK ONLY

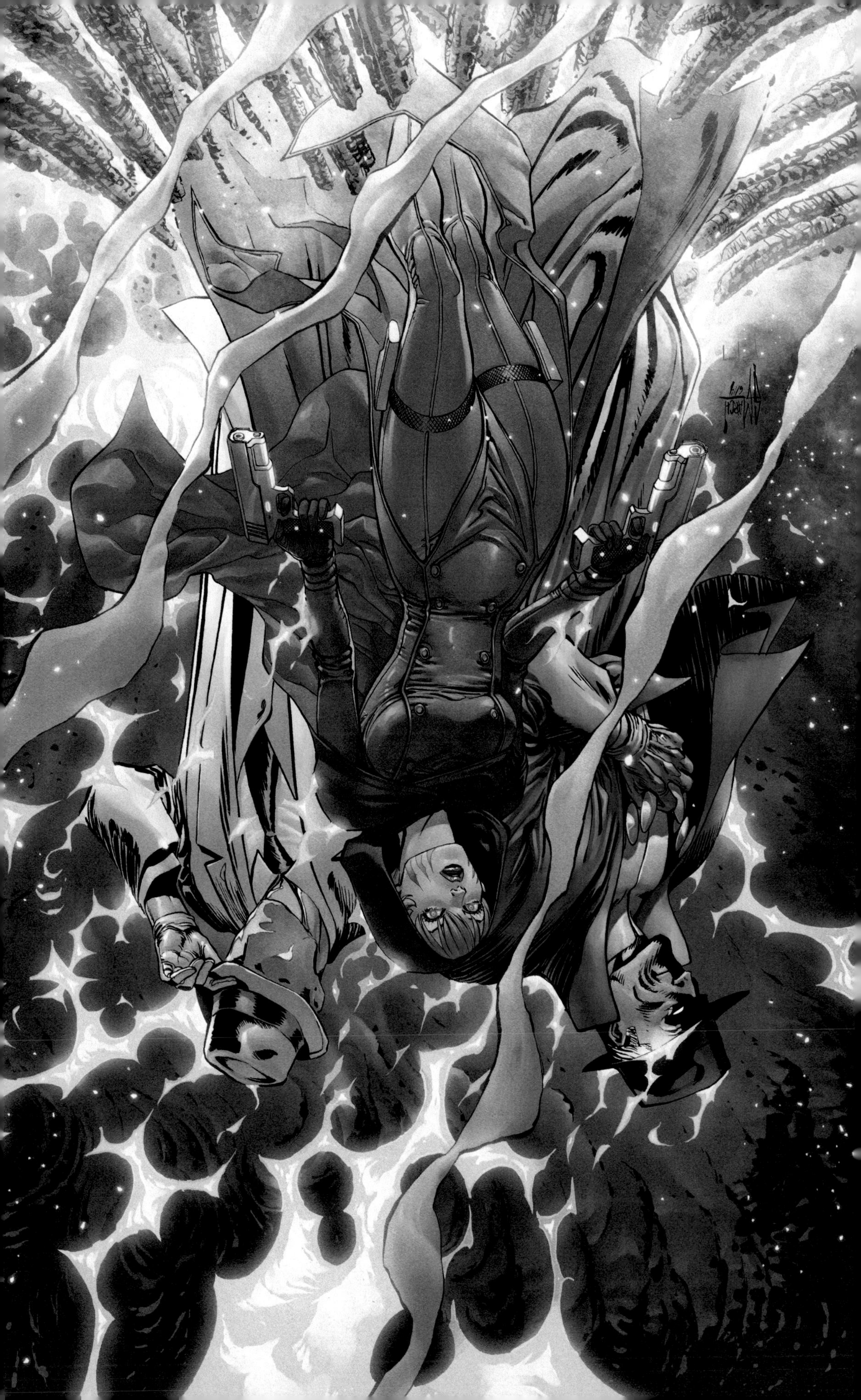

PART ONE: NIGHTFALL

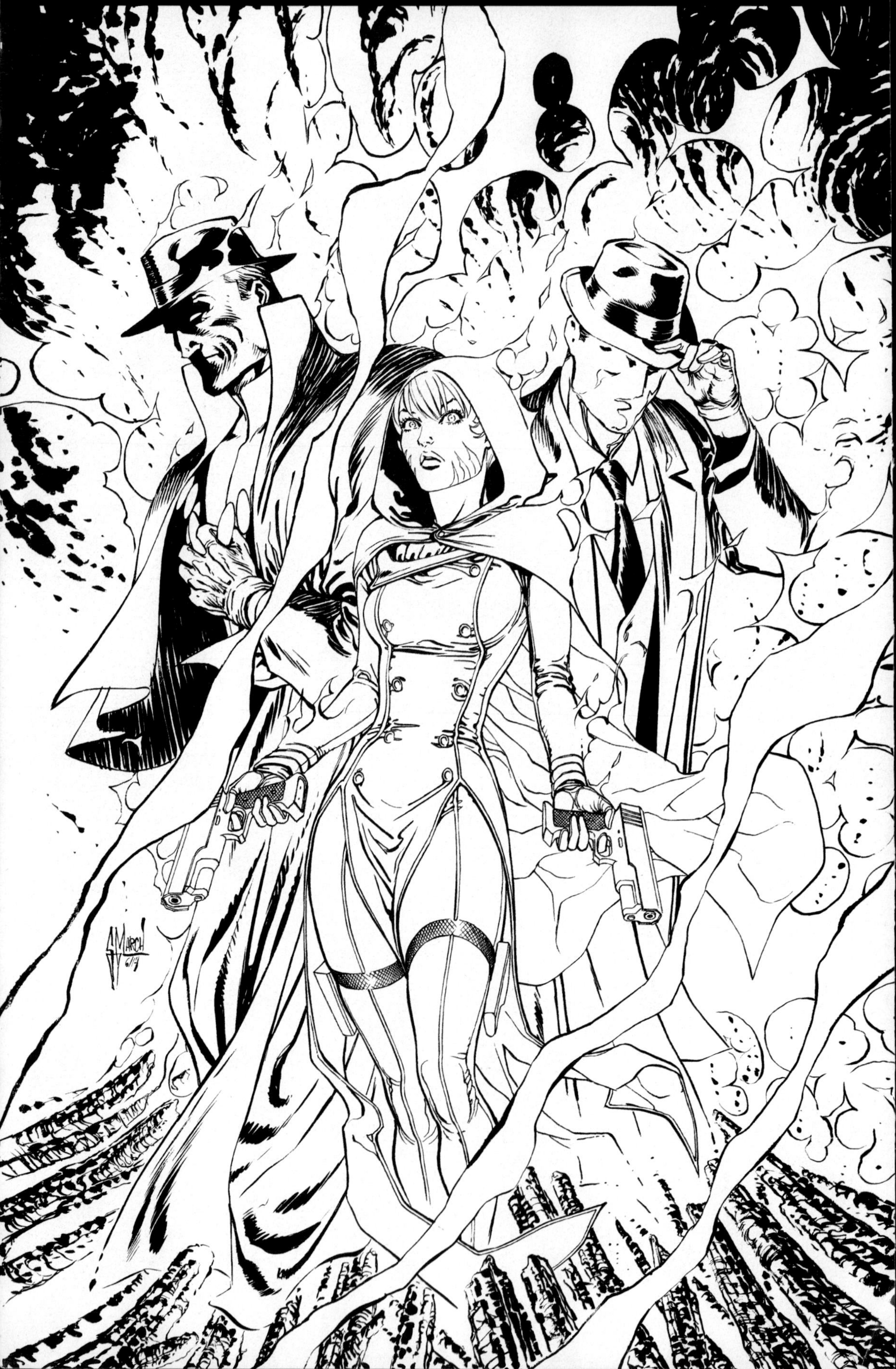

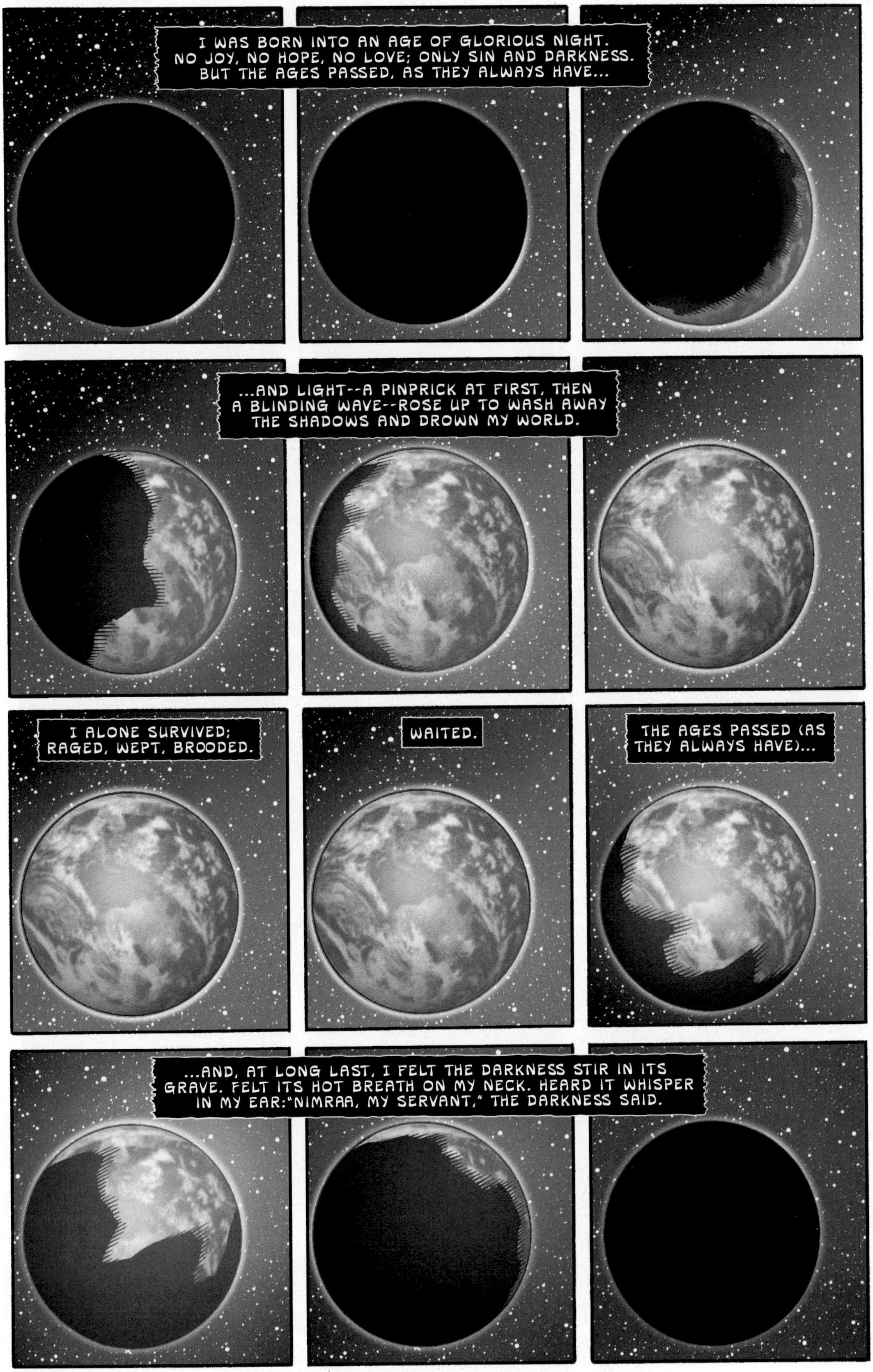
I WAS BORN INTO AN AGE OF GLORIOUS NIGHT. NO JOY, NO HOPE, NO LOVE; ONLY SIN AND DARKNESS. BUT THE AGES PASSED, AS THEY ALWAYS HAVE...
...AND LIGHT--A PINPRICK AT FIRST, THEN A BLINDING WAVE--ROSE UP TO WASH AWAY THE SHADOWS AND DROWN MY WORLD.
I ALONE SURVIVED; RAGED, WEPT, BROODED.
WAITED.
THE AGES PASSED (AS THEY ALWAYS HAVE)...
...AND, AT LONG LAST, I FELT THE DARKNESS STIR IN ITS GRAVE. FELT ITS HOT BREATH ON MY NECK. HEARD IT WHISPER IN MY EAR: "NIMRAA, MY SERVANT," THE DARKNESS SAID.

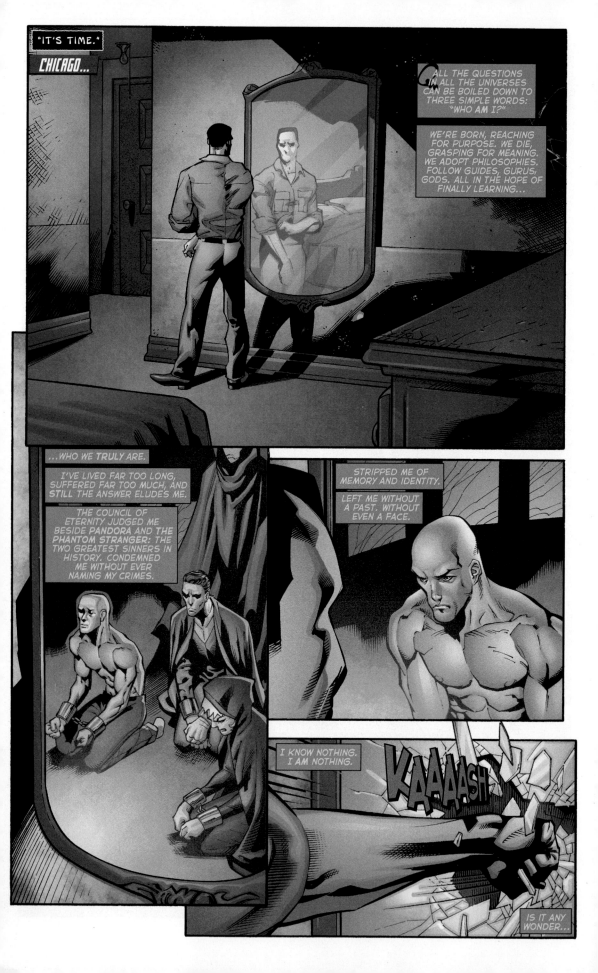

"IT'S TIME."

CHICAGO...

ALL THE QUESTIONS IN ALL THE UNIVERSES CAN BE BOILED DOWN TO THREE SIMPLE WORDS: "WHO AM I?"

WE'RE BORN, REACHING FOR PURPOSE. WE DIE, GRASPING FOR MEANING. WE ADOPT PHILOSOPHIES. FOLLOW GUIDES, GURUS, GODS. ALL IN THE HOPE OF FINALLY LEARNING...

...WHO WE TRULY ARE.

I'VE LIVED FAR TOO LONG, SUFFERED FAR TOO MUCH, AND STILL THE ANSWER ELUDES ME.

THE COUNCIL OF ETERNITY JUDGED ME BESIDE PANDORA AND THE PHANTOM STRANGER: THE TWO GREATEST SINNERS IN HISTORY. CONDEMNED ME WITHOUT EVER NAMING MY CRIMES.

STRIPPED ME OF MEMORY AND IDENTITY.

LEFT ME WITHOUT A PAST. WITHOUT EVEN A FACE.

I KNOW NOTHING. I AM NOTHING.

KAAAASH

IS IT ANY WONDER...

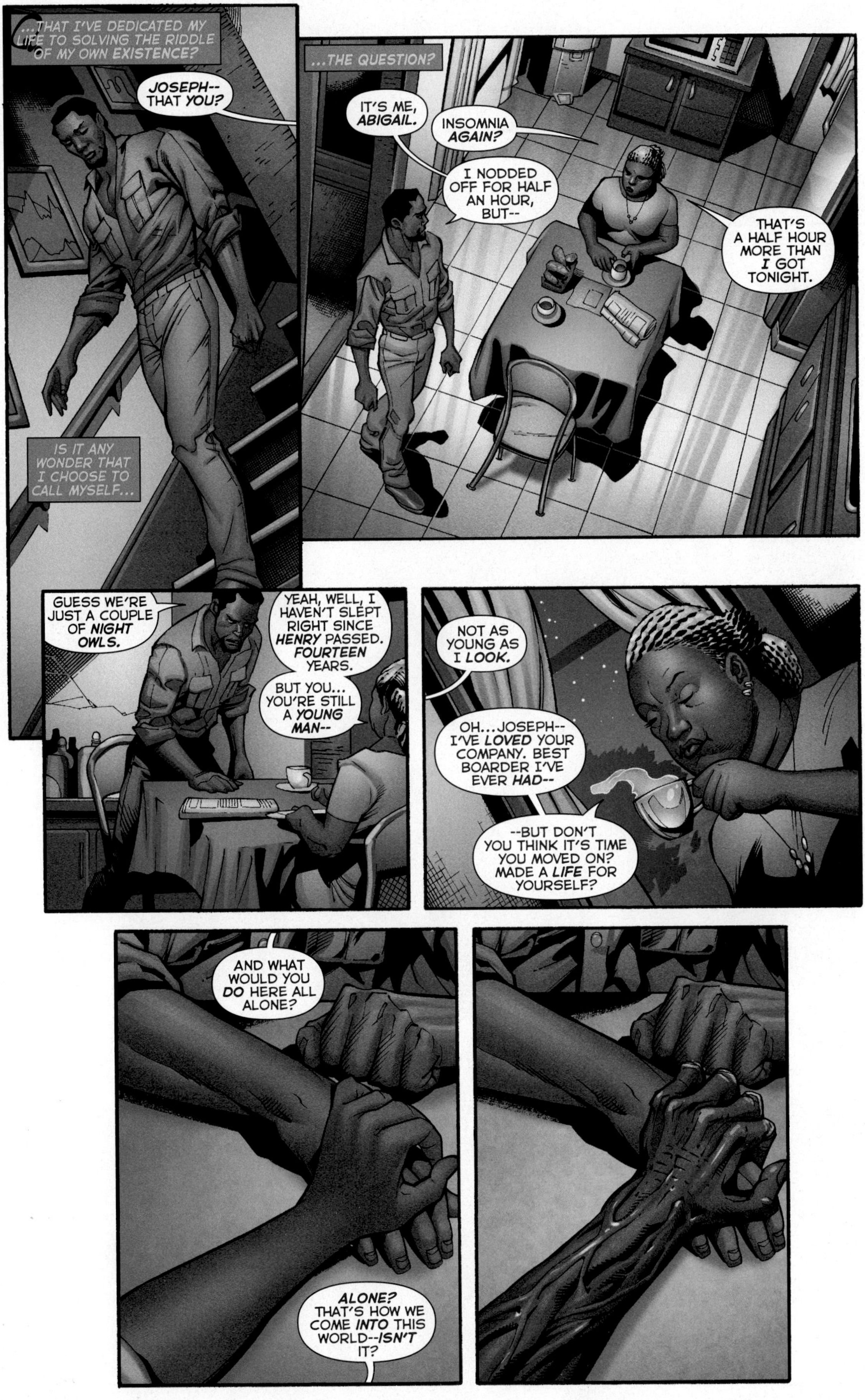
...THAT I'VE DEDICATED MY LIFE TO SOLVING THE RIDDLE OF MY OWN EXISTENCE?
JOSEPH-- THAT YOU?
IS IT ANY WONDER THAT I CHOOSE TO CALL MYSELF...
...THE QUESTION?
IT'S ME, ABIGAIL.
INSOMNIA AGAIN?
I NODDED OFF FOR HALF AN HOUR, BUT--
THAT'S A HALF HOUR MORE THAN I GOT TONIGHT.
GUESS WE'RE JUST A COUPLE OF NIGHT OWLS.
YEAH, WELL, I HAVEN'T SLEPT RIGHT SINCE HENRY PASSED. FOURTEEN YEARS.
BUT YOU... YOU'RE STILL A YOUNG MAN--
NOT AS YOUNG AS I LOOK.
OH...JOSEPH-- I'VE LOVED YOUR COMPANY. BEST BOARDER I'VE EVER HAD--
--BUT DON'T YOU THINK IT'S TIME YOU MOVED ON? MADE A LIFE FOR YOURSELF?
AND WHAT WOULD YOU DO HERE ALL ALONE?
ALONE? THAT'S HOW WE COME INTO THIS WORLD--ISN'T IT?

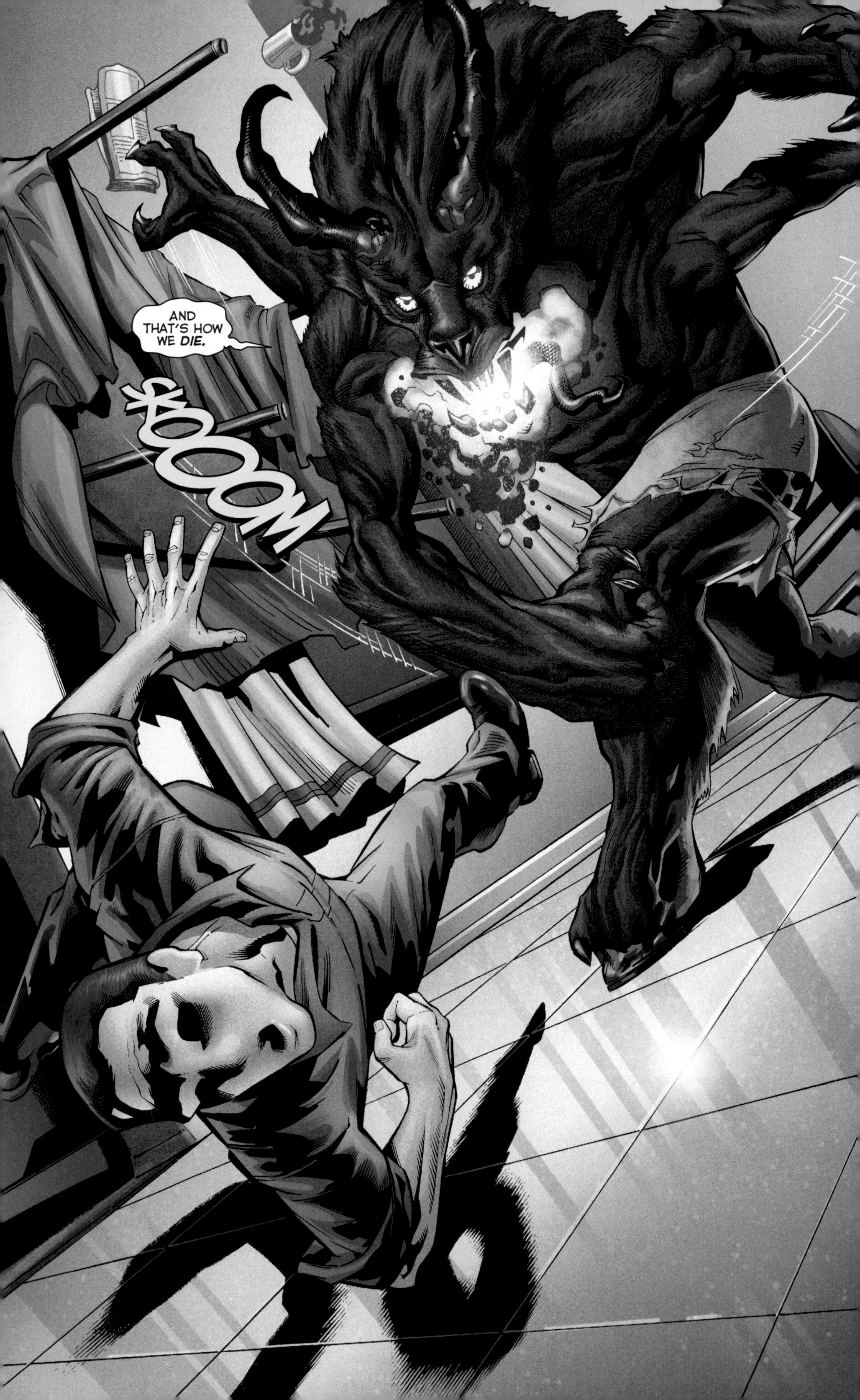
AND THAT'S HOW WE *DIE.*
SKOOOOM

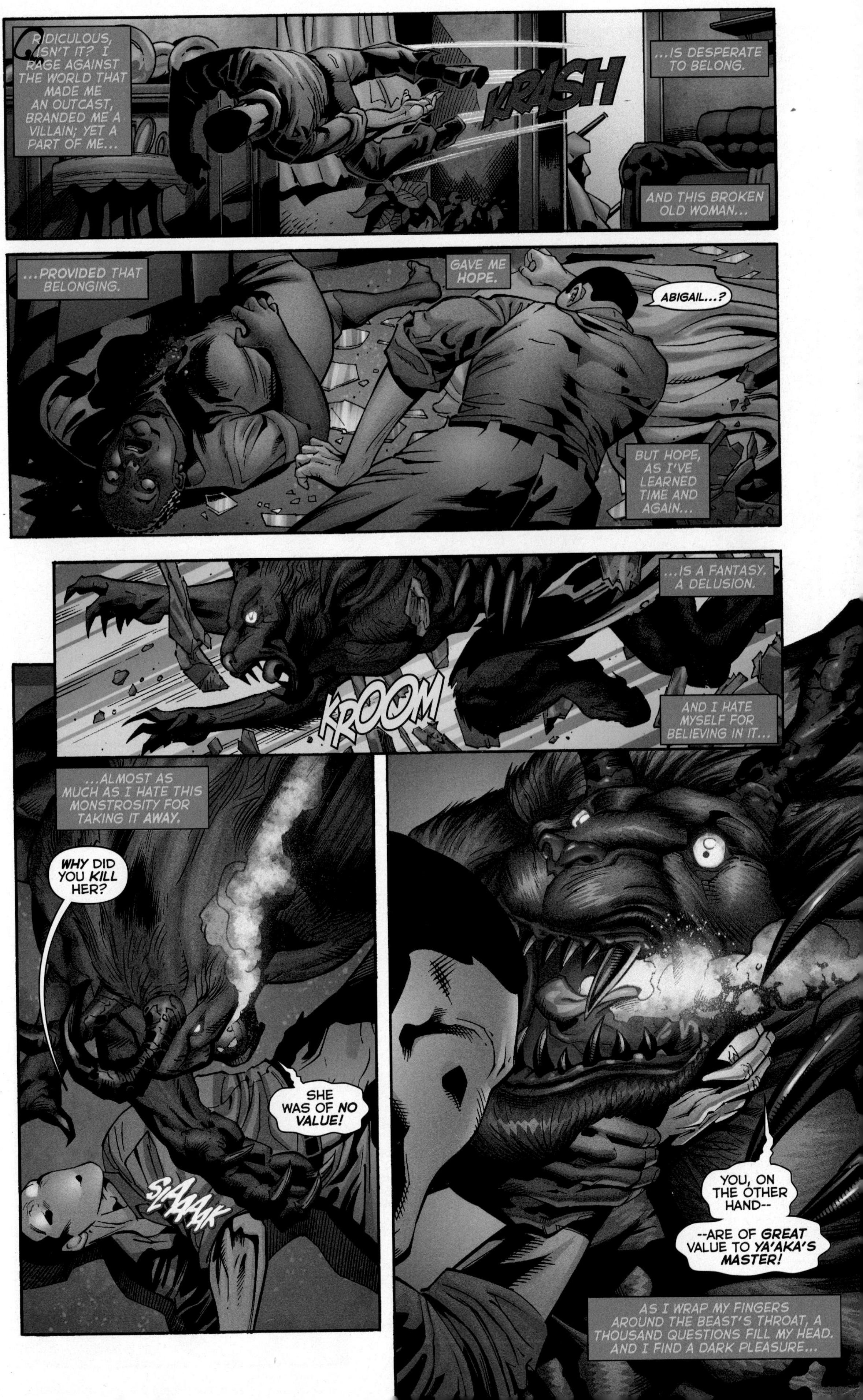
RIDICULOUS, ISN'T IT? I RAGE AGAINST THE WORLD THAT MADE ME AN OUTCAST, BRANDED ME A VILLAIN; YET A PART OF ME...
KRASH
...IS DESPERATE TO BELONG.
AND THIS BROKEN OLD WOMAN...
...PROVIDED THAT BELONGING.
GAVE ME HOPE.
ABIGAIL...?
BUT HOPE, AS I'VE LEARNED TIME AND AGAIN...
...IS A FANTASY. A DELUSION.
KROOM
AND I HATE MYSELF FOR BELIEVING IN IT...
...ALMOST AS MUCH AS I HATE THIS MONSTROSITY FOR TAKING IT AWAY.
WHY DID YOU KILL HER?
SHE WAS OF NO VALUE!
SLAAAAK
YOU, ON THE OTHER HAND--
--ARE OF GREAT VALUE TO YA'AKA'S MASTER!
AS I WRAP MY FINGERS AROUND THE BEAST'S THROAT, A THOUSAND QUESTIONS FILL MY HEAD. AND I FIND A DARK PLEASURE...

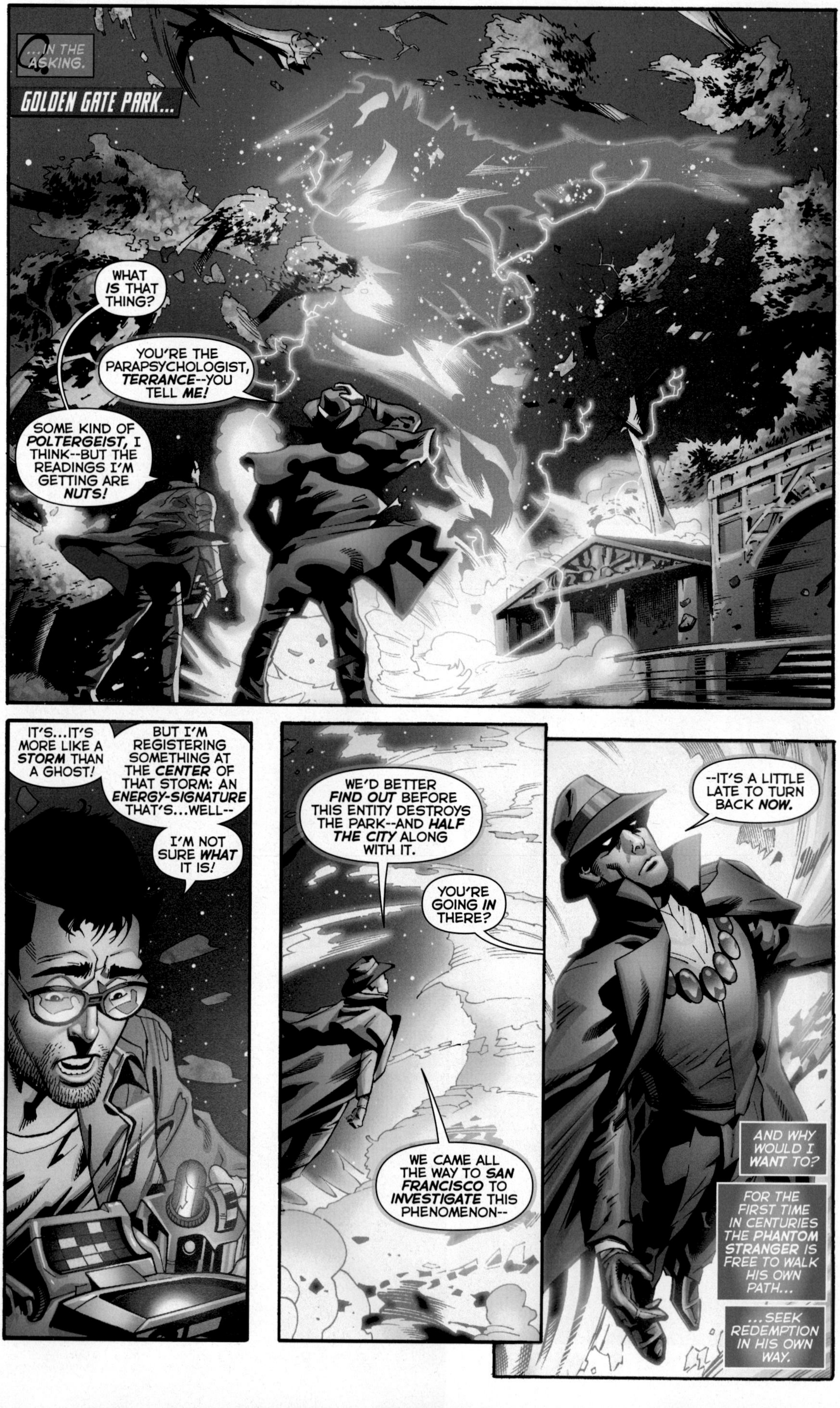

...IN THE ASKING.
GOLDEN GATE PARK...
WHAT IS THAT THING?
YOU'RE THE PARAPSYCHOLOGIST, TERRANCE--YOU TELL ME!
SOME KIND OF POLTERGEIST, I THINK--BUT THE READINGS I'M GETTING ARE NUTS!
IT'S...IT'S MORE LIKE A STORM THAN A GHOST!
BUT I'M REGISTERING SOMETHING AT THE CENTER OF THAT STORM: AN ENERGY-SIGNATURE THAT'S...WELL--
I'M NOT SURE WHAT IT IS!
WE'D BETTER FIND OUT BEFORE THIS ENTITY DESTROYS THE PARK--AND HALF THE CITY ALONG WITH IT.
YOU'RE GOING IN THERE?
WE CAME ALL THE WAY TO SAN FRANCISCO TO INVESTIGATE THIS PHENOMENON--
--IT'S A LITTLE LATE TO TURN BACK NOW.
AND WHY WOULD I WANT TO?
FOR THE FIRST TIME IN CENTURIES THE PHANTOM STRANGER IS FREE TO WALK HIS OWN PATH...
...SEEK REDEMPTION IN HIS OWN WAY.

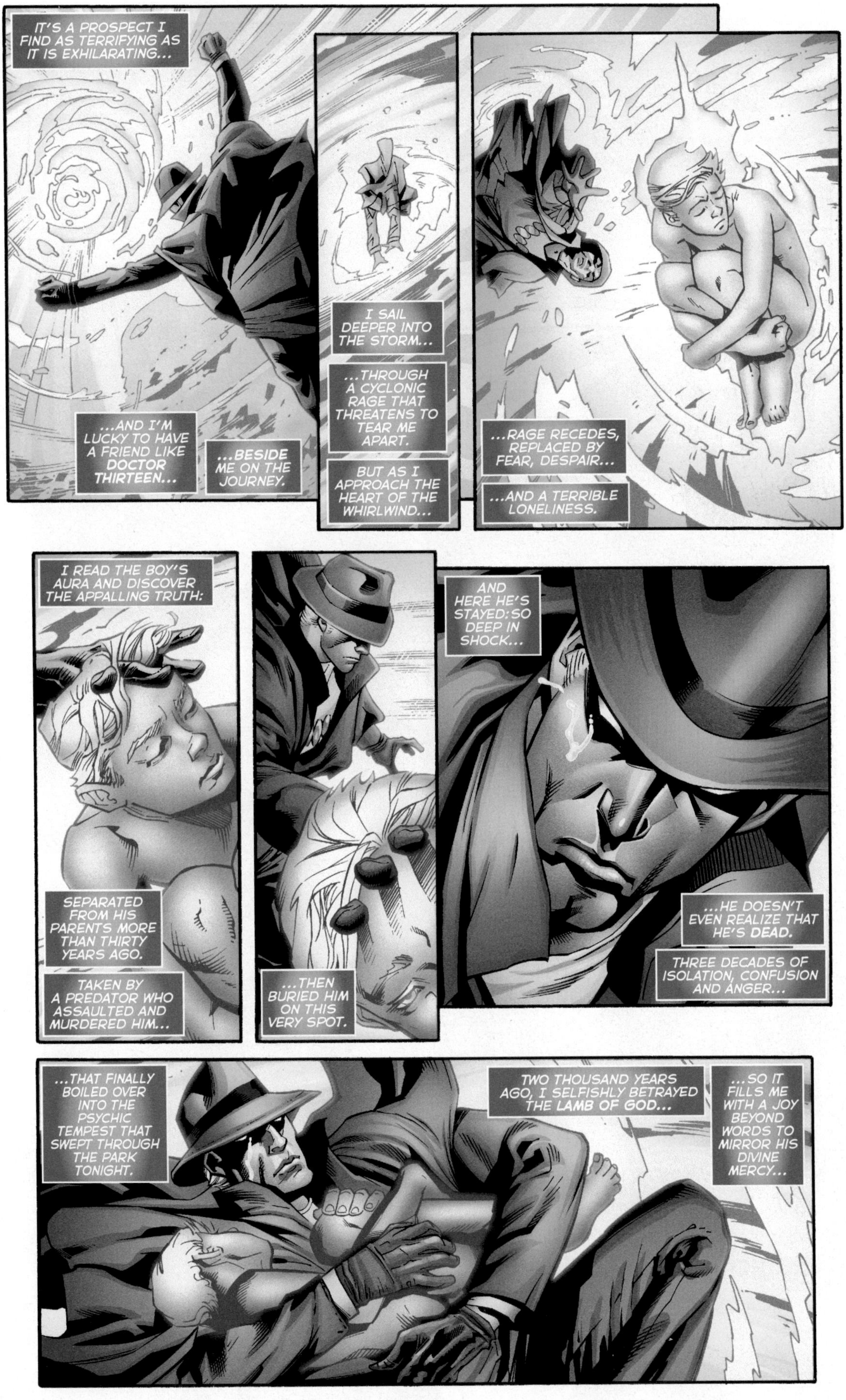
IT'S A PROSPECT I FIND AS TERRIFYING AS IT IS EXHILARATING...
...AND I'M LUCKY TO HAVE A FRIEND LIKE DOCTOR THIRTEEN...
...BESIDE ME ON THE JOURNEY.
I SAIL DEEPER INTO THE STORM...
...THROUGH A CYCLONIC RAGE THAT THREATENS TO TEAR ME APART.
BUT AS I APPROACH THE HEART OF THE WHIRLWIND...
...RAGE RECEDES, REPLACED BY FEAR, DESPAIR...
...AND A TERRIBLE LONELINESS.
I READ THE BOY'S AURA AND DISCOVER THE APPALLING TRUTH:
SEPARATED FROM HIS PARENTS MORE THAN THIRTY YEARS AGO.
TAKEN BY A PREDATOR WHO ASSAULTED AND MURDERED HIM...
...THEN BURIED HIM ON THIS VERY SPOT.
AND HERE HE'S STAYED: SO DEEP IN SHOCK...
...HE DOESN'T EVEN REALIZE THAT HE'S DEAD.
THREE DECADES OF ISOLATION, CONFUSION AND ANGER...
...THAT FINALLY BOILED OVER INTO THE PSYCHIC TEMPEST THAT SWEPT THROUGH THE PARK TONIGHT.
TWO THOUSAND YEARS AGO, I SELFISHLY BETRAYED THE LAMB OF GOD...
...SO IT FILLS ME WITH A JOY BEYOND WORDS TO MIRROR HIS DIVINE MERCY...

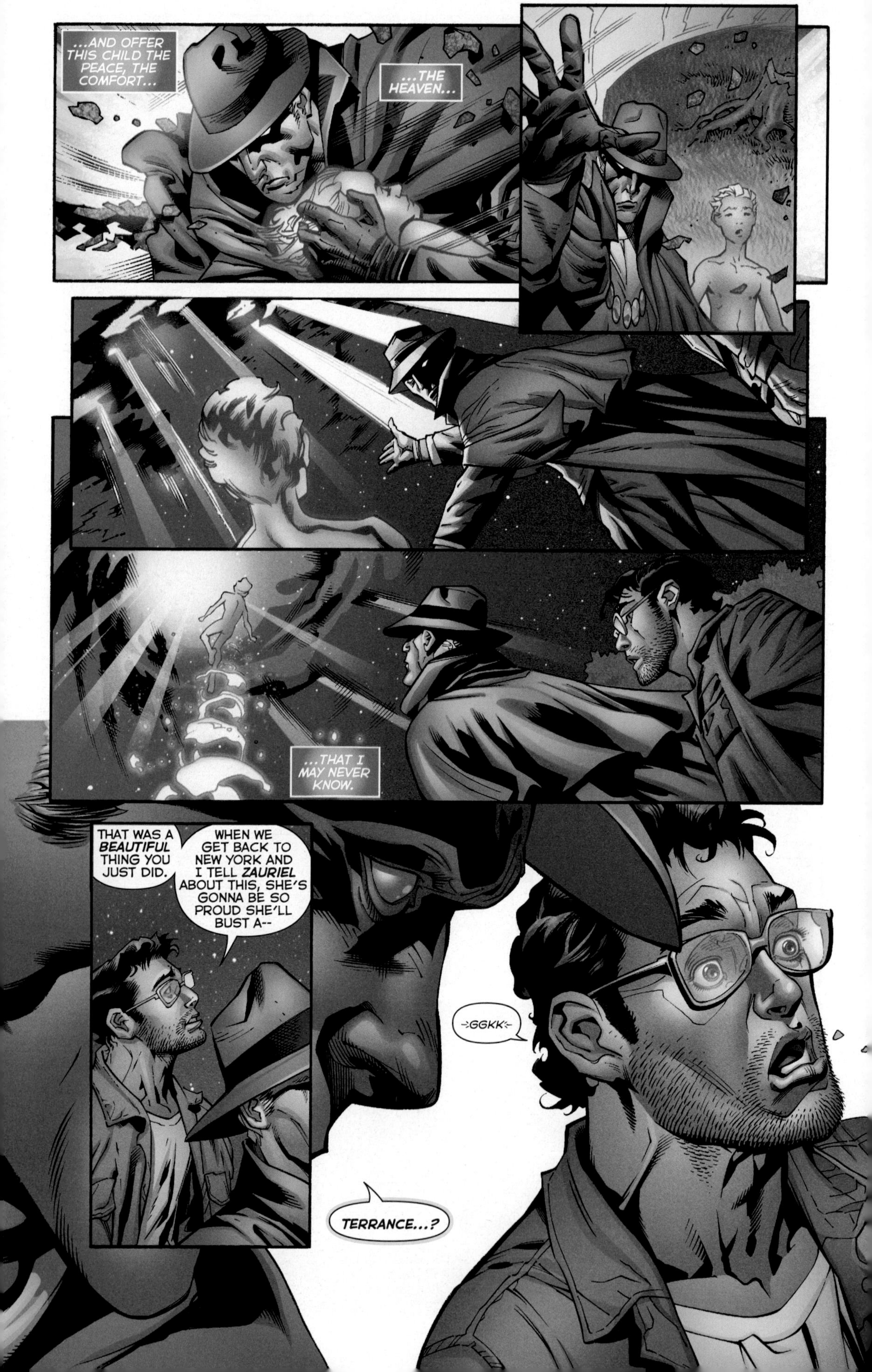
...AND OFFER THIS CHILD THE PEACE, THE COMFORT...
...THE HEAVEN...
...THAT I MAY NEVER KNOW.
THAT WAS A *BEAUTIFUL* THING YOU JUST DID.
WHEN WE GET BACK TO NEW YORK AND I TELL *ZAURIEL* ABOUT THIS, SHE'S GONNA BE SO PROUD SHE'LL BUST A--
GGKK
TERRANCE...?

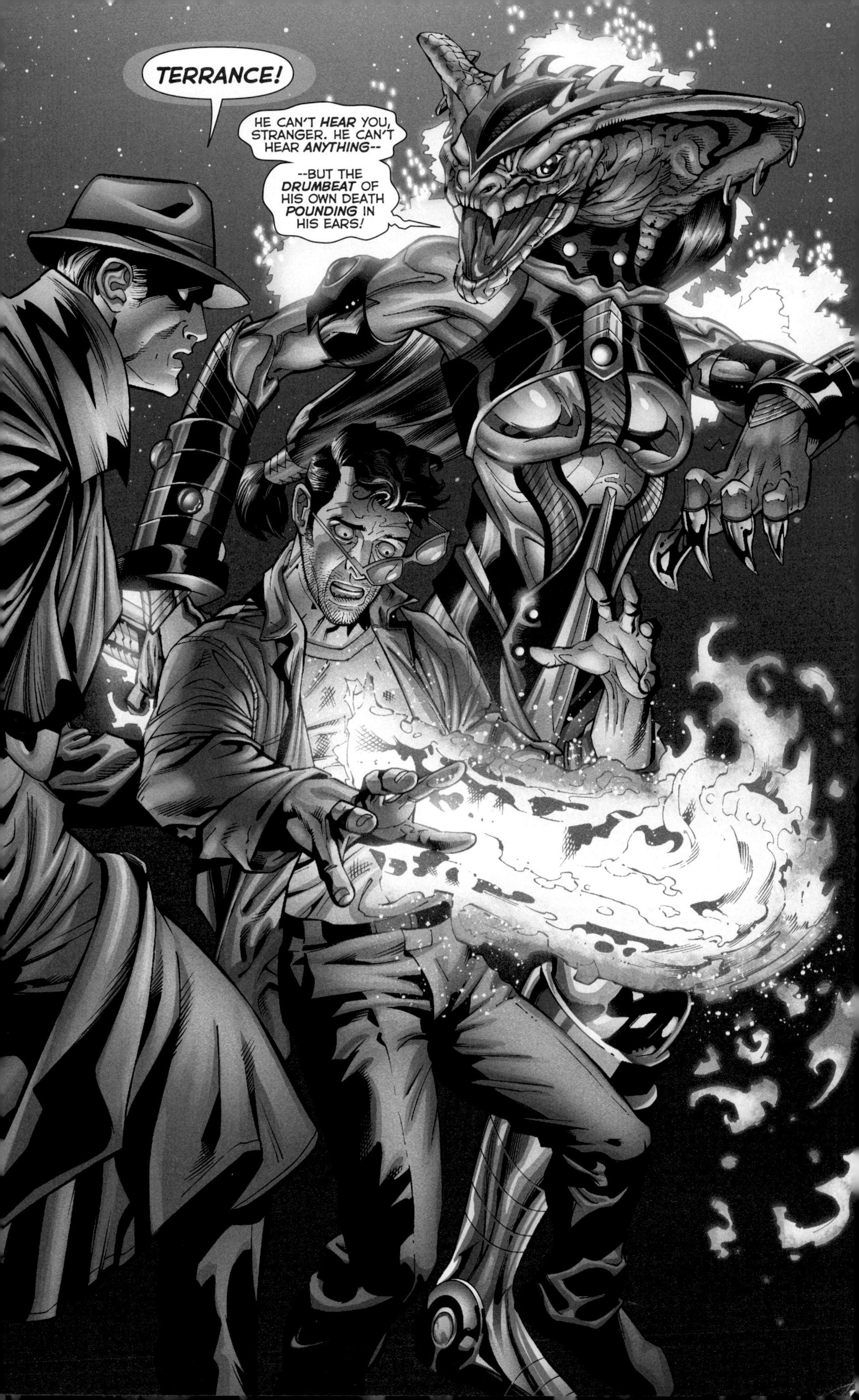
TERRANCE!
HE CAN'T HEAR YOU, STRANGER. HE CAN'T HEAR ANYTHING--
--BUT THE DRUMBEAT OF HIS OWN DEATH POUNDING IN HIS EARS!

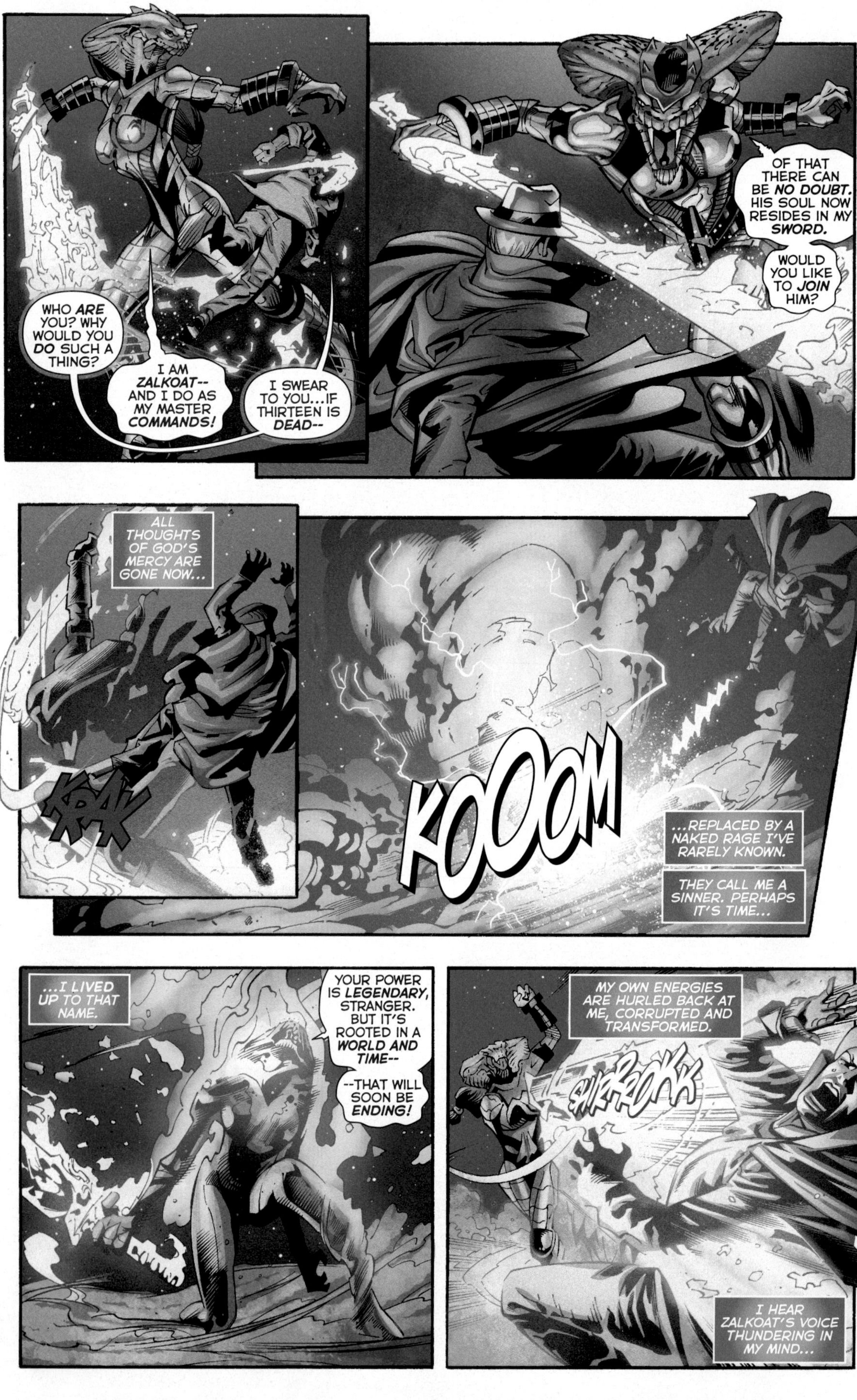
WHO ARE YOU? WHY WOULD YOU DO SUCH A THING?
I AM ZALKOAT--AND I DO AS MY MASTER COMMANDS!
I SWEAR TO YOU...IF THIRTEEN IS DEAD--
OF THAT THERE CAN BE NO DOUBT. HIS SOUL NOW RESIDES IN MY SWORD.
WOULD YOU LIKE TO JOIN HIM?
ALL THOUGHTS OF GOD'S MERCY ARE GONE NOW...
KRAK
KOOOM
...REPLACED BY A NAKED RAGE I'VE RARELY KNOWN.
THEY CALL ME A SINNER. PERHAPS IT'S TIME...
...I LIVED UP TO THAT NAME.
YOUR POWER IS LEGENDARY, STRANGER. BUT IT'S ROOTED IN A WORLD AND TIME--
--THAT WILL SOON BE ENDING!
MY OWN ENERGIES ARE HURLED BACK AT ME, CORRUPTED AND TRANSFORMED.
SHRROKK
I HEAR ZALKOAT'S VOICE THUNDERING IN MY MIND...

...AND SHE'S LAUGHING.

SOUTHERN INDIA...

WHEN **MARCUS** SUGGESTED I TAKE A FEW DAYS FOR MYSELF TO GET AWAY, REFRESH AND RENEW, I THOUGHT HE WAS CRAZY.

I HAVEN'T DONE THAT ONCE IN ALL THE CENTURIES SINCE I INADVERTENTLY OPENED **THE BOX** THAT UNLEASHED A TIDE OF EVIL ON THE WORLD.

BUT COMING BACK HERE TO **GOA**, TO THIS SACRED LAND I FIRST VISITED HUNDREDS OF YEARS AGO...

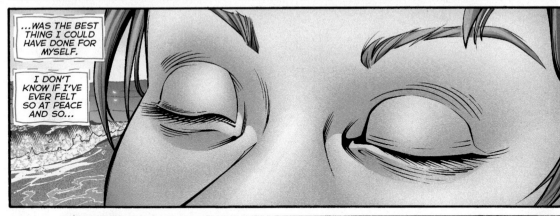

...WAS THE BEST THING I COULD HAVE DONE FOR MYSELF.

I DON'T KNOW IF I'VE EVER FELT SO AT PEACE AND SO...

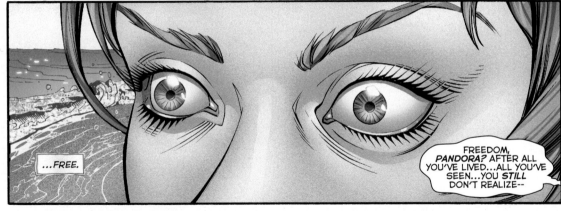

...FREE.

FREEDOM, *PANDORA?* AFTER ALL YOU'VE LIVED...ALL YOU'VE SEEN...YOU *STILL* DON'T REALIZE--

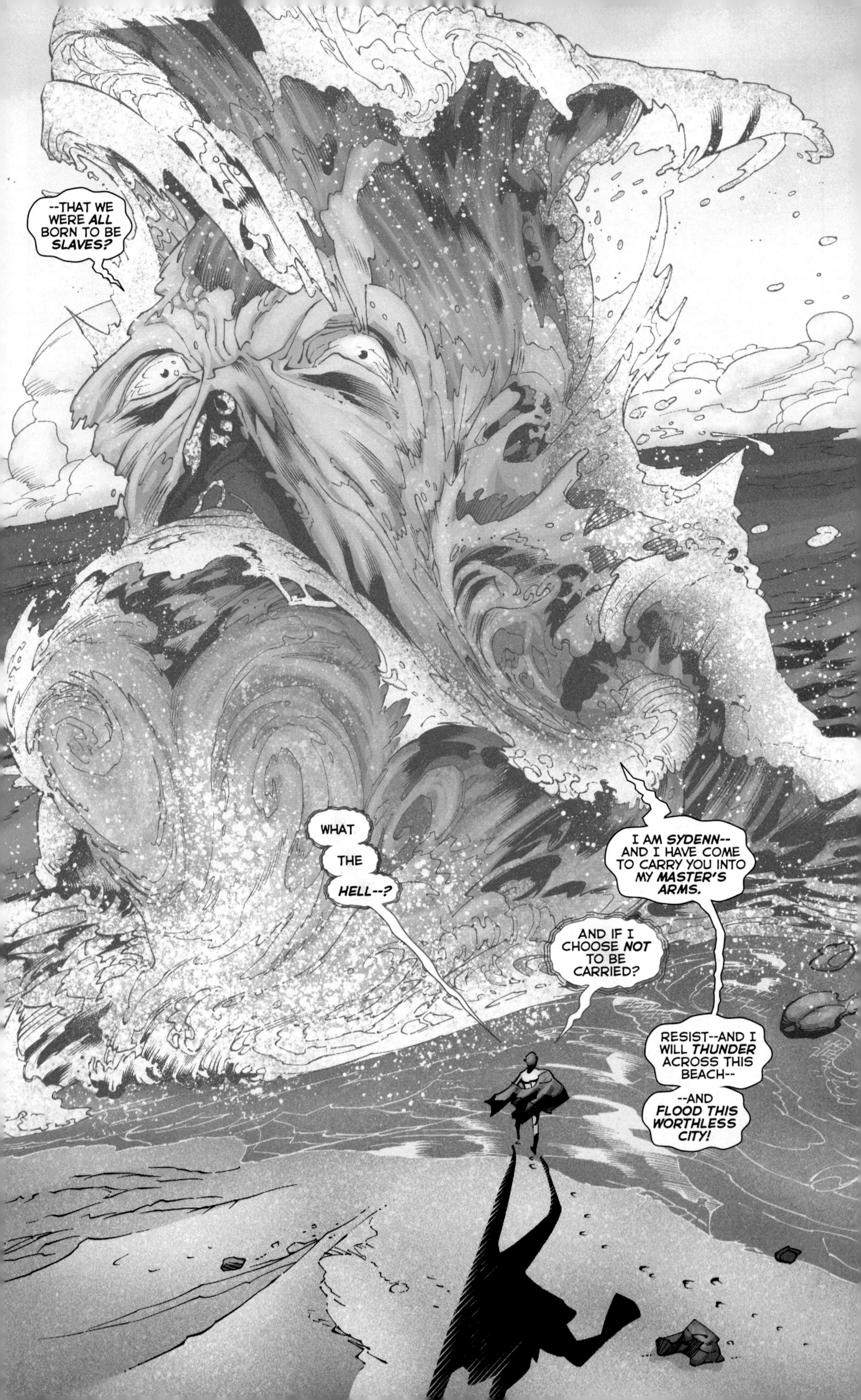
--THAT WE WERE ALL BORN TO BE SLAVES?
WHAT THE HELL--?
I AM SYDENN--AND I HAVE COME TO CARRY YOU INTO MY MASTER'S ARMS.
AND IF I CHOOSE NOT TO BE CARRIED?
RESIST--AND I WILL THUNDER ACROSS THIS BEACH--
--AND FLOOD THIS WORTHLESS CITY!

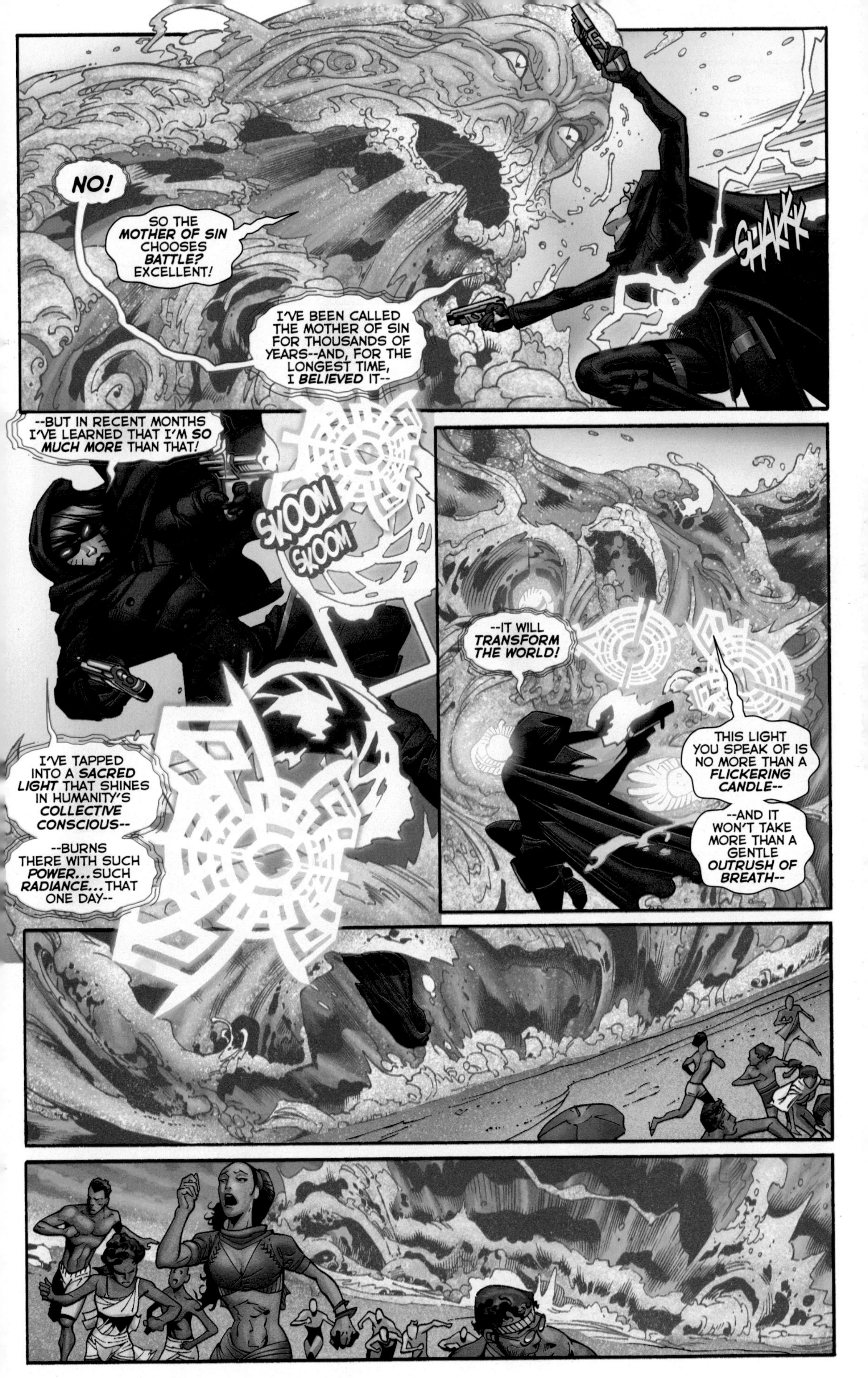
NO!
SO THE MOTHER OF SIN CHOOSES BATTLE? EXCELLENT!
SHAKKK
I'VE BEEN CALLED THE MOTHER OF SIN FOR THOUSANDS OF YEARS--AND, FOR THE LONGEST TIME, I BELIEVED IT--
--BUT IN RECENT MONTHS I'VE LEARNED THAT I'M SO MUCH MORE THAN THAT!
SKOOM
SKOOM
I'VE TAPPED INTO A SACRED LIGHT THAT SHINES IN HUMANITY'S COLLECTIVE CONSCIOUS--
--BURNS THERE WITH SUCH POWER... SUCH RADIANCE... THAT ONE DAY--
--IT WILL TRANSFORM THE WORLD!
THIS LIGHT YOU SPEAK OF IS NO MORE THAN A FLICKERING CANDLE--
--AND IT WON'T TAKE MORE THAN A GENTLE OUTRUSH OF BREATH--

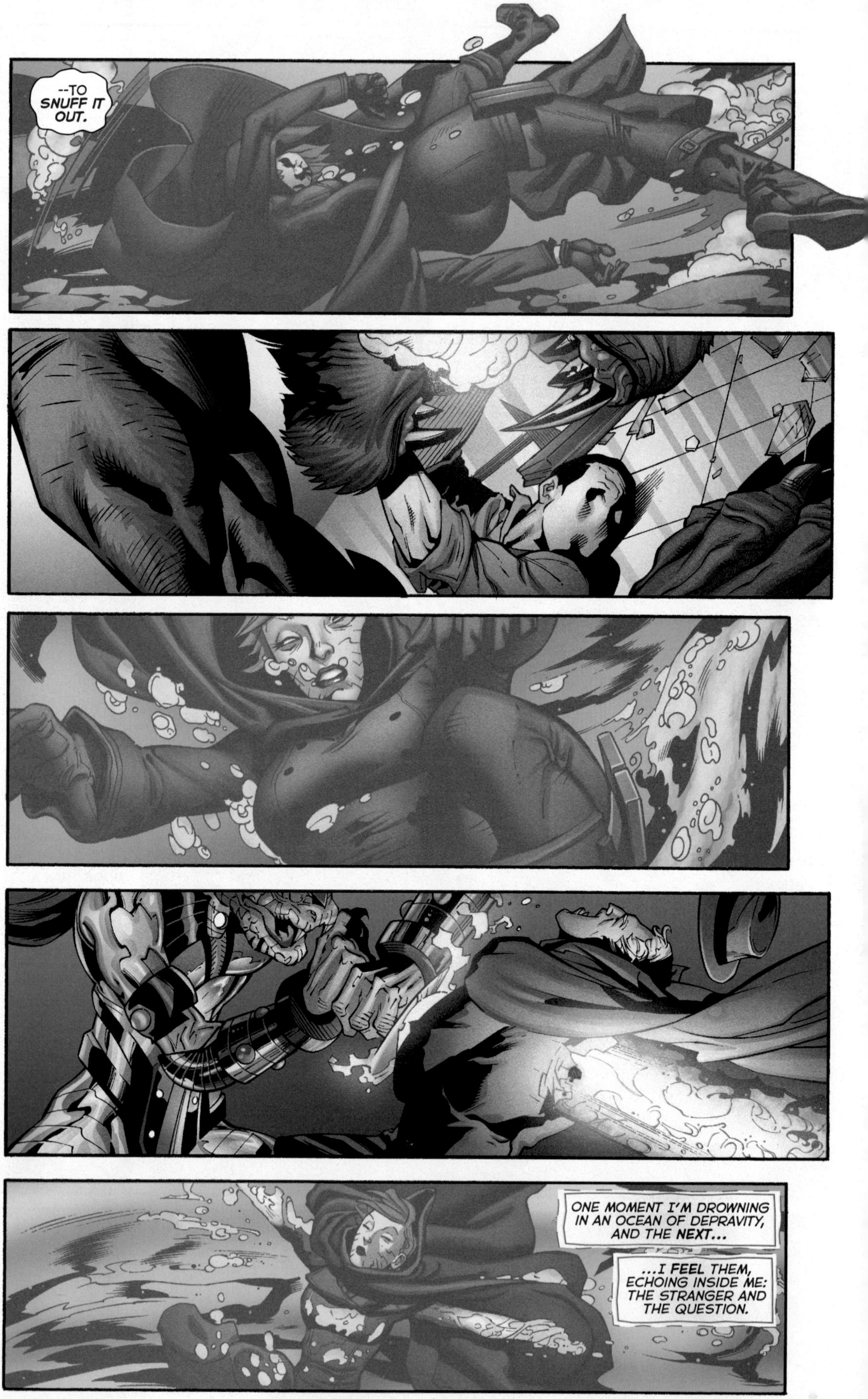
--TO SNUFF IT OUT.
ONE MOMENT I'M DROWNING IN AN OCEAN OF DEPRAVITY, AND THE NEXT...
...I FEEL THEM, ECHOING INSIDE ME: THE STRANGER AND THE QUESTION.

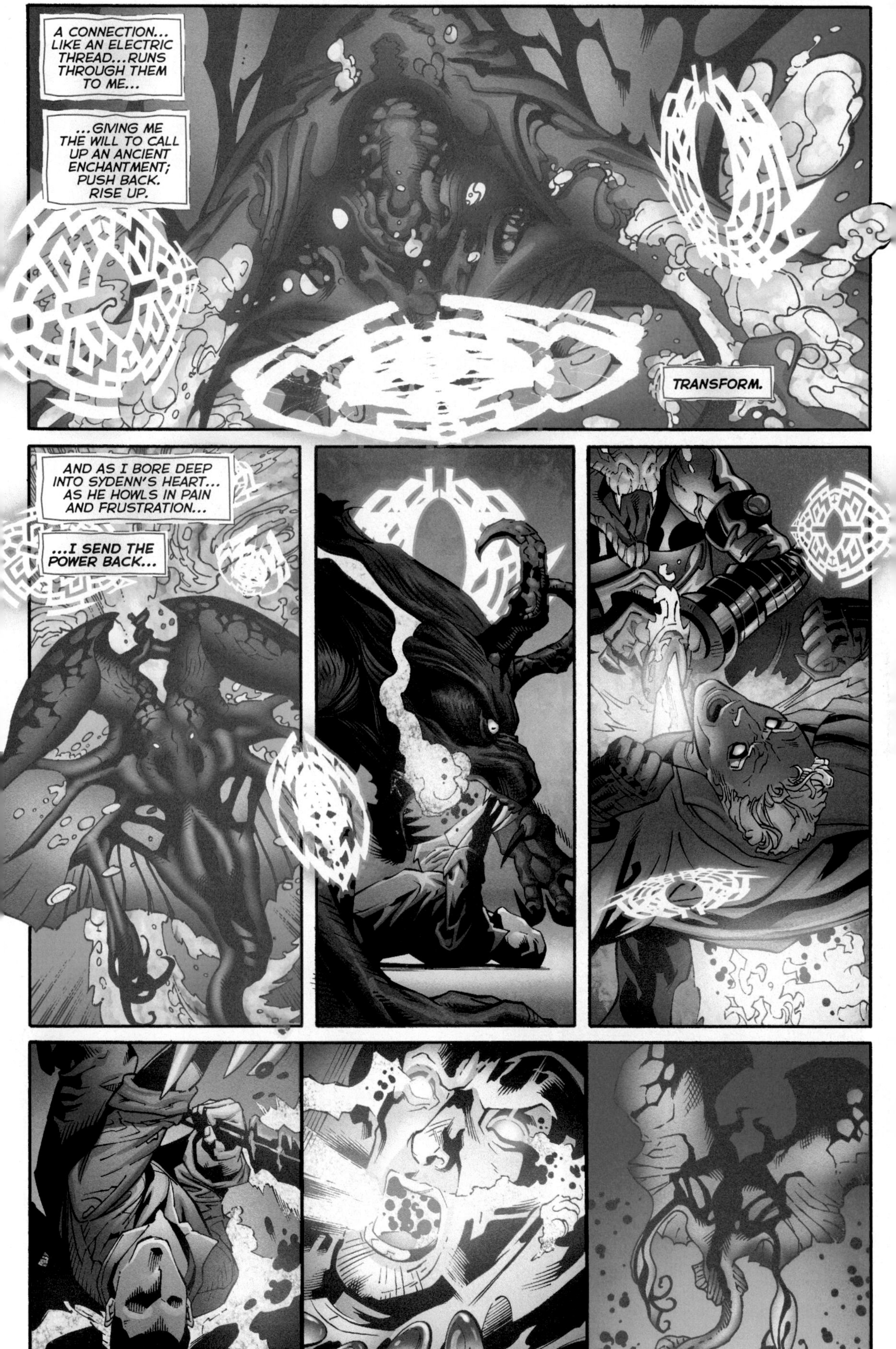
A CONNECTION... LIKE AN ELECTRIC THREAD...RUNS THROUGH THEM TO ME...
...GIVING ME THE WILL TO CALL UP AN ANCIENT ENCHANTMENT; PUSH BACK. RISE UP.
TRANSFORM.
AND AS I BORE DEEP INTO SYDENN'S HEART... AS HE HOWLS IN PAIN AND FRUSTRATION...
...I SEND THE POWER BACK...

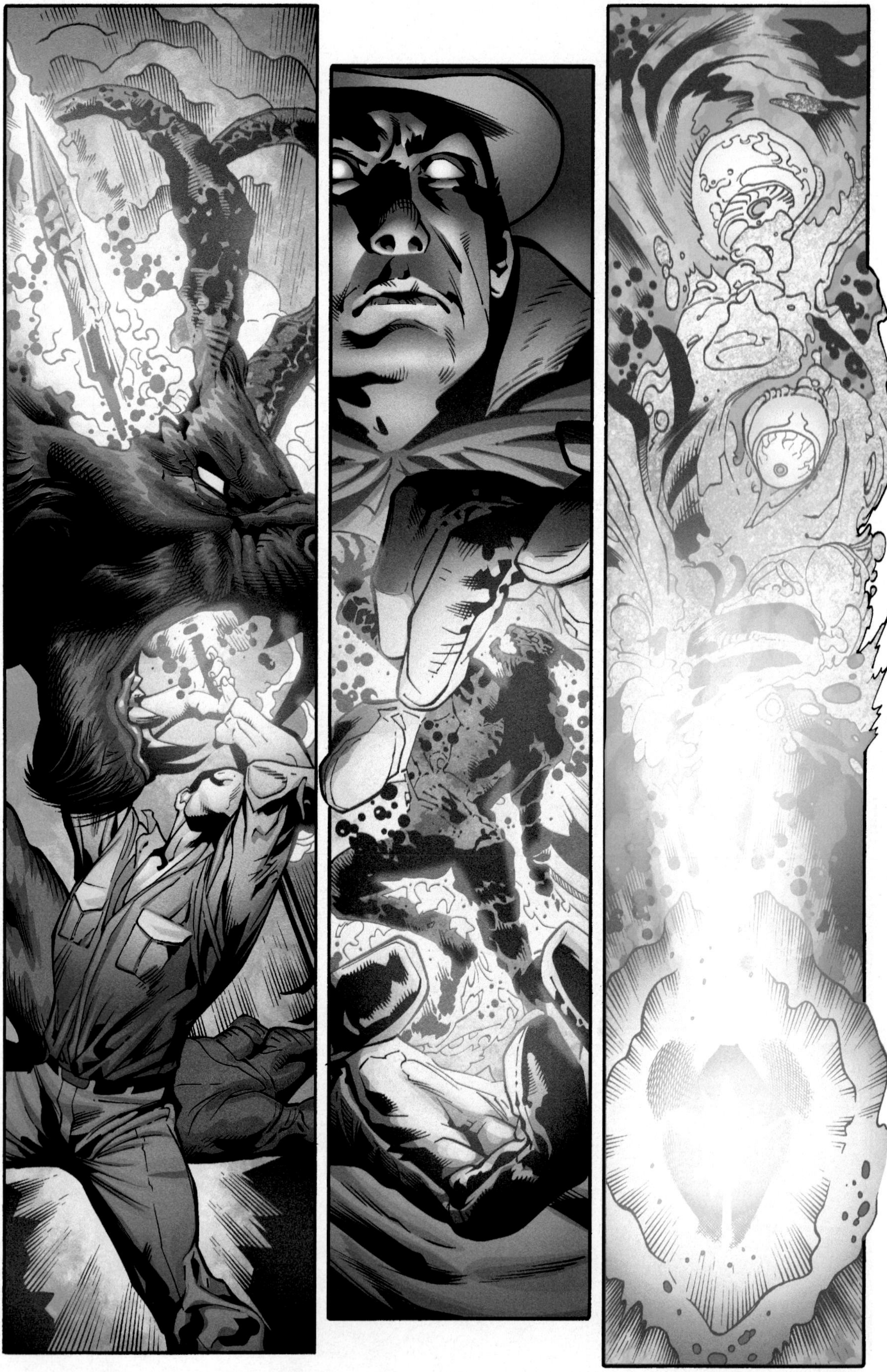

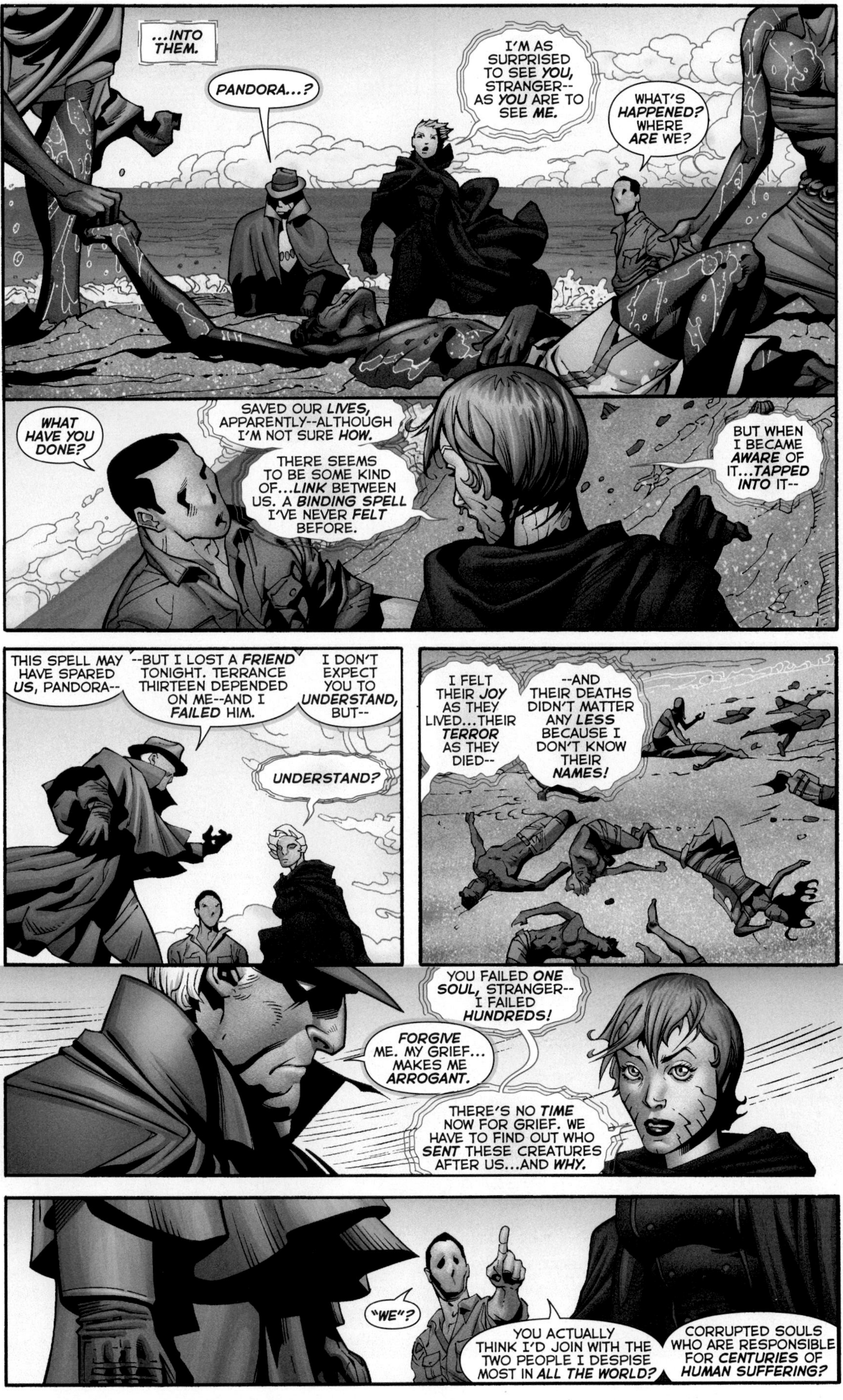

...INTO THEM.
PANDORA...?
I'M AS SURPRISED TO SEE YOU, STRANGER-- AS YOU ARE TO SEE ME.
WHAT'S HAPPENED? WHERE ARE WE?
WHAT HAVE YOU DONE?
SAVED OUR LIVES, APPARENTLY--ALTHOUGH I'M NOT SURE HOW.
THERE SEEMS TO BE SOME KIND OF...LINK BETWEEN US. A BINDING SPELL I'VE NEVER FELT BEFORE.
BUT WHEN I BECAME AWARE OF IT...TAPPED INTO IT--
THIS SPELL MAY HAVE SPARED US, PANDORA--
--BUT I LOST A FRIEND TONIGHT. TERRANCE THIRTEEN DEPENDED ON ME--AND I FAILED HIM.
I DON'T EXPECT YOU TO UNDERSTAND, BUT--
UNDERSTAND?
I FELT THEIR JOY AS THEY LIVED...THEIR TERROR AS THEY DIED--
--AND THEIR DEATHS DIDN'T MATTER ANY LESS BECAUSE I DON'T KNOW THEIR NAMES!
YOU FAILED ONE SOUL, STRANGER-- I FAILED HUNDREDS!
FORGIVE ME. MY GRIEF... MAKES ME ARROGANT.
THERE'S NO TIME NOW FOR GRIEF. WE HAVE TO FIND OUT WHO SENT THESE CREATURES AFTER US...AND WHY.
"WE"?
YOU ACTUALLY THINK I'D JOIN WITH THE TWO PEOPLE I DESPISE MOST IN ALL THE WORLD?
CORRUPTED SOULS WHO ARE RESPONSIBLE FOR CENTURIES OF HUMAN SUFFERING?

WHO SOMEHOW *DRAGGED ME DOWN* INTO THE CESSPOOL *WITH* THEM--

--AND CONVINCED THE *COUNCIL OF ETERNITY* TO CONDEMN--

--A *BLAMELESS MAN?*

IT'S BEEN MY EXPERIENCE THAT PEOPLE WHO CONSTANTLY *PROTEST THEIR INNOCENCE*-- ARE OFTEN THE *GUILTIEST* OF ALL.

MAYBE *SO.* BUT HE'S *POWERFUL.* AND GIVEN WHAT WE'VE *FACED* TODAY--WE COULD *USE* HIM.

HE'D ONLY TURN *AGAINST* US. IF THERE'S ONE THING I KNOW ABOUT THE QUESTION--IT'S THAT HE'S *COLD...* HEARTLESS--

"--AND DRIVEN ONLY BY *HATE.*"

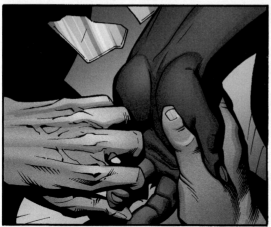

THE *NEW YORK CITY* PENTHOUSE OF DOCTOR THIRTEEN...

WE SHOULD *BURY* HIM.

NO. ZALKOAT SAID THAT TERRANCE'S SOUL WAS *WITHIN* HER SWORD. IF I CAN GET IT *BACK*--

YOU DON'T KNOW IF THAT'S *TRUE.* SHE MIGHT HAVE BEEN *TAUNTING* YOU OR--

I'LL HAVE THAT *WITCH'S HEAD*--

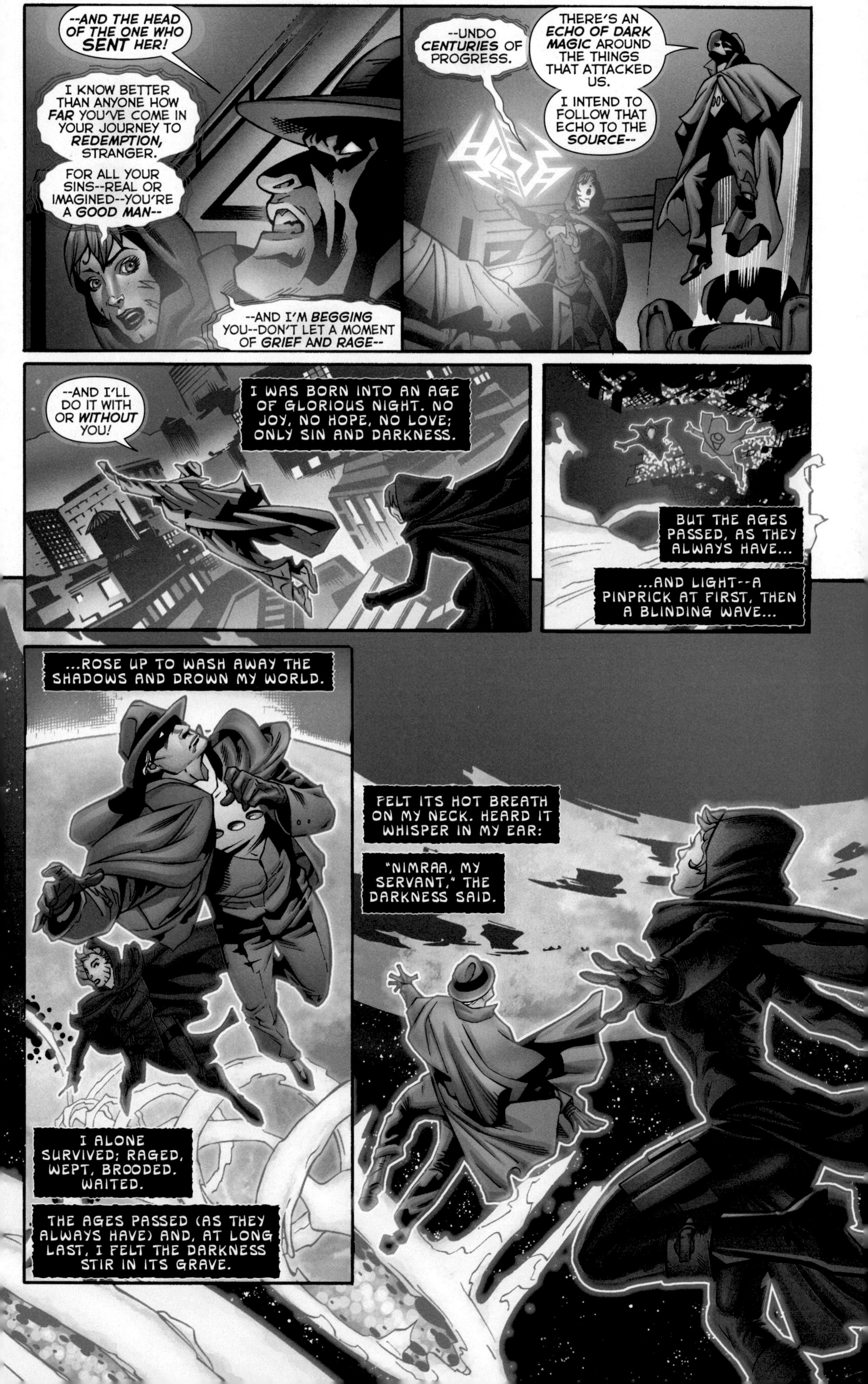
--AND THE HEAD OF THE ONE WHO SENT HER!
I KNOW BETTER THAN ANYONE HOW FAR YOU'VE COME IN YOUR JOURNEY TO REDEMPTION, STRANGER.
FOR ALL YOUR SINS--REAL OR IMAGINED--YOU'RE A GOOD MAN--
--AND I'M BEGGING YOU--DON'T LET A MOMENT OF GRIEF AND RAGE--
--UNDO CENTURIES OF PROGRESS.
THERE'S AN ECHO OF DARK MAGIC AROUND THE THINGS THAT ATTACKED US.
I INTEND TO FOLLOW THAT ECHO TO THE SOURCE--
--AND I'LL DO IT WITH OR WITHOUT YOU!
I WAS BORN INTO AN AGE OF GLORIOUS NIGHT. NO JOY, NO HOPE, NO LOVE; ONLY SIN AND DARKNESS.
BUT THE AGES PASSED, AS THEY ALWAYS HAVE...
...AND LIGHT--A PINPRICK AT FIRST, THEN A BLINDING WAVE...
...ROSE UP TO WASH AWAY THE SHADOWS AND DROWN MY WORLD.
I ALONE SURVIVED; RAGED, WEPT, BROODED. WAITED.
THE AGES PASSED (AS THEY ALWAYS HAVE) AND, AT LONG LAST, I FELT THE DARKNESS STIR IN ITS GRAVE.
FELT ITS HOT BREATH ON MY NECK. HEARD IT WHISPER IN MY EAR:
"NIMRAA, MY SERVANT," THE DARKNESS SAID.

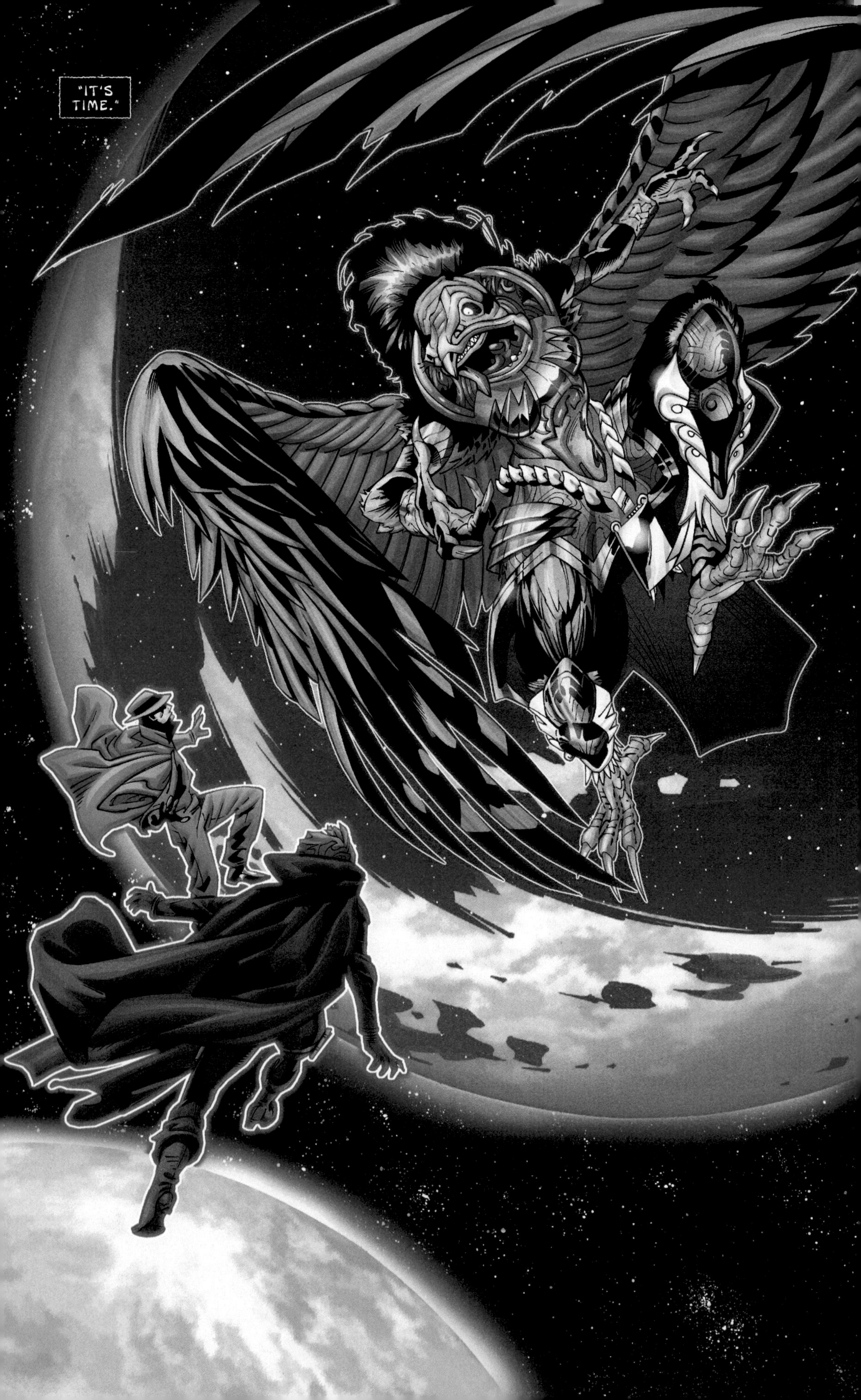
"IT'S TIME."

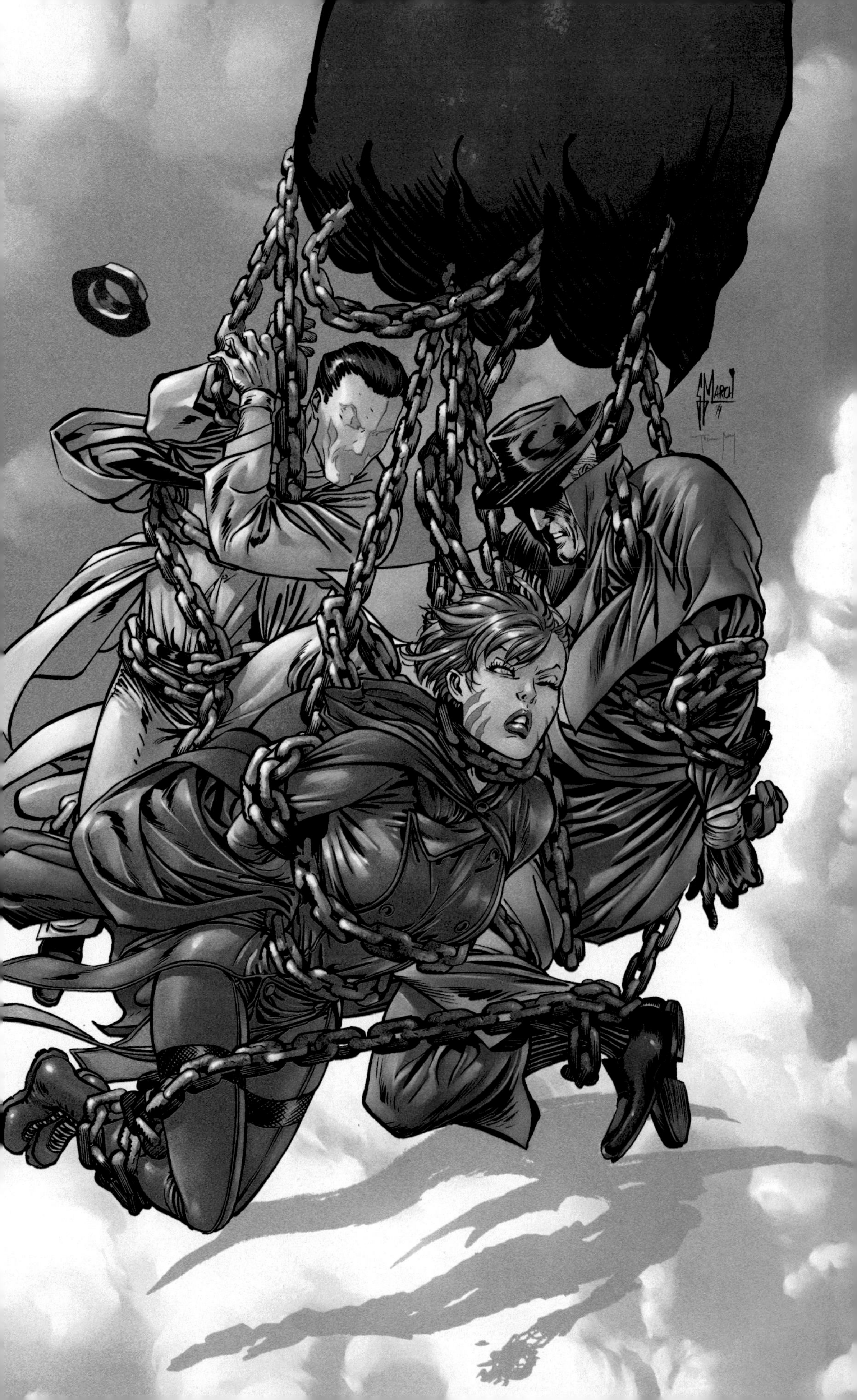

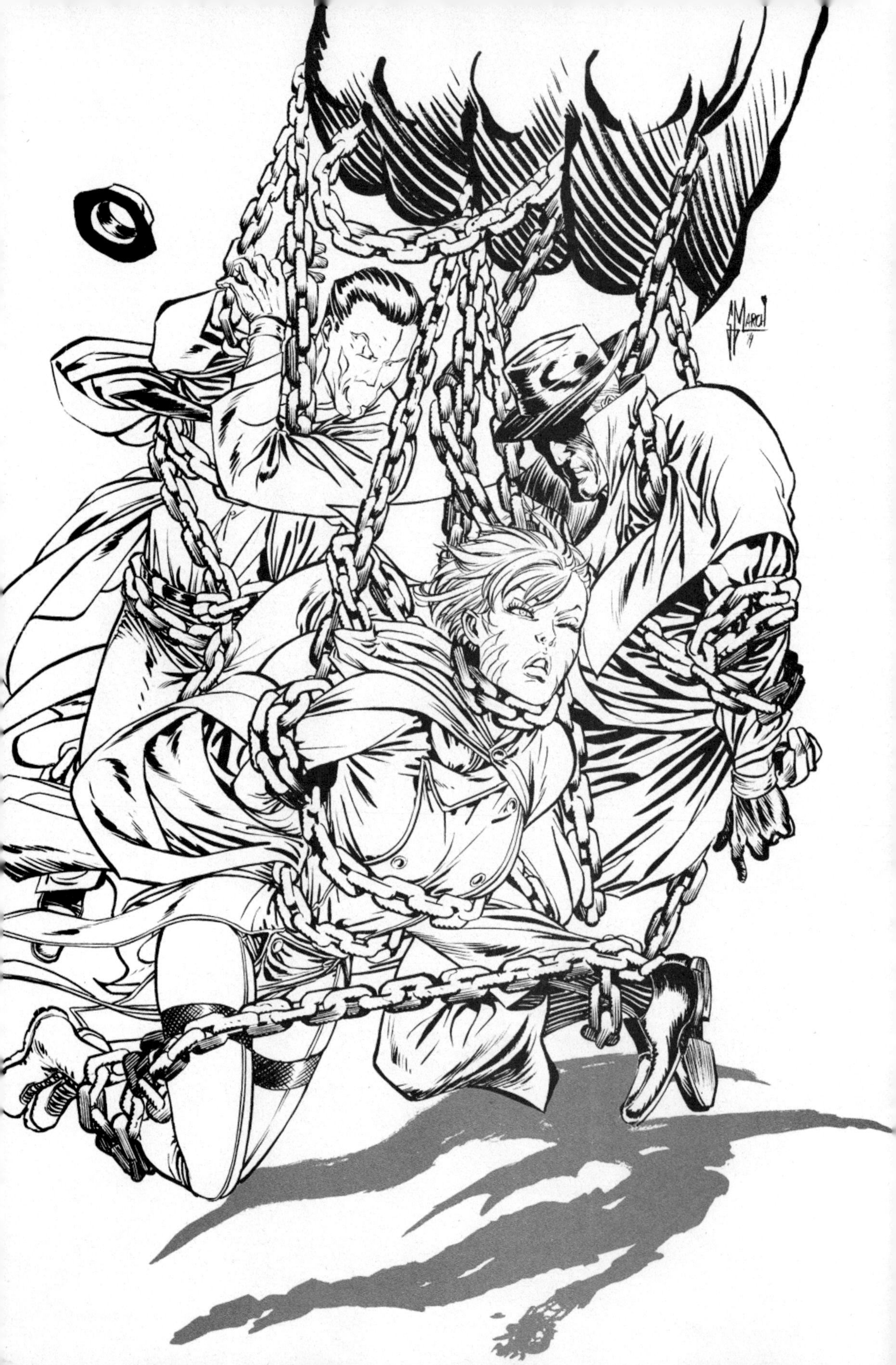

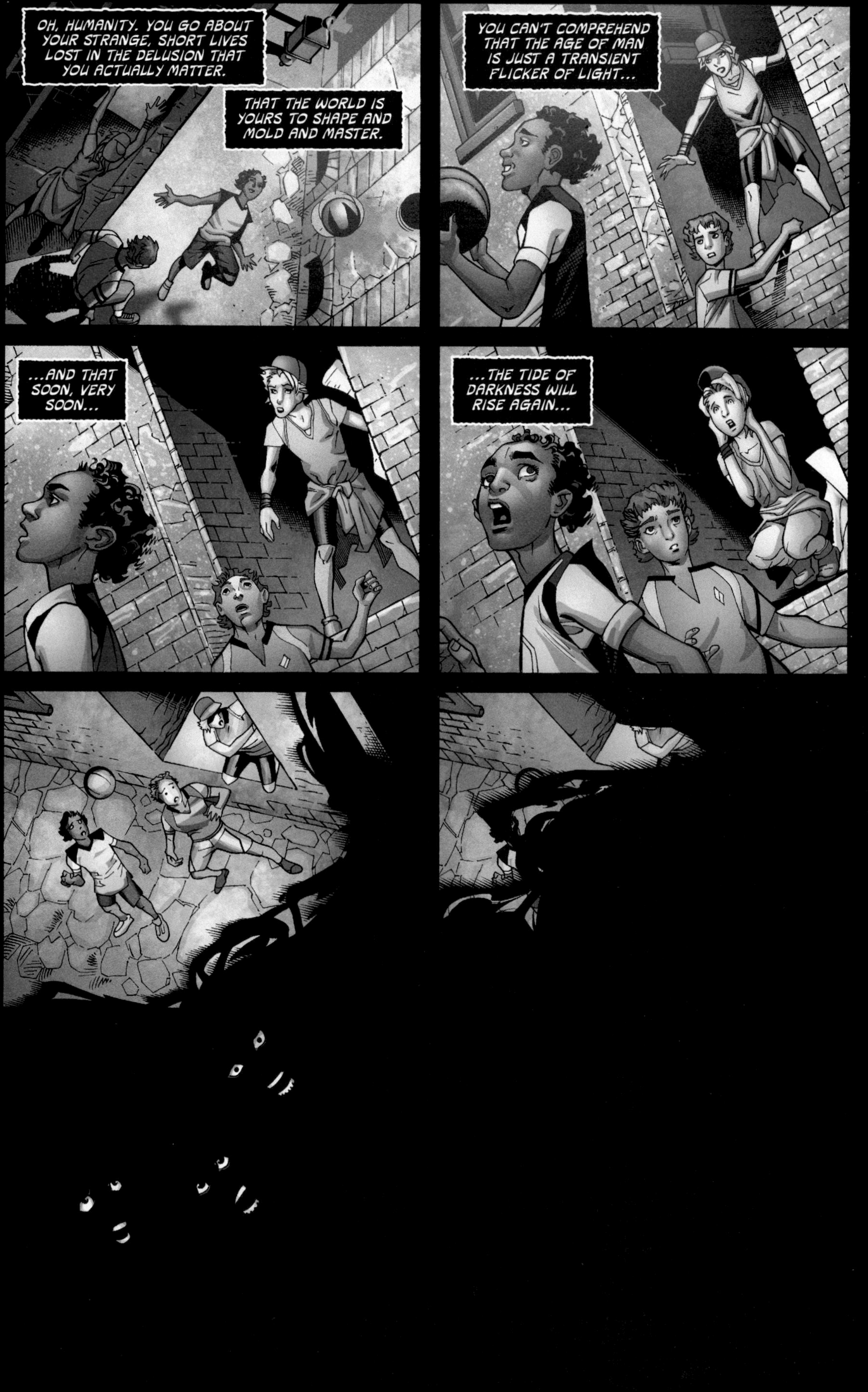
OH, HUMANITY. YOU GO ABOUT YOUR STRANGE, SHORT LIVES LOST IN THE DELUSION THAT YOU ACTUALLY MATTER.
THAT THE WORLD IS YOURS TO SHAPE AND MOLD AND MASTER.
YOU CAN'T COMPREHEND THAT THE AGE OF MAN IS JUST A TRANSIENT FLICKER OF LIGHT...
...AND THAT SOON, VERY SOON...
...THE TIDE OF DARKNESS WILL RISE AGAIN...

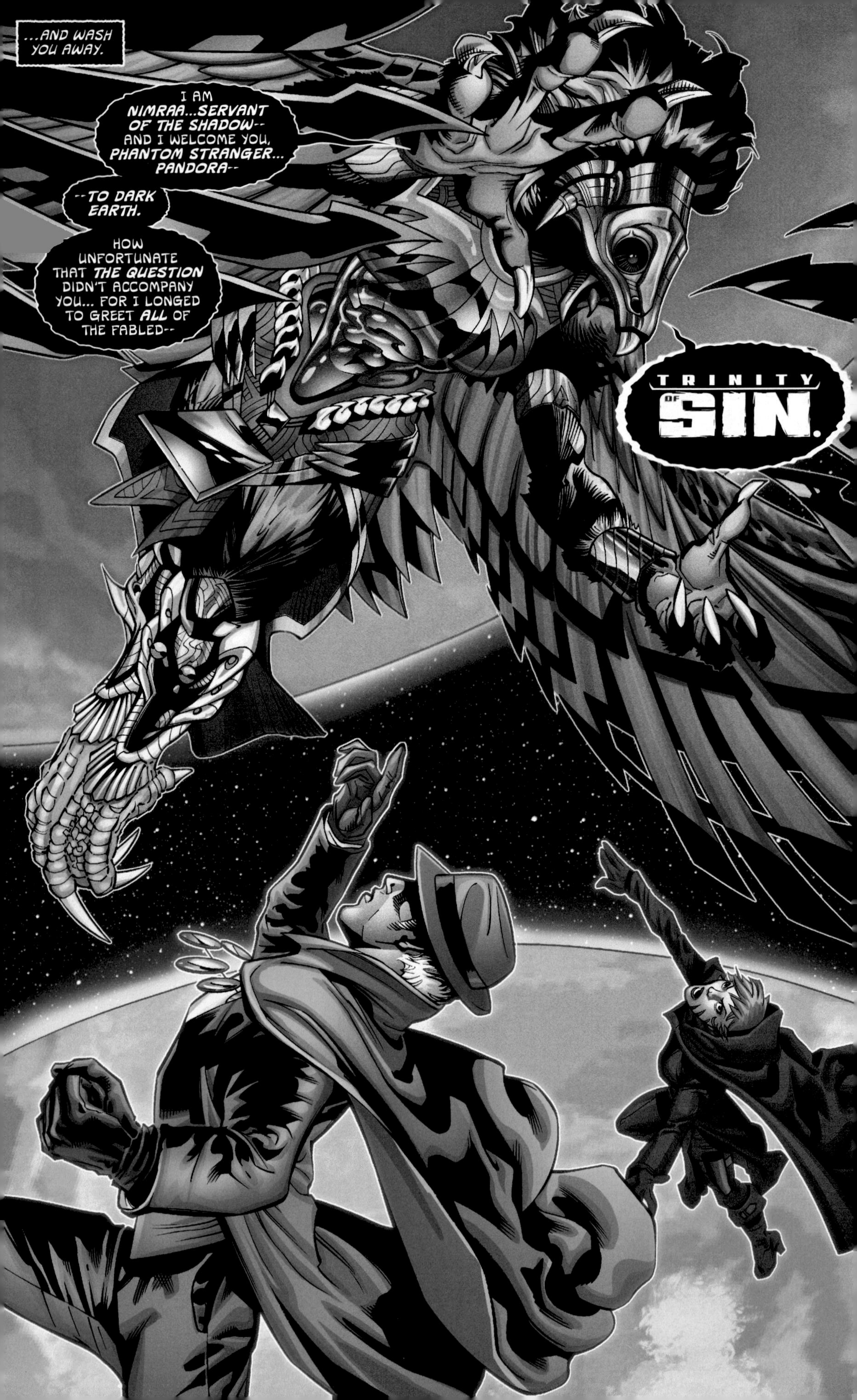
...AND WASH YOU AWAY.
I AM NIMRAA...SERVANT OF THE SHADOW-- AND I WELCOME YOU, PHANTOM STRANGER... PANDORA--
--TO DARK EARTH.
HOW UNFORTUNATE THAT THE QUESTION DIDN'T ACCOMPANY YOU... FOR I LONGED TO GREET ALL OF THE FABLED--
TRINITY OF SIN.

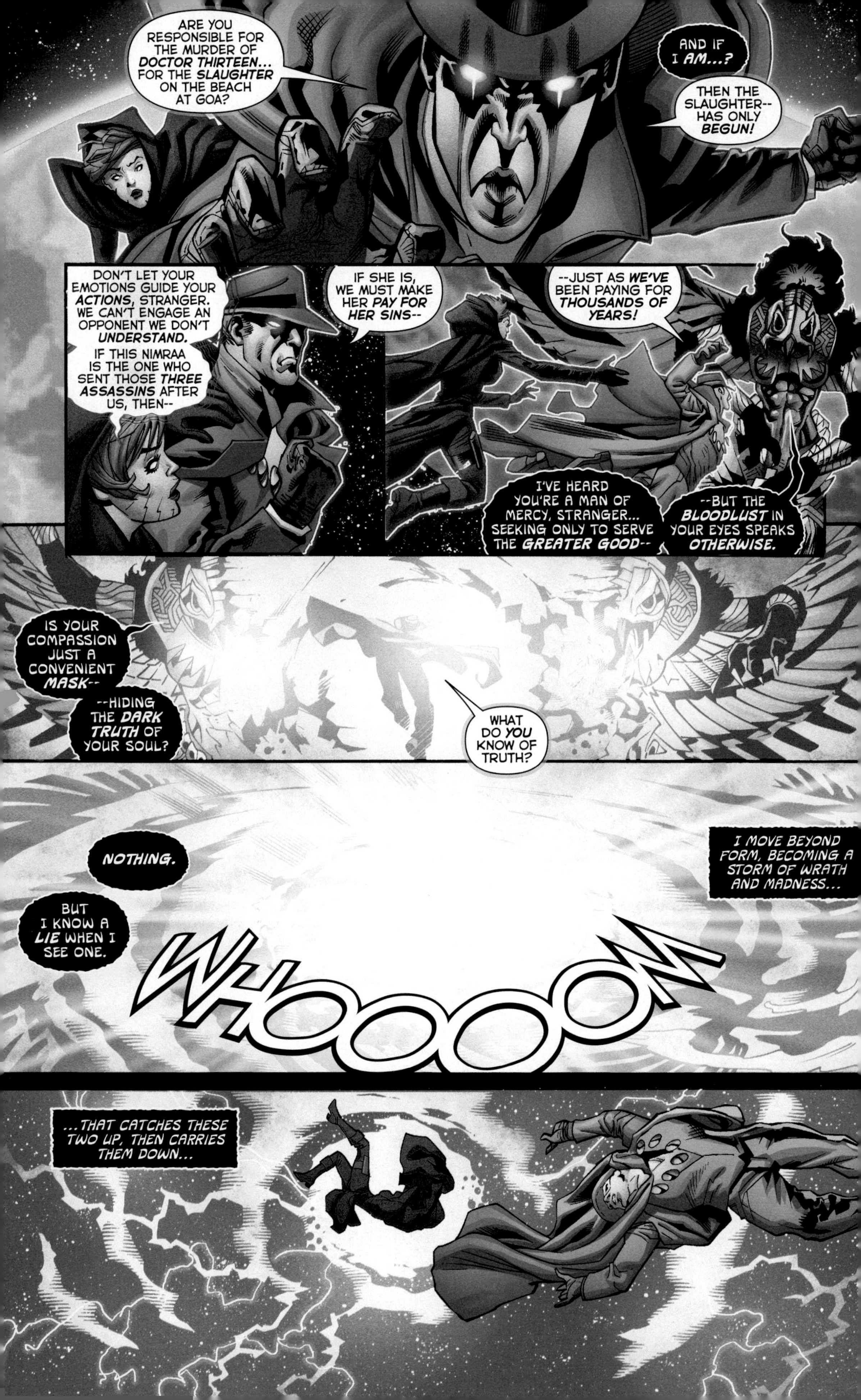
ARE YOU RESPONSIBLE FOR THE MURDER OF *DOCTOR THIRTEEN...* FOR THE *SLAUGHTER* ON THE BEACH AT GOA?
AND IF I *AM...?*
THEN THE SLAUGHTER--HAS ONLY *BEGUN!*
DON'T LET YOUR EMOTIONS GUIDE YOUR *ACTIONS,* STRANGER. WE CAN'T ENGAGE AN OPPONENT WE DON'T *UNDERSTAND.*
IF THIS NIMRAA IS THE ONE WHO SENT THOSE *THREE ASSASSINS* AFTER US, THEN--
IF SHE IS, WE MUST MAKE HER *PAY FOR HER SINS--*
--JUST AS *WE'VE* BEEN PAYING FOR *THOUSANDS OF YEARS!*
I'VE HEARD YOU'RE A MAN OF MERCY, STRANGER... SEEKING ONLY TO SERVE THE *GREATER GOOD--*
--BUT THE *BLOODLUST* IN YOUR EYES SPEAKS *OTHERWISE.*
IS YOUR COMPASSION JUST A CONVENIENT *MASK--*
--HIDING THE *DARK TRUTH* OF YOUR SOUL?
WHAT DO *YOU* KNOW OF TRUTH?
NOTHING.
BUT I KNOW A *LIE* WHEN I SEE ONE.
I MOVE BEYOND FORM, BECOMING A STORM OF WRATH AND MADNESS...
WHOOOOOM
...THAT CATCHES THESE TWO UP, THEN CARRIES THEM DOWN...

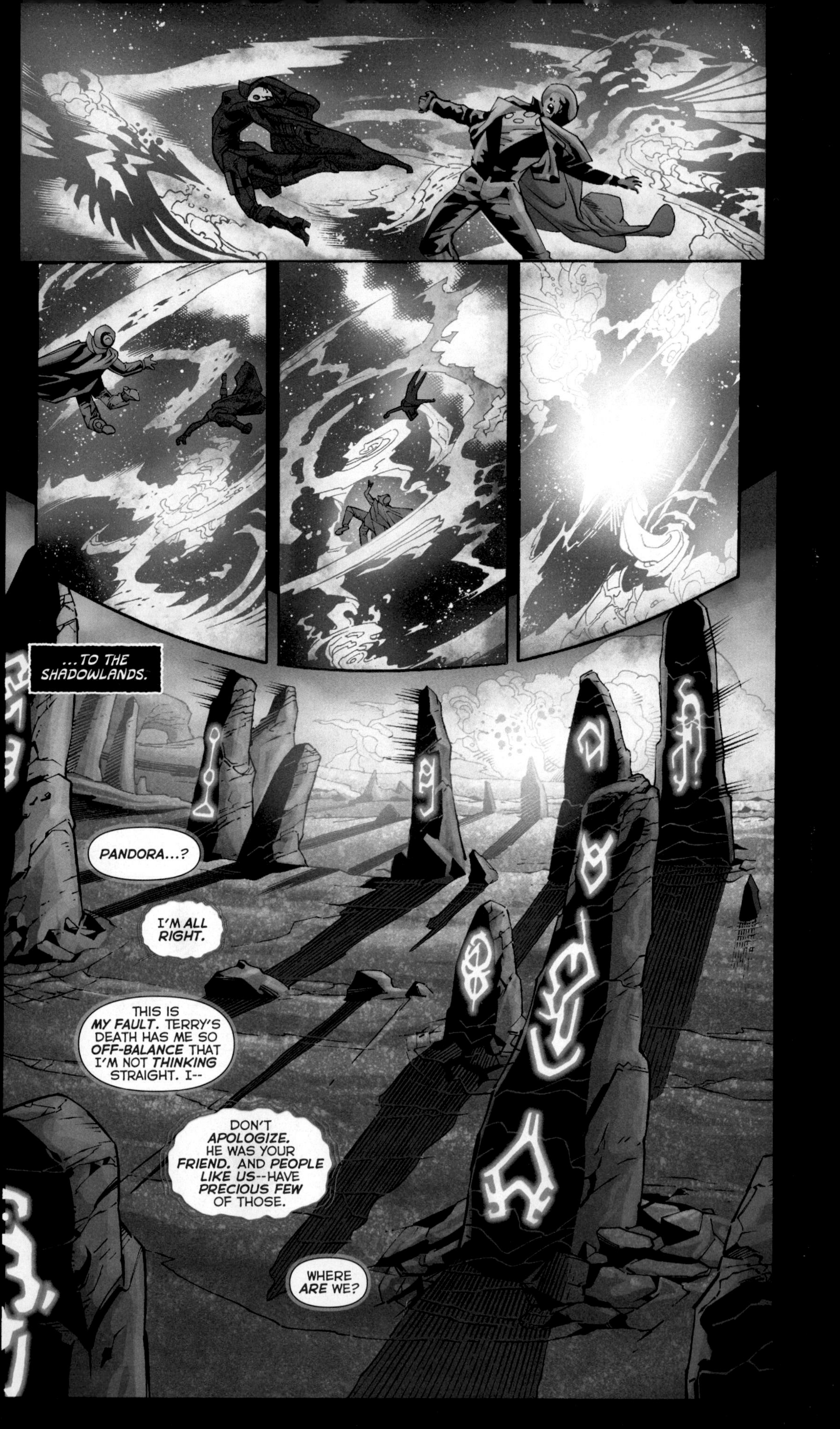
...TO THE SHADOWLANDS.
PANDORA...?
I'M ALL RIGHT.
THIS IS MY FAULT. TERRY'S DEATH HAS ME SO OFF-BALANCE THAT I'M NOT THINKING STRAIGHT. I--
DON'T APOLOGIZE. HE WAS YOUR FRIEND. AND PEOPLE LIKE US--HAVE PRECIOUS FEW OF THOSE.
WHERE ARE WE?

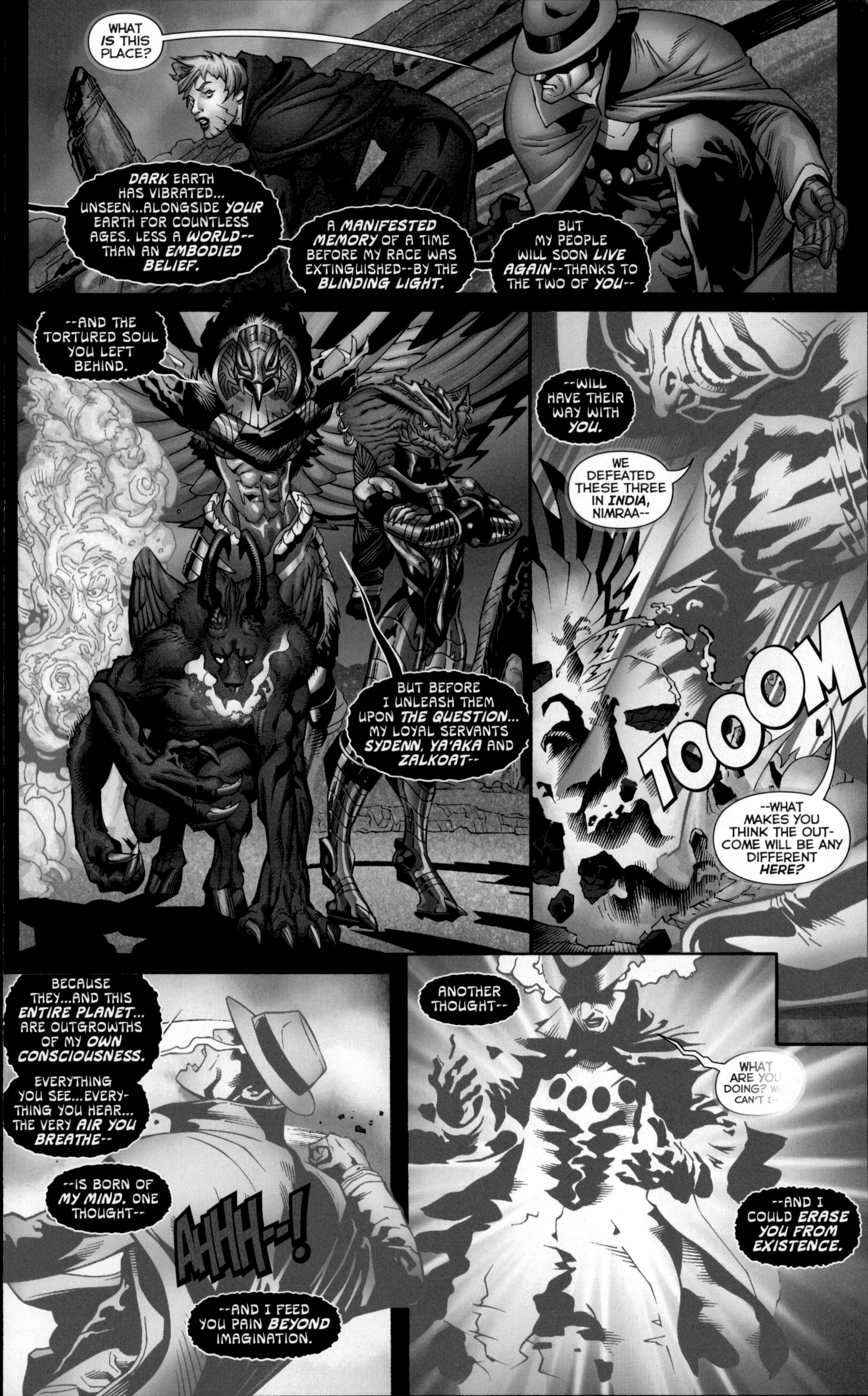
WHAT IS THIS PLACE?
DARK EARTH HAS VIBRATED... UNSEEN...ALONGSIDE YOUR EARTH FOR COUNTLESS AGES. LESS A WORLD-- THAN AN EMBODIED BELIEF.
A MANIFESTED MEMORY OF A TIME BEFORE MY RACE WAS EXTINGUISHED--BY THE BLINDING LIGHT.
BUT MY PEOPLE WILL SOON LIVE AGAIN--THANKS TO THE TWO OF YOU--
--AND THE TORTURED SOUL YOU LEFT BEHIND.
BUT BEFORE I UNLEASH THEM UPON THE QUESTION... MY LOYAL SERVANTS SYDENN, YA'AKA AND ZALKOAT--
--WILL HAVE THEIR WAY WITH YOU.
WE DEFEATED THESE THREE IN INDIA, NIMRAA--
TOOOM
--WHAT MAKES YOU THINK THE OUT-COME WILL BE ANY DIFFERENT HERE?
BECAUSE THEY...AND THIS ENTIRE PLANET... ARE OUTGROWTHS OF MY OWN CONSCIOUSNESS.
EVERYTHING YOU SEE...EVERY-THING YOU HEAR... THE VERY AIR YOU BREATHE--
--IS BORN OF MY MIND. ONE THOUGHT--
AHHH--!
--AND I FEED YOU PAIN BEYOND IMAGINATION.
ANOTHER THOUGHT--
WHAT ARE YOU DOING?
--AND I COULD ERASE YOU FROM EXISTENCE.

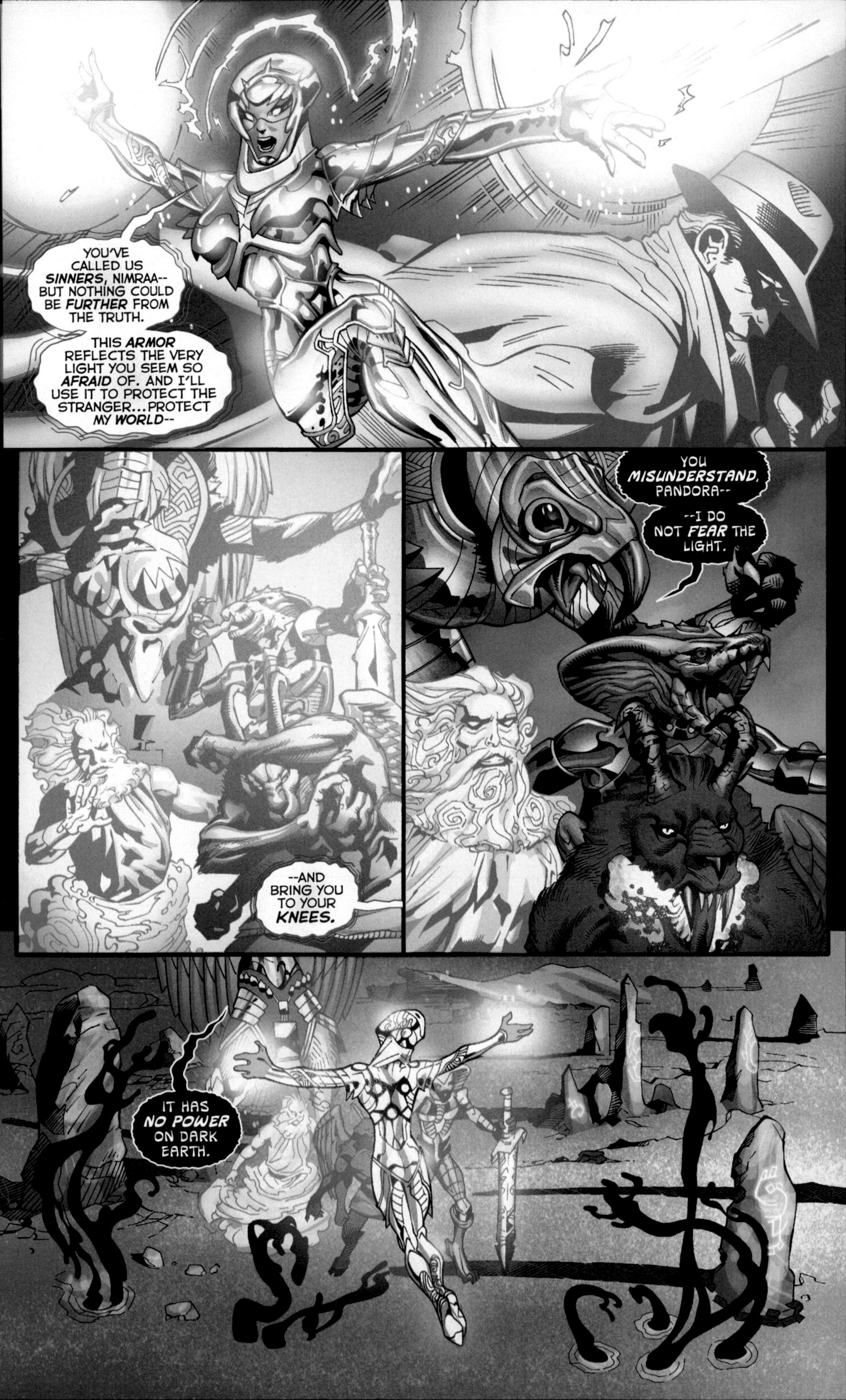
YOU'VE CALLED US SINNERS, NIMRAA-- BUT NOTHING COULD BE FURTHER FROM THE TRUTH.
THIS ARMOR REFLECTS THE VERY LIGHT YOU SEEM SO AFRAID OF. AND I'LL USE IT TO PROTECT THE STRANGER...PROTECT MY WORLD--
--AND BRING YOU TO YOUR KNEES.
YOU MISUNDERSTAND, PANDORA--
--I DO NOT FEAR THE LIGHT.
IT HAS NO POWER ON DARK EARTH.

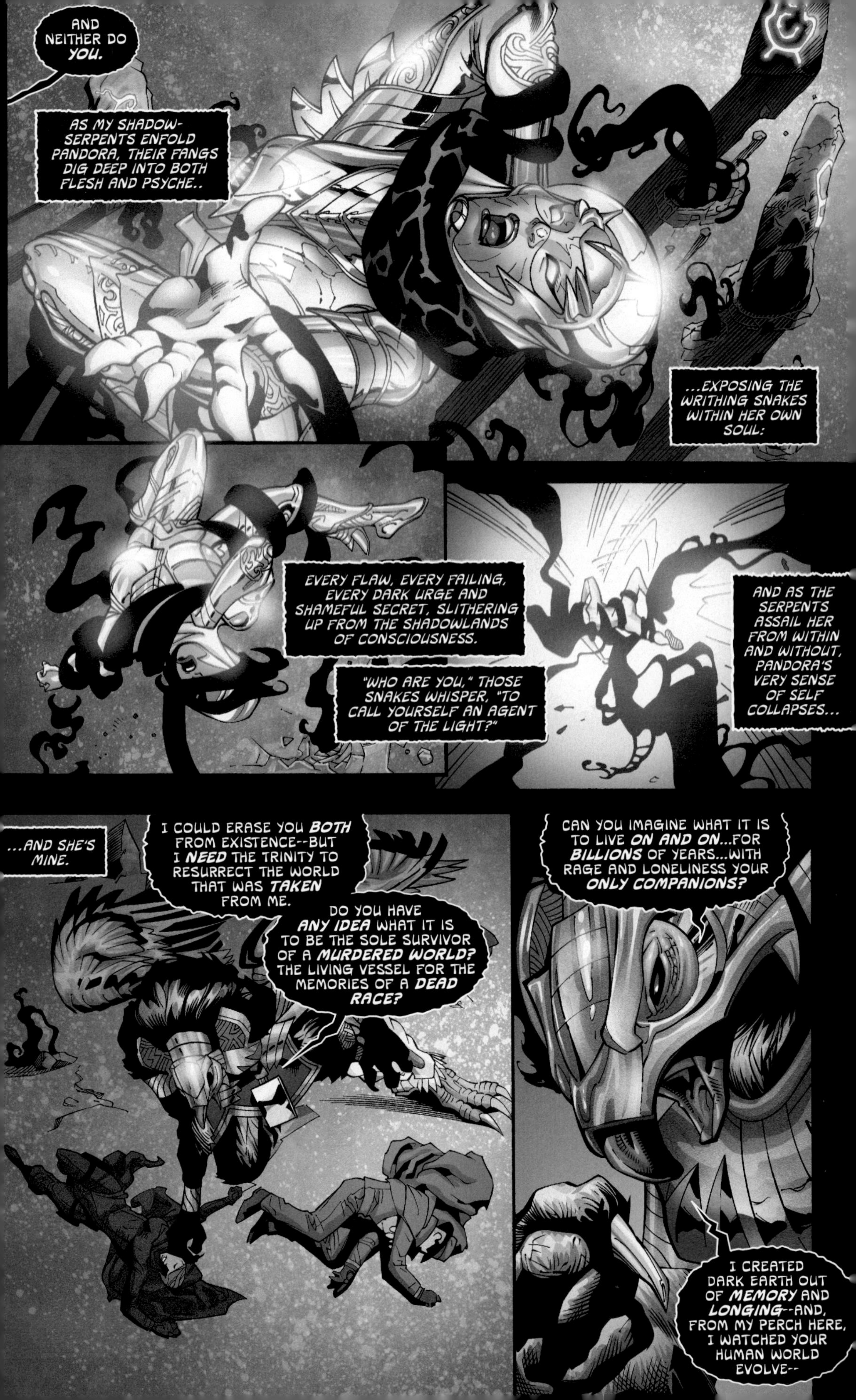
AND NEITHER DO YOU.
AS MY SHADOW-SERPENTS ENFOLD PANDORA, THEIR FANGS DIG DEEP INTO BOTH FLESH AND PSYCHE..
...EXPOSING THE WRITHING SNAKES WITHIN HER OWN SOUL:
EVERY FLAW, EVERY FAILING, EVERY DARK URGE AND SHAMEFUL SECRET, SLITHERING UP FROM THE SHADOWLANDS OF CONSCIOUSNESS.
"WHO ARE YOU," THOSE SNAKES WHISPER, "TO CALL YOURSELF AN AGENT OF THE LIGHT?"
AND AS THE SERPENTS ASSAIL HER FROM WITHIN AND WITHOUT, PANDORA'S VERY SENSE OF SELF COLLAPSES...
...AND SHE'S MINE.
I COULD ERASE YOU BOTH FROM EXISTENCE--BUT I NEED THE TRINITY TO RESURRECT THE WORLD THAT WAS TAKEN FROM ME.
DO YOU HAVE ANY IDEA WHAT IT IS TO BE THE SOLE SURVIVOR OF A MURDERED WORLD? THE LIVING VESSEL FOR THE MEMORIES OF A DEAD RACE?
CAN YOU IMAGINE WHAT IT IS TO LIVE ON AND ON...FOR BILLIONS OF YEARS...WITH RAGE AND LONELINESS YOUR ONLY COMPANIONS?
I CREATED DARK EARTH OUT OF MEMORY AND LONGING--AND, FROM MY PERCH HERE, I WATCHED YOUR HUMAN WORLD EVOLVE--

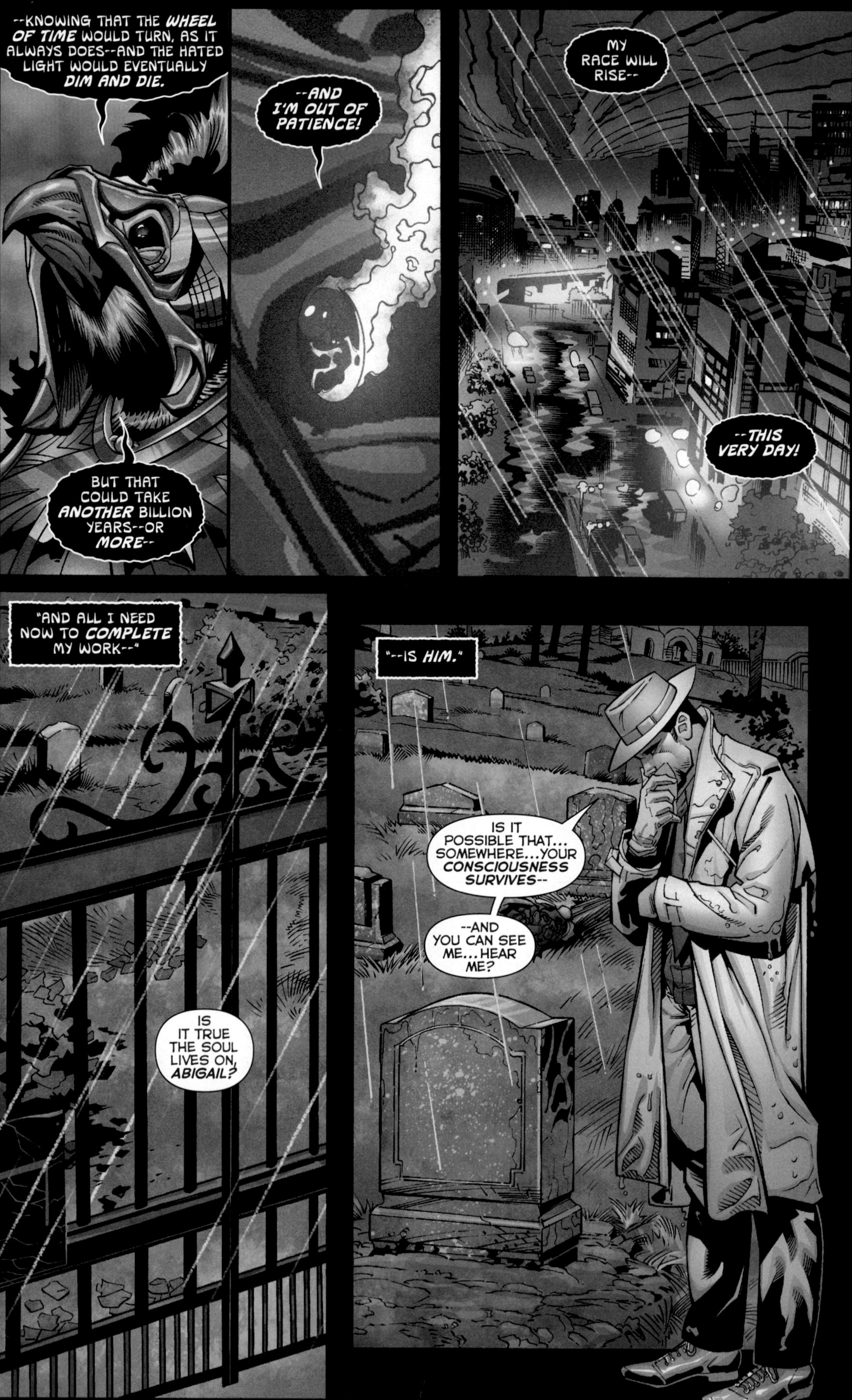
--KNOWING THAT THE WHEEL OF TIME WOULD TURN, AS IT ALWAYS DOES--AND THE HATED LIGHT WOULD EVENTUALLY DIM AND DIE.
BUT THAT COULD TAKE ANOTHER BILLION YEARS--OR MORE--
--AND I'M OUT OF PATIENCE!
MY RACE WILL RISE--
--THIS VERY DAY!
"AND ALL I NEED NOW TO COMPLETE MY WORK--"
"--IS HIM."
IS IT POSSIBLE THAT... SOMEWHERE...YOUR CONSCIOUSNESS SURVIVES--
--AND YOU CAN SEE ME...HEAR ME?
IS IT TRUE THE SOUL LIVES ON, ABIGAIL?

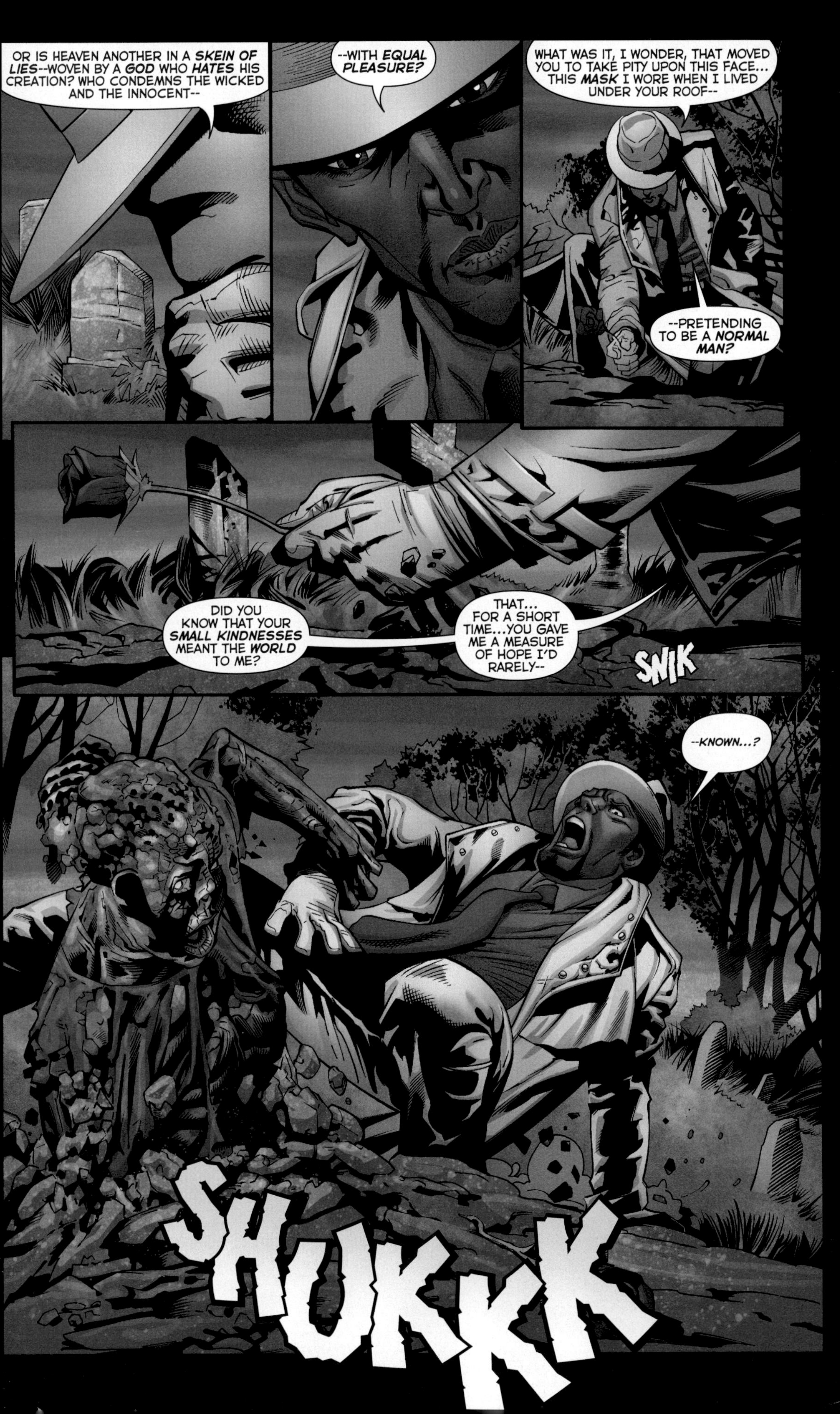
OR IS HEAVEN ANOTHER IN A SKEIN OF LIES--WOVEN BY A GOD WHO HATES HIS CREATION? WHO CONDEMNS THE WICKED AND THE INNOCENT--
--WITH EQUAL PLEASURE?
WHAT WAS IT, I WONDER, THAT MOVED YOU TO TAKE PITY UPON THIS FACE... THIS MASK I WORE WHEN I LIVED UNDER YOUR ROOF--
--PRETENDING TO BE A NORMAL MAN?
DID YOU KNOW THAT YOUR SMALL KINDNESSES MEANT THE WORLD TO ME?
THAT... FOR A SHORT TIME...YOU GAVE ME A MEASURE OF HOPE I'D RARELY--
SNIK
--KNOWN...?
SHUKKK

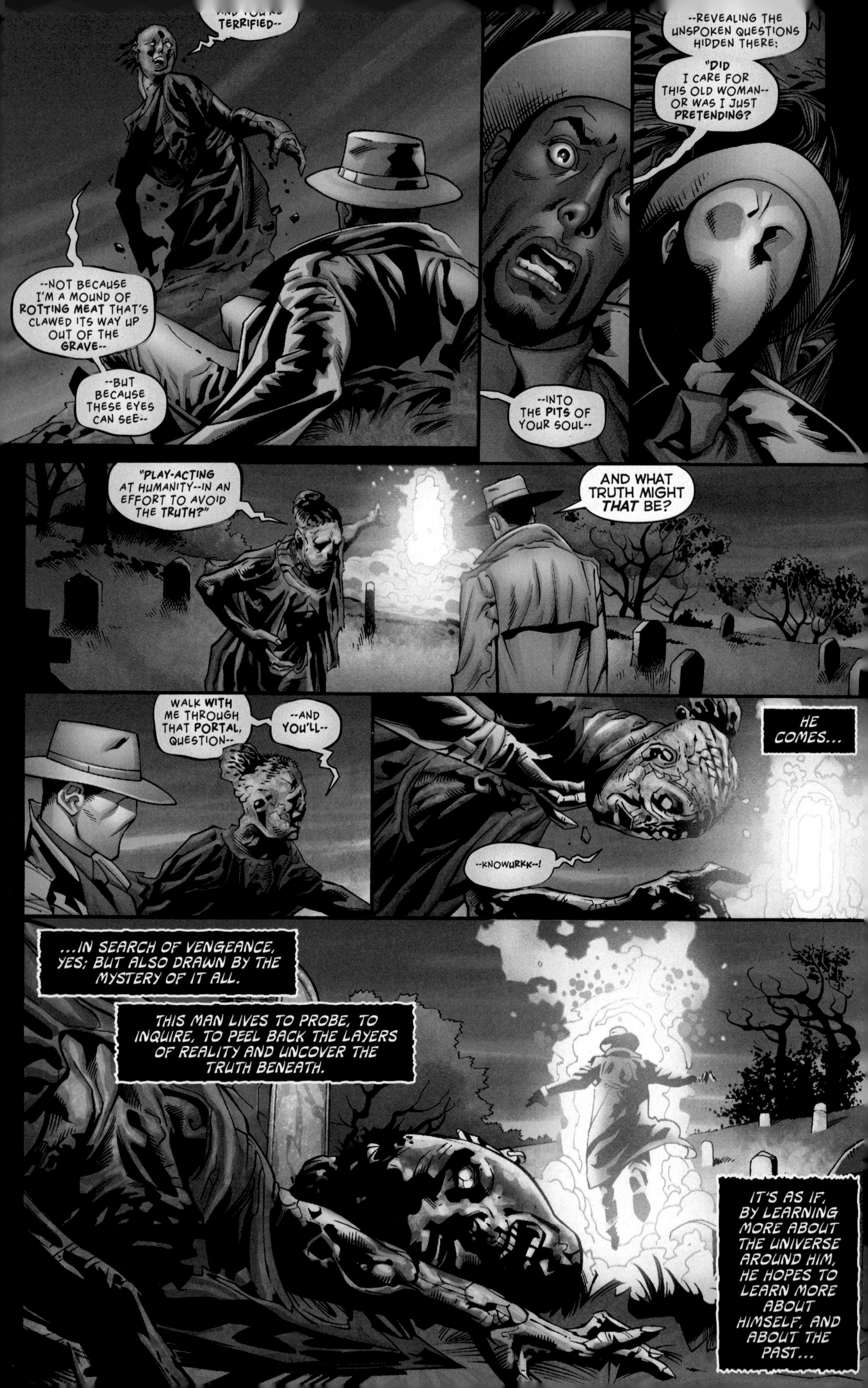

TERRIFIED--
--NOT BECAUSE I'M A MOUND OF ROTTING MEAT THAT'S CLAWED ITS WAY UP OUT OF THE GRAVE--
--BUT BECAUSE THESE EYES CAN SEE--
--INTO THE PITS OF YOUR SOUL--
--REVEALING THE UNSPOKEN QUESTIONS HIDDEN THERE:
"DID I CARE FOR THIS OLD WOMAN--OR WAS I JUST PRETENDING?
"PLAY-ACTING AT HUMANITY--IN AN EFFORT TO AVOID THE TRUTH?"
AND WHAT TRUTH MIGHT THAT BE?
WALK WITH ME THROUGH THAT PORTAL, QUESTION--
--AND YOU'LL--
--KNOWURKK--!
HE COMES...
...IN SEARCH OF VENGEANCE, YES; BUT ALSO DRAWN BY THE MYSTERY OF IT ALL.
THIS MAN LIVES TO PROBE, TO INQUIRE, TO PEEL BACK THE LAYERS OF REALITY AND UNCOVER THE TRUTH BENEATH.
IT'S AS IF, BY LEARNING MORE ABOUT THE UNIVERSE AROUND HIM, HE HOPES TO LEARN MORE ABOUT HIMSELF, AND ABOUT THE PAST...

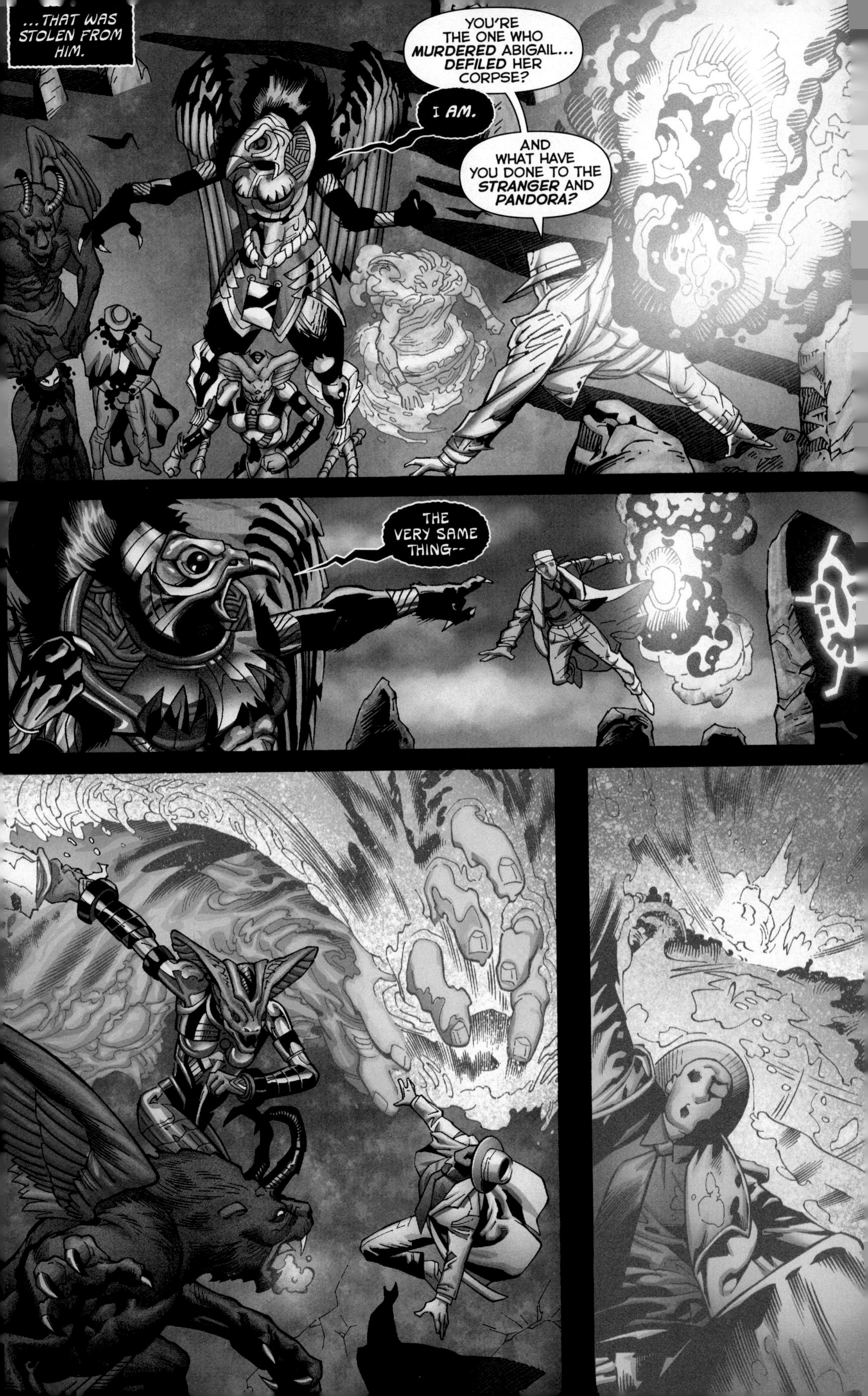
...THAT WAS STOLEN FROM HIM.
YOU'RE THE ONE WHO MURDERED ABIGAIL... DEFILED HER CORPSE?
I AM.
AND WHAT HAVE YOU DONE TO THE STRANGER AND PANDORA?
THE VERY SAME THING--

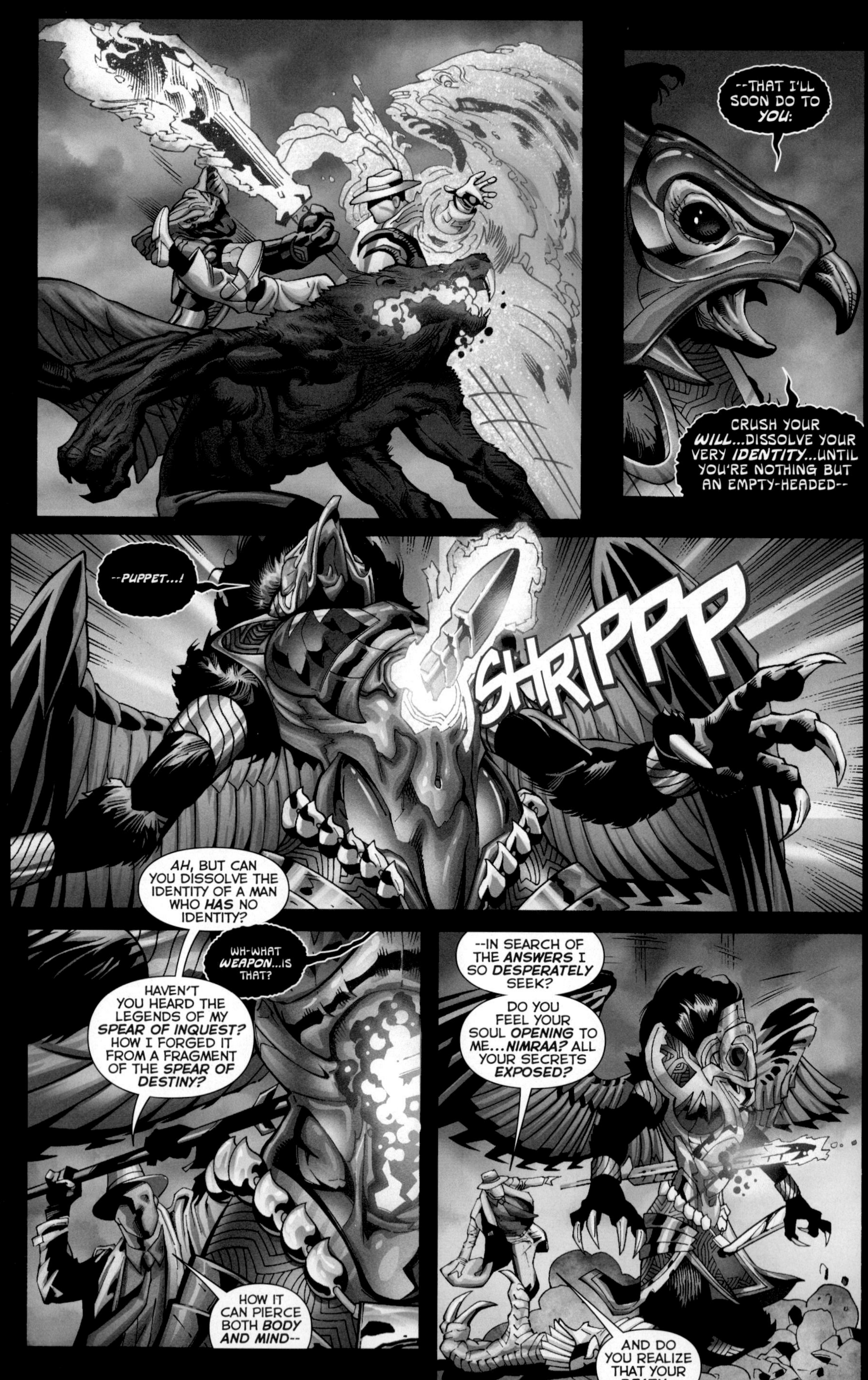
--THAT I'LL SOON DO TO YOU:
CRUSH YOUR WILL...DISSOLVE YOUR VERY IDENTITY...UNTIL YOU'RE NOTHING BUT AN EMPTY-HEADED--
--PUPPET...!
SHRIPPP
AH, BUT CAN YOU DISSOLVE THE IDENTITY OF A MAN WHO HAS NO IDENTITY?
WH-WHAT WEAPON...IS THAT?
HAVEN'T YOU HEARD THE LEGENDS OF MY SPEAR OF INQUEST? HOW I FORGED IT FROM A FRAGMENT OF THE SPEAR OF DESTINY?
HOW IT CAN PIERCE BOTH BODY AND MIND--
--IN SEARCH OF THE ANSWERS I SO DESPERATELY SEEK?
DO YOU FEEL YOUR SOUL OPENING TO ME...NIMRAA? ALL YOUR SECRETS EXPOSED?
AND DO YOU REALIZE THAT YOUR DEATH--

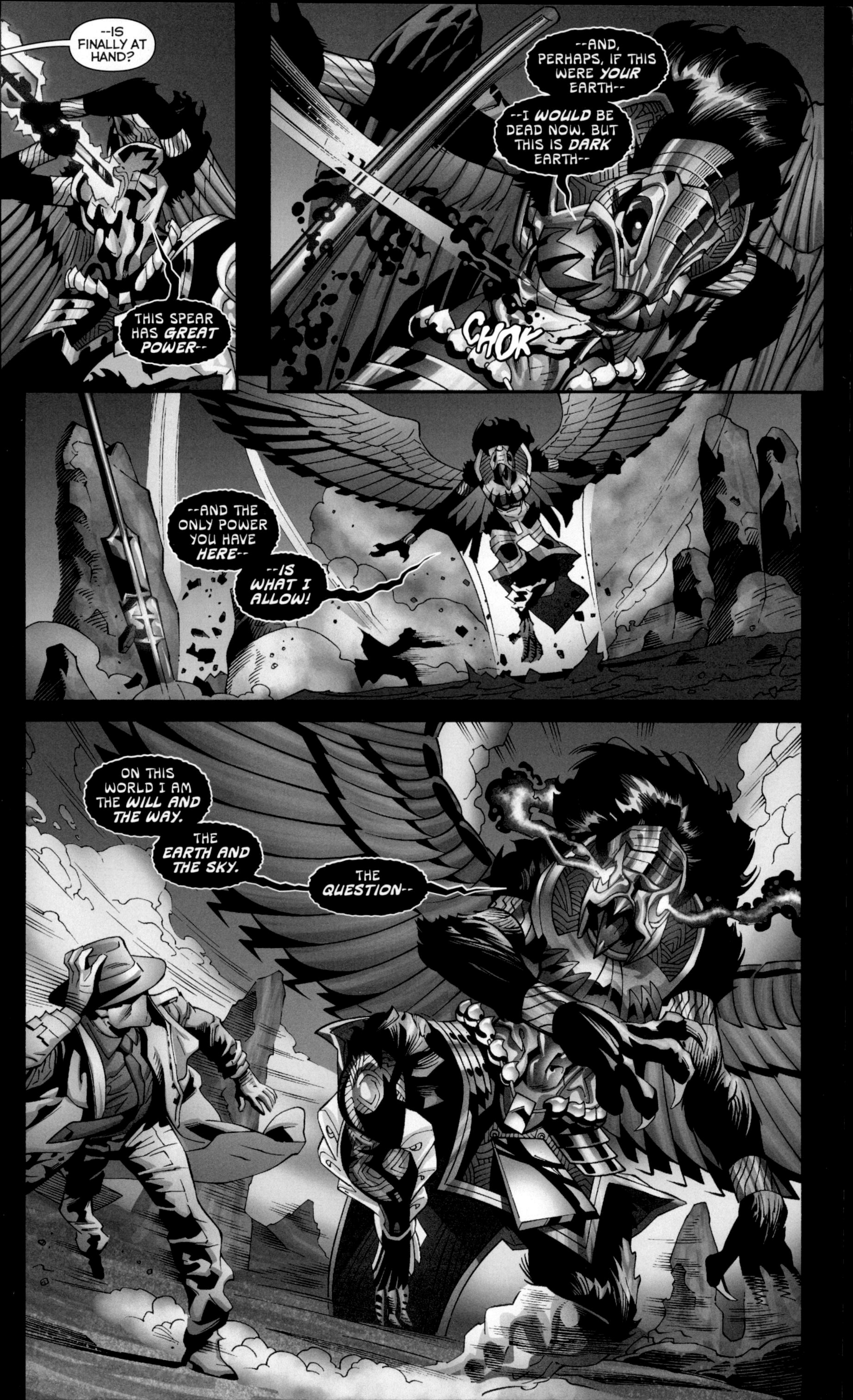
--IS FINALLY AT HAND?
THIS SPEAR HAS GREAT POWER--
--AND, PERHAPS, IF THIS WERE YOUR EARTH--
--I WOULD BE DEAD NOW. BUT THIS IS DARK EARTH--
CHOK
--AND THE ONLY POWER YOU HAVE HERE--
--IS WHAT I ALLOW!
ON THIS WORLD I AM THE WILL AND THE WAY.
THE EARTH AND THE SKY.
THE QUESTION--

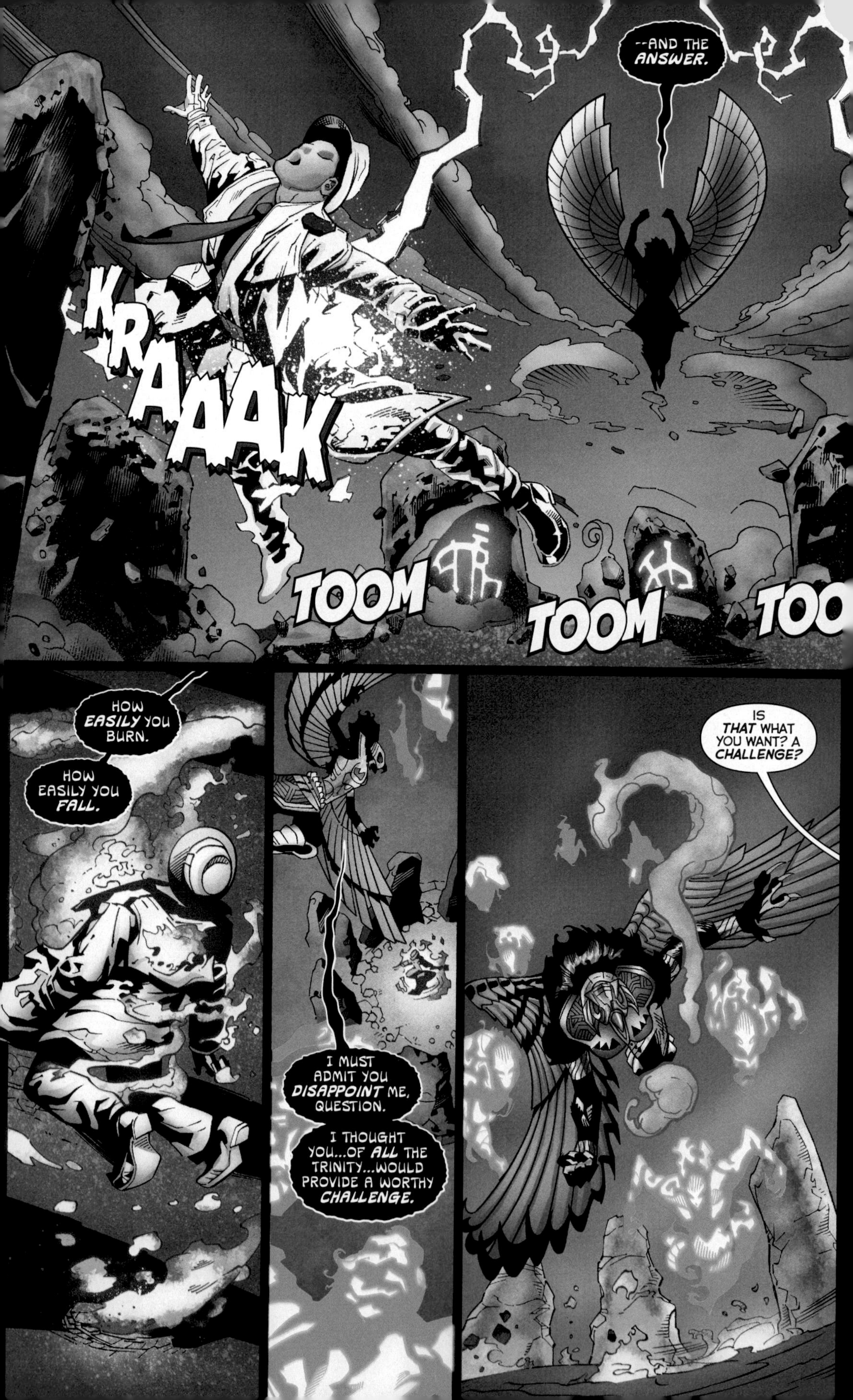
--AND THE ANSWER.
KRRAAAK
TOOM
TOOM
TOO
HOW EASILY YOU BURN.
HOW EASILY YOU FALL.
I MUST ADMIT YOU DISAPPOINT ME, QUESTION.
I THOUGHT YOU...OF ALL THE TRINITY...WOULD PROVIDE A WORTHY CHALLENGE.
IS THAT WHAT YOU WANT? A CHALLENGE?

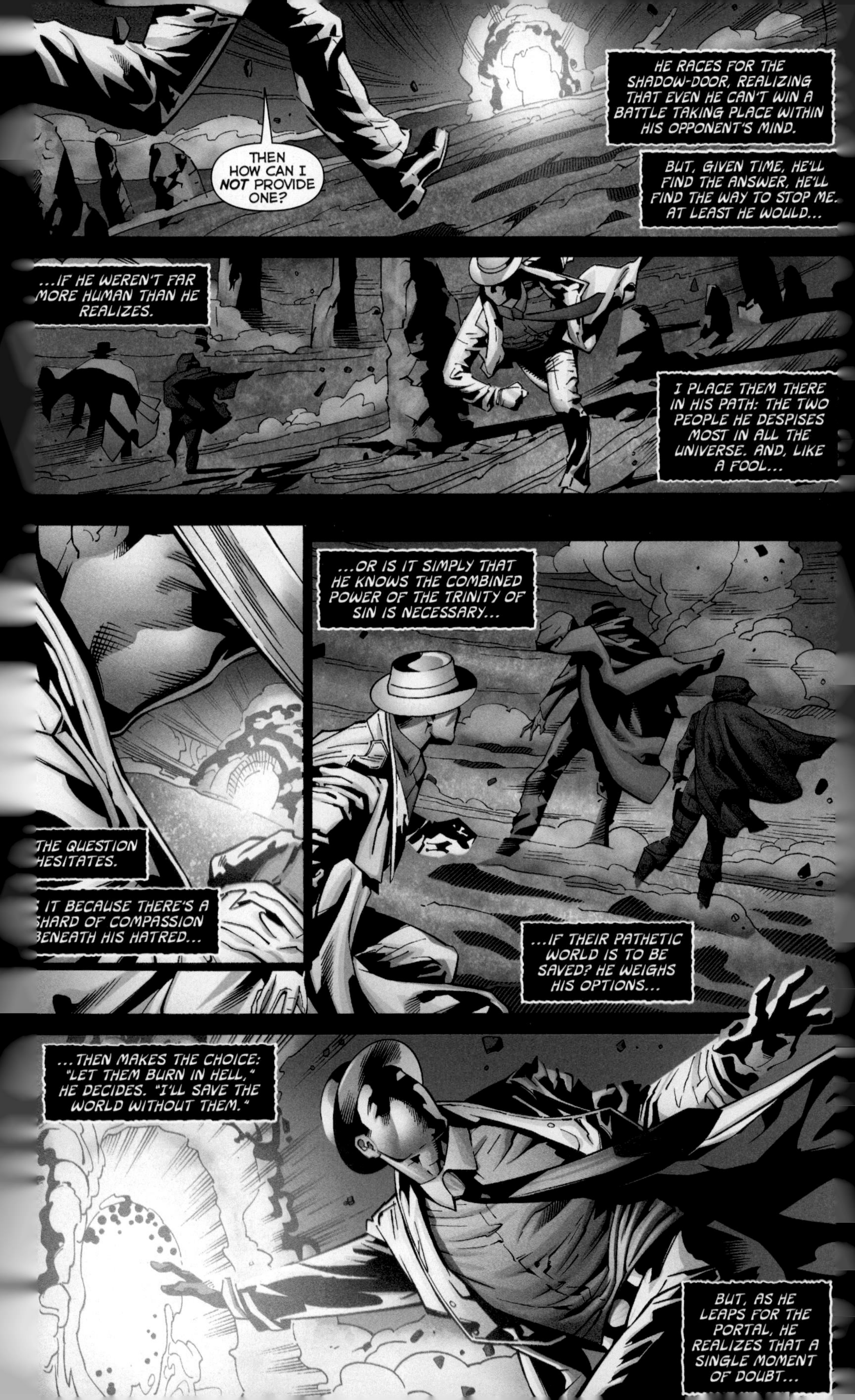
THEN HOW CAN I NOT PROVIDE ONE?
HE RACES FOR THE SHADOW-DOOR, REALIZING THAT EVEN HE CAN'T WIN A BATTLE TAKING PLACE WITHIN HIS OPPONENT'S MIND.
BUT, GIVEN TIME, HE'LL FIND THE ANSWER, HE'LL FIND THE WAY TO STOP ME. AT LEAST HE WOULD...
...IF HE WEREN'T FAR MORE HUMAN THAN HE REALIZES.
I PLACE THEM THERE IN HIS PATH: THE TWO PEOPLE HE DESPISES MOST IN ALL THE UNIVERSE. AND, LIKE A FOOL...
THE QUESTION HESITATES.
IT BECAUSE THERE'S A HARD OF COMPASSION ENEATH HIS HATRED...
...OR IS IT SIMPLY THAT HE KNOWS THE COMBINED POWER OF THE TRINITY OF SIN IS NECESSARY...
...IF THEIR PATHETIC WORLD IS TO BE SAVED? HE WEIGHS HIS OPTIONS...
...THEN MAKES THE CHOICE: "LET THEM BURN IN HELL," HE DECIDES. "I'LL SAVE THE WORLD WITHOUT THEM."
BUT, AS HE LEAPS FOR THE PORTAL, HE REALIZES THAT A SINGLE MOMENT OF DOUBT...

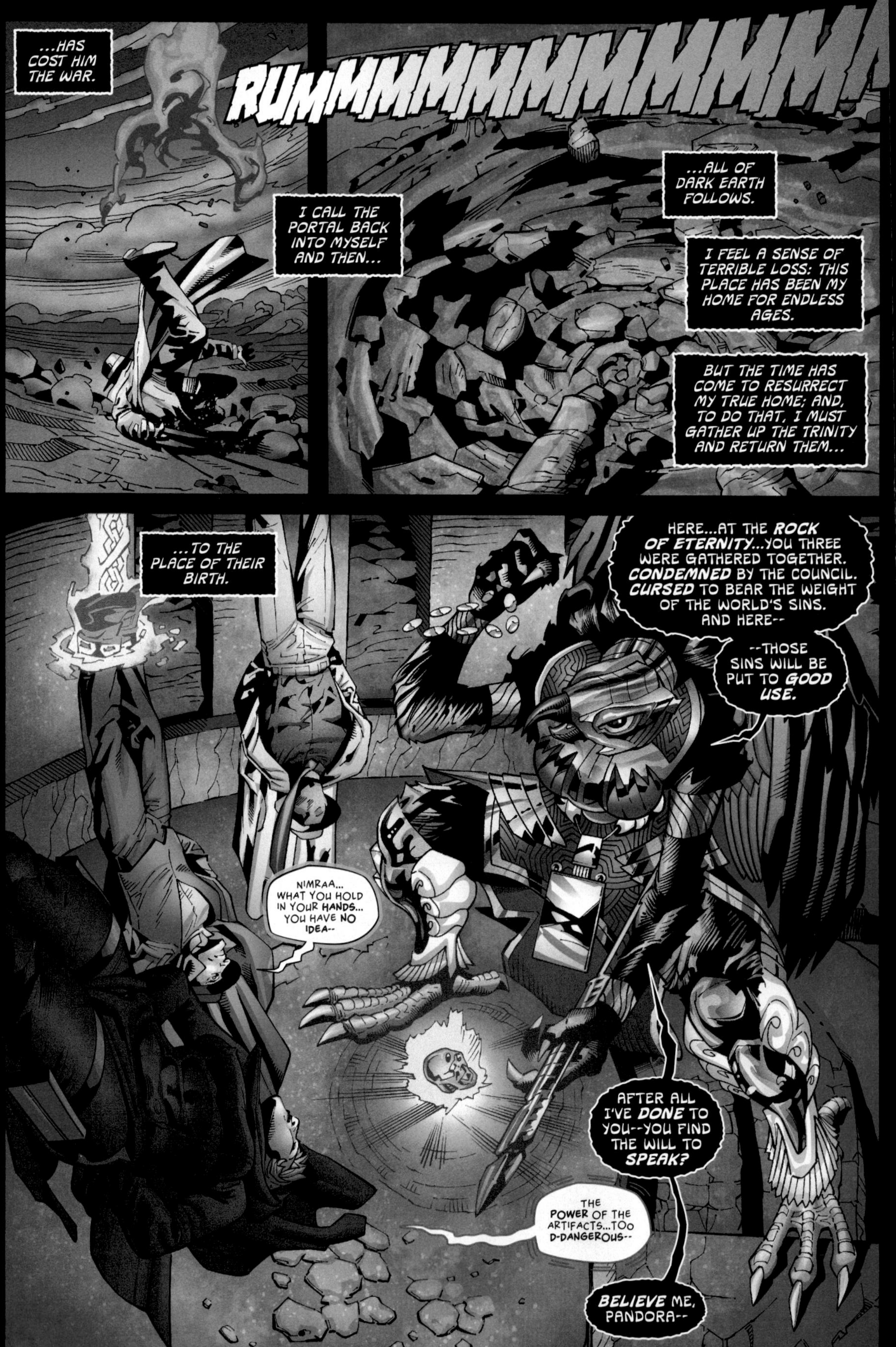
...HAS COST HIM THE WAR.
RUMMMMMMMMMMMMMM
I CALL THE PORTAL BACK INTO MYSELF AND THEN...
...ALL OF DARK EARTH FOLLOWS.
I FEEL A SENSE OF TERRIBLE LOSS: THIS PLACE HAS BEEN MY HOME FOR ENDLESS AGES.
BUT THE TIME HAS COME TO RESURRECT MY TRUE HOME; AND, TO DO THAT, I MUST GATHER UP THE TRINITY AND RETURN THEM...
...TO THE PLACE OF THEIR BIRTH.
HERE...AT THE ROCK OF ETERNITY...YOU THREE WERE GATHERED TOGETHER. CONDEMNED BY THE COUNCIL. CURSED TO BEAR THE WEIGHT OF THE WORLD'S SINS. AND HERE--
--THOSE SINS WILL BE PUT TO GOOD USE.
NIMRAA... WHAT YOU HOLD IN YOUR HANDS... YOU HAVE NO IDEA--
AFTER ALL I'VE DONE TO YOU--YOU FIND THE WILL TO SPEAK?
THE POWER OF THE ARTIFACTS...TOO D-DANGEROUS--
BELIEVE ME, PANDORA--

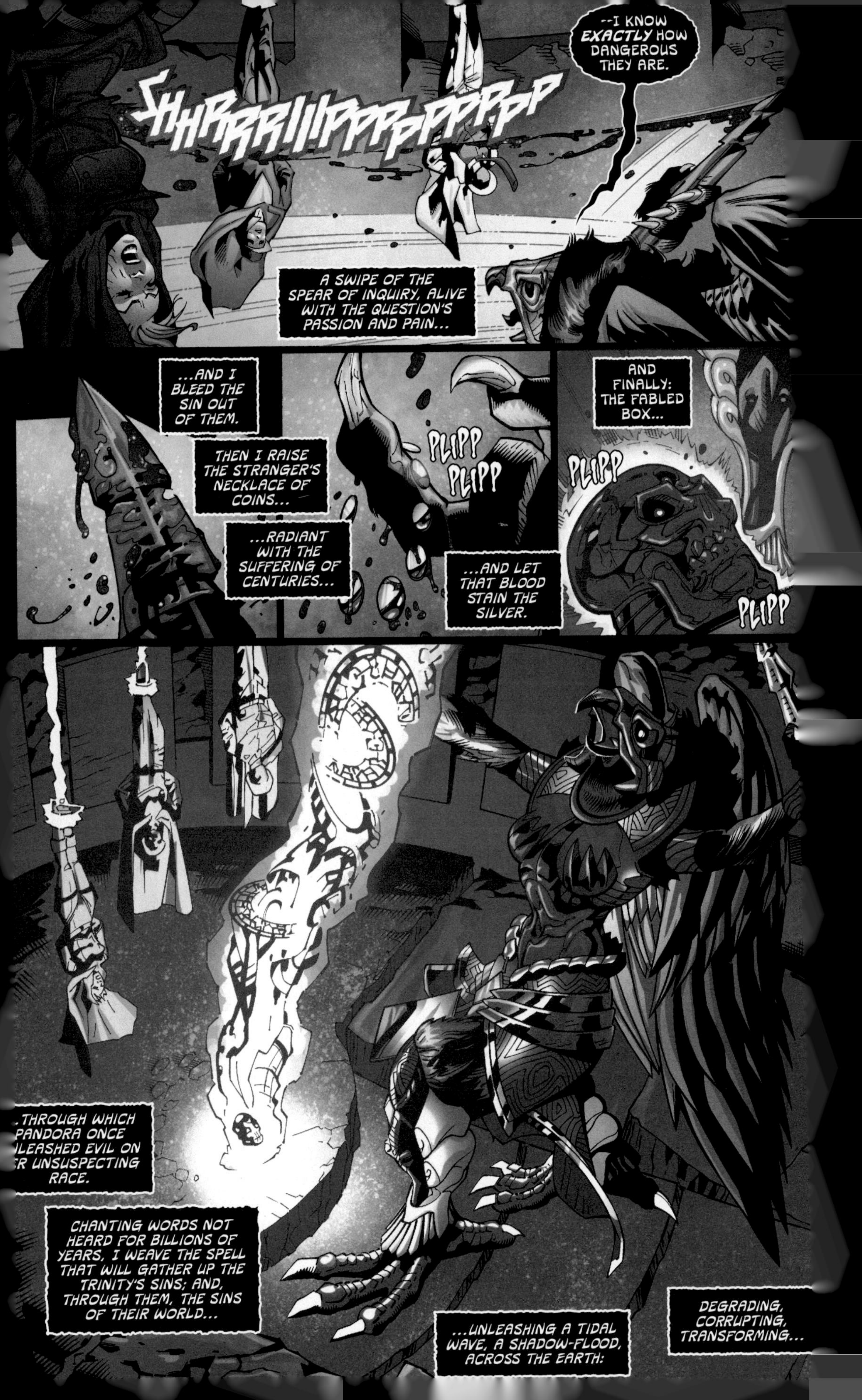
--I KNOW EXACTLY HOW DANGEROUS THEY ARE.
SHHRRRIIIIPPPPPPPPP
A SWIPE OF THE SPEAR OF INQUIRY, ALIVE WITH THE QUESTION'S PASSION AND PAIN...
...AND I BLEED THE SIN OUT OF THEM.
THEN I RAISE THE STRANGER'S NECKLACE OF COINS...
...RADIANT WITH THE SUFFERING OF CENTURIES...
PLIPP PLIPP
...AND LET THAT BLOOD STAIN THE SILVER.
AND FINALLY: THE FABLED BOX...
PLIPP
PLIPP
.THROUGH WHICH PANDORA ONCE UNLEASHED EVIL ON ER UNSUSPECTING RACE.
CHANTING WORDS NOT HEARD FOR BILLIONS OF YEARS, I WEAVE THE SPELL THAT WILL GATHER UP THE TRINITY'S SINS; AND, THROUGH THEM, THE SINS OF THEIR WORLD...
...UNLEASHING A TIDAL WAVE, A SHADOW-FLOOD, ACROSS THE EARTH:
DEGRADING, CORRUPTING, TRANSFORMING...

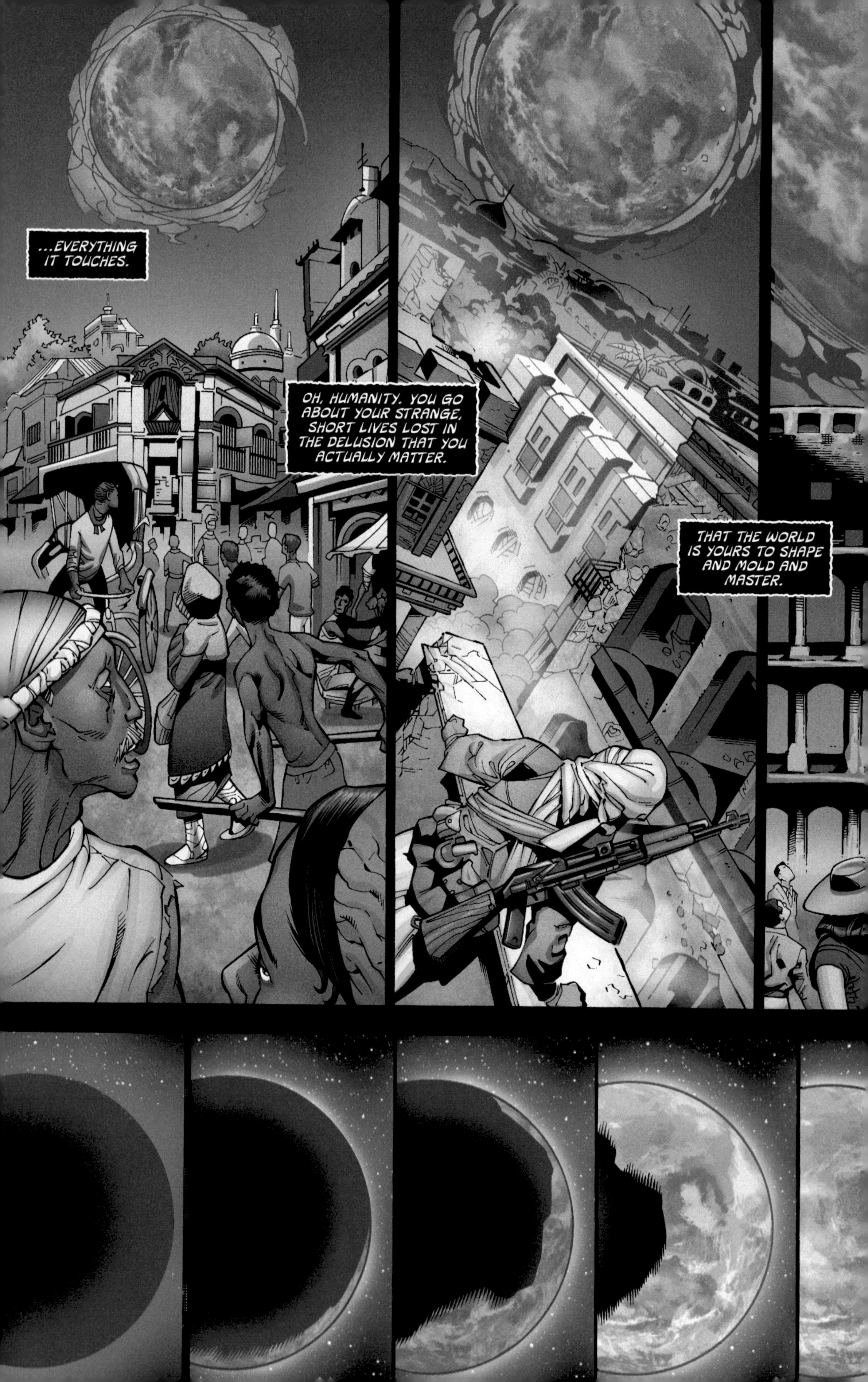
...EVERYTHING IT TOUCHES.
OH, HUMANITY. YOU GO ABOUT YOUR STRANGE, SHORT LIVES LOST IN THE DELUSION THAT YOU ACTUALLY MATTER.
THAT THE WORLD IS YOURS TO SHAPE AND MOLD AND MASTER.

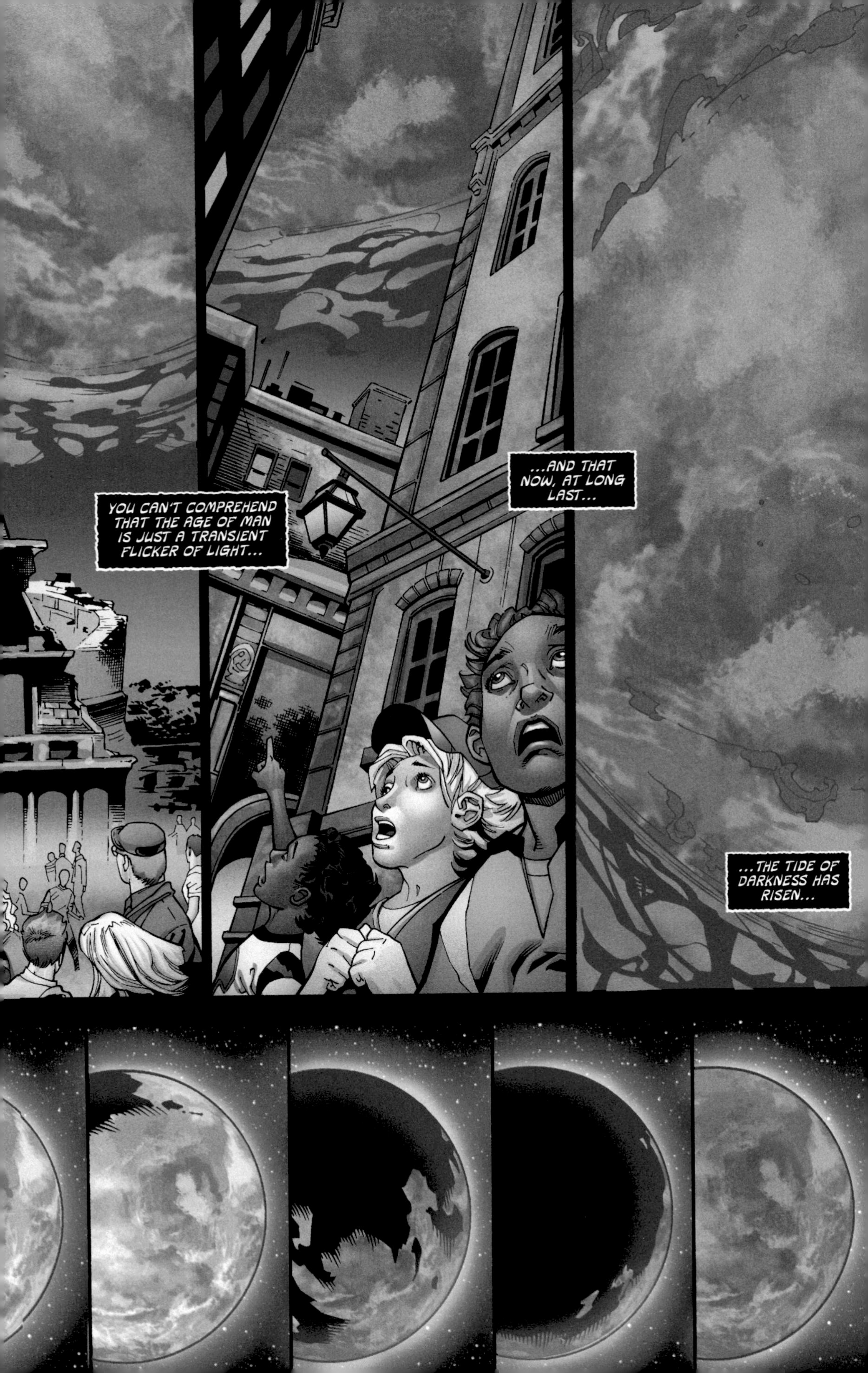
YOU CAN'T COMPREHEND THAT THE AGE OF MAN IS JUST A TRANSIENT FLICKER OF LIGHT...
...AND THAT NOW, AT LONG LAST...
...THE TIDE OF DARKNESS HAS RISEN...

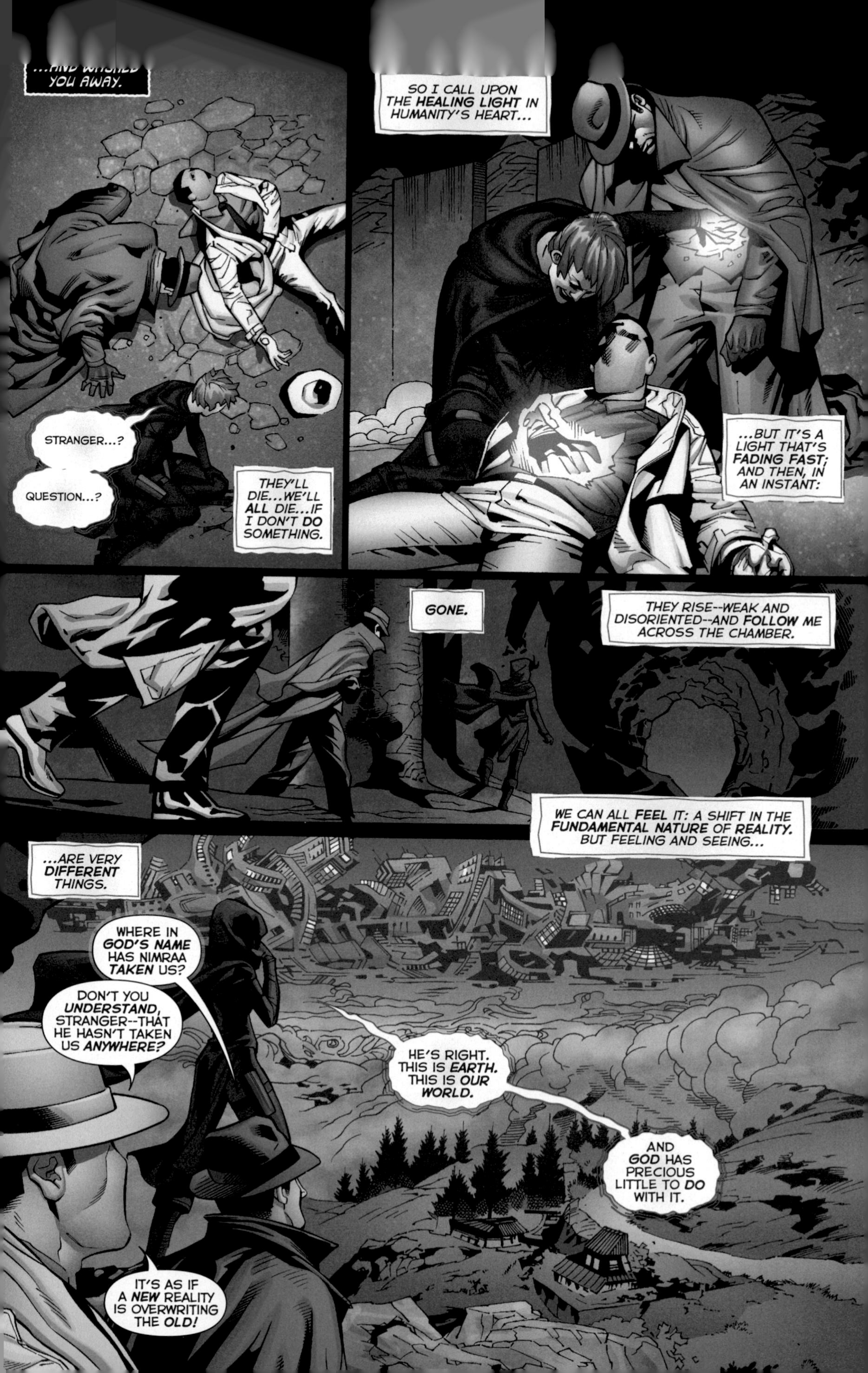
...AND WHISKED YOU AWAY.
STRANGER...?
QUESTION...?
THEY'LL DIE...WE'LL ALL DIE...IF I DON'T DO SOMETHING.
SO I CALL UPON THE HEALING LIGHT IN HUMANITY'S HEART...
...BUT IT'S A LIGHT THAT'S FADING FAST; AND THEN, IN AN INSTANT:
GONE.
THEY RISE--WEAK AND DISORIENTED--AND FOLLOW ME ACROSS THE CHAMBER.
WE CAN ALL FEEL IT: A SHIFT IN THE FUNDAMENTAL NATURE OF REALITY. BUT FEELING AND SEEING...
...ARE VERY DIFFERENT THINGS.
WHERE IN GOD'S NAME HAS NIMRAA TAKEN US?
DON'T YOU UNDERSTAND, STRANGER--THAT HE HASN'T TAKEN US ANYWHERE?
HE'S RIGHT. THIS IS EARTH. THIS IS OUR WORLD.
AND GOD HAS PRECIOUS LITTLE TO DO WITH IT.
IT'S AS IF A NEW REALITY IS OVERWRITING THE OLD!

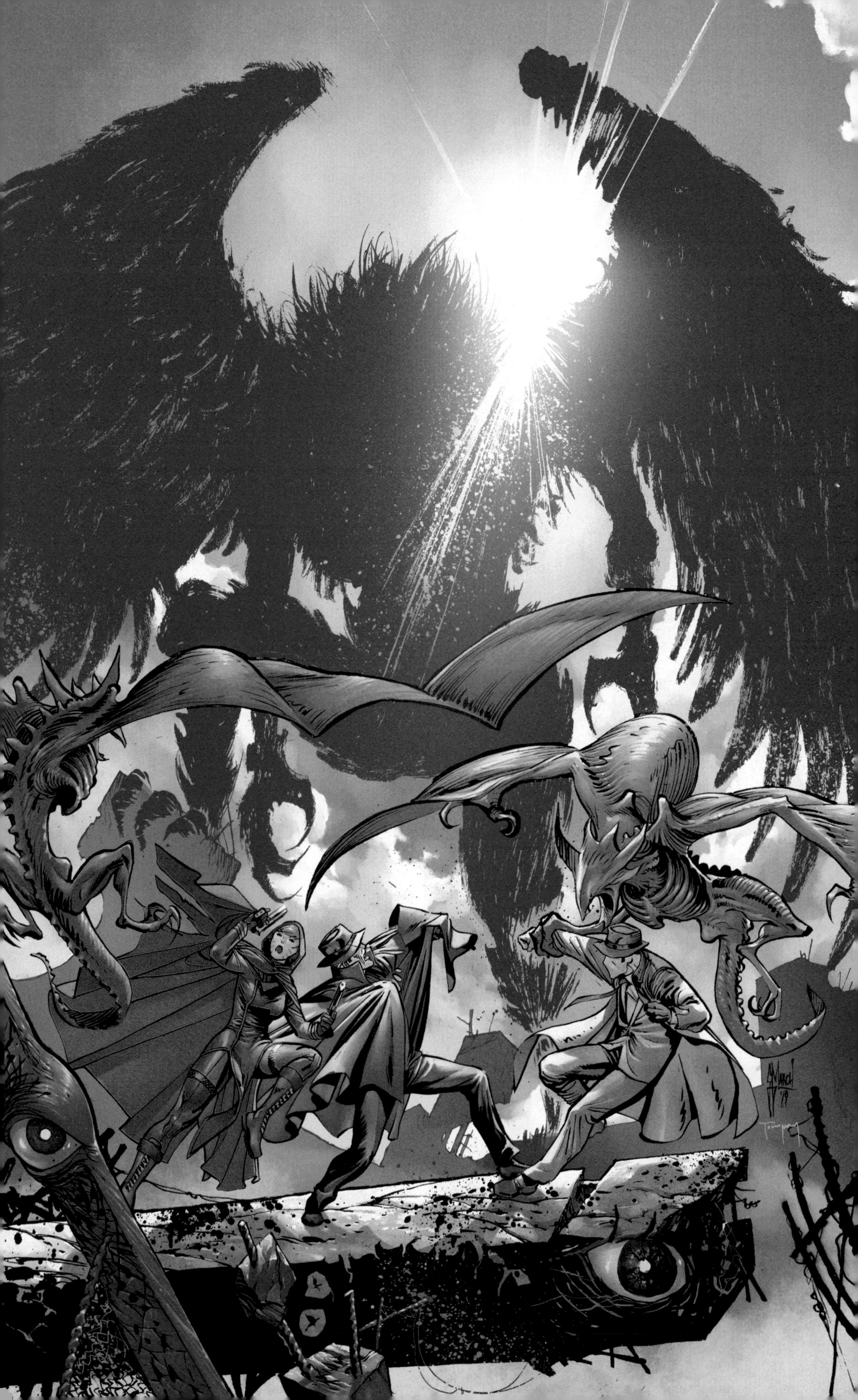

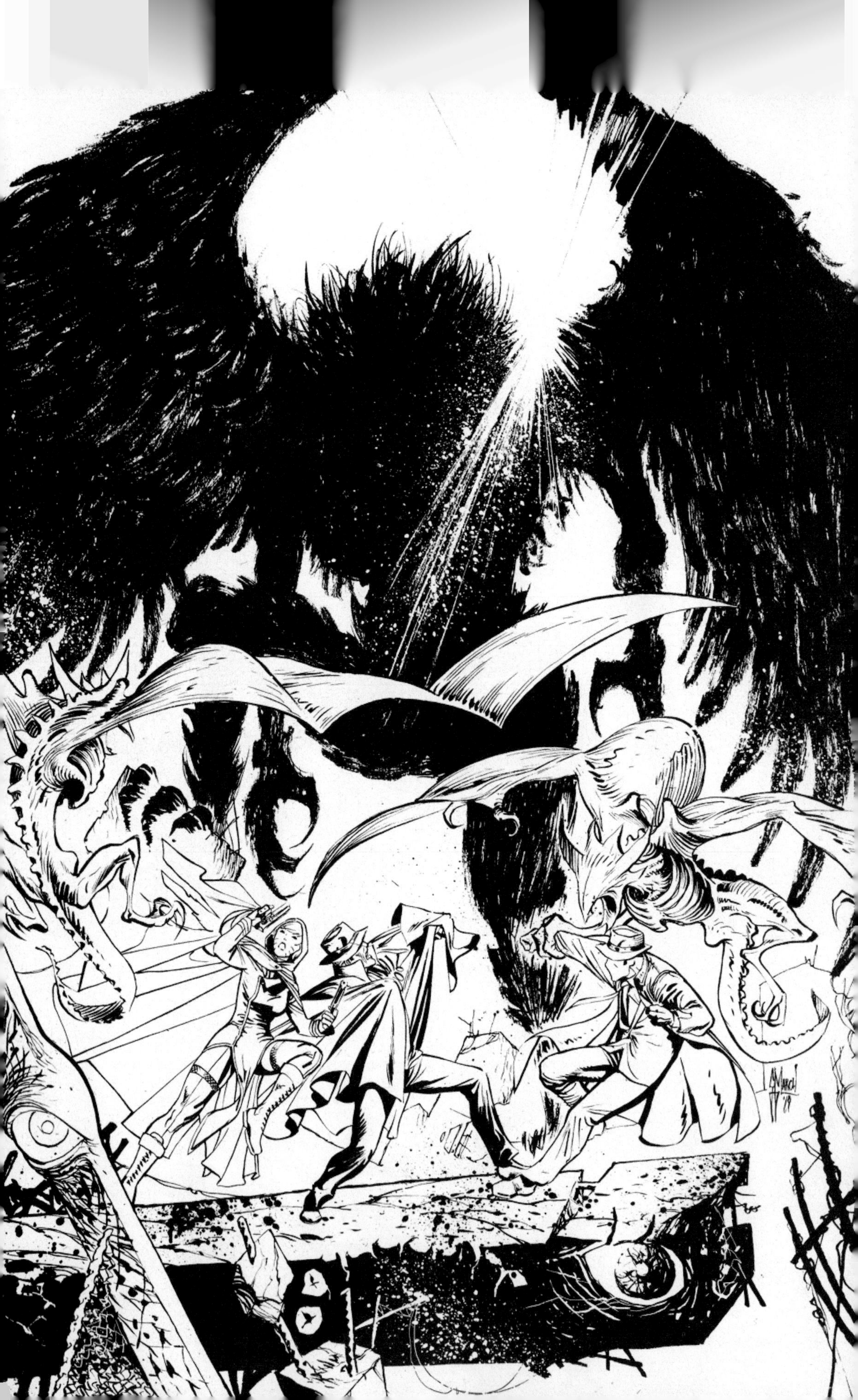

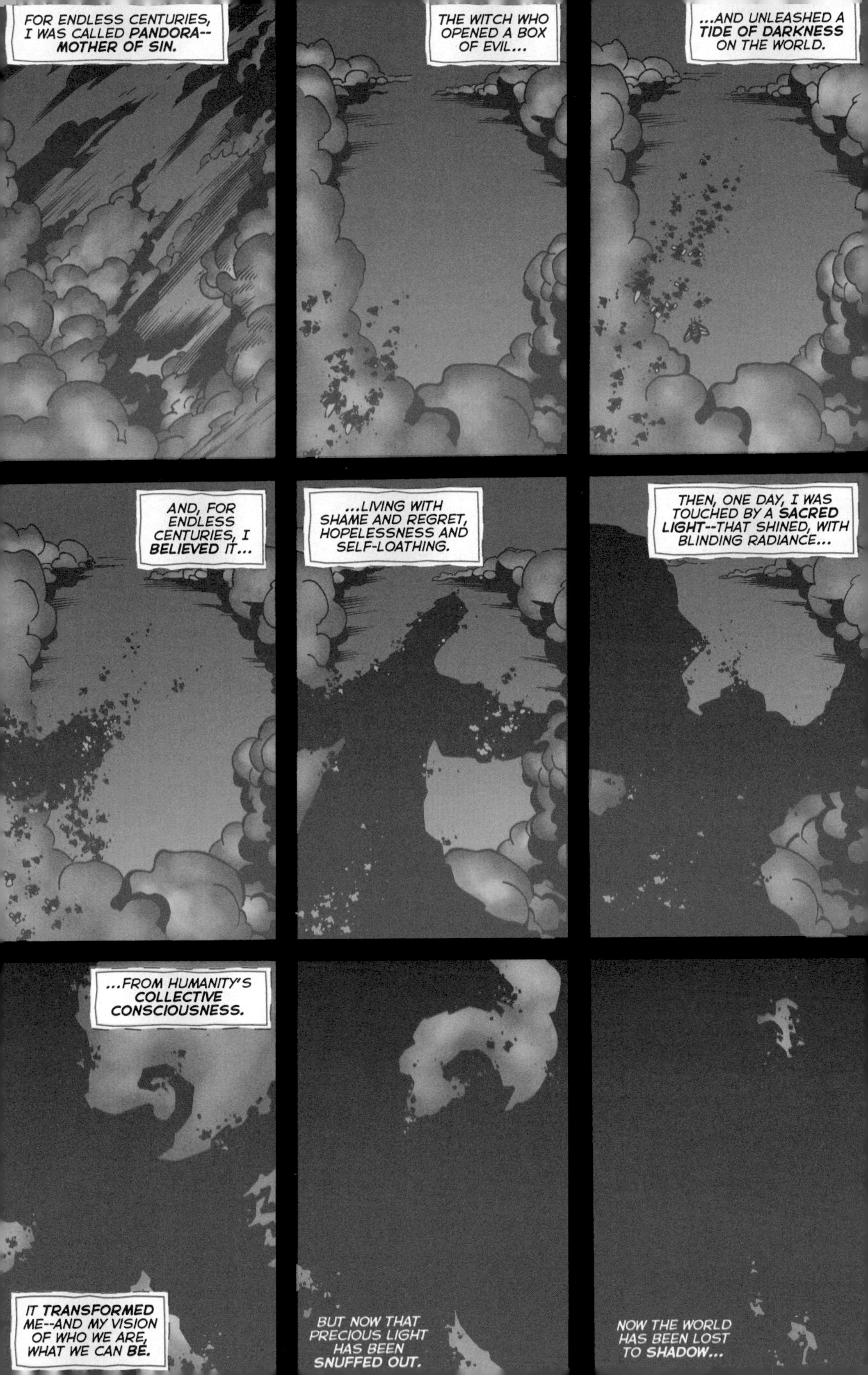
FOR ENDLESS CENTURIES, I WAS CALLED PANDORA-- MOTHER OF SIN.
THE WITCH WHO OPENED A BOX OF EVIL...
...AND UNLEASHED A TIDE OF DARKNESS ON THE WORLD.
AND, FOR ENDLESS CENTURIES, I BELIEVED IT...
...LIVING WITH SHAME AND REGRET, HOPELESSNESS AND SELF-LOATHING.
THEN, ONE DAY, I WAS TOUCHED BY A SACRED LIGHT--THAT SHINED, WITH BLINDING RADIANCE...
...FROM HUMANITY'S COLLECTIVE CONSCIOUSNESS.
IT TRANSFORMED ME--AND MY VISION OF WHO WE ARE, WHAT WE CAN BE.
BUT NOW THAT PRECIOUS LIGHT HAS BEEN SNUFFED OUT.
NOW THE WORLD HAS BEEN LOST TO SHADOW...

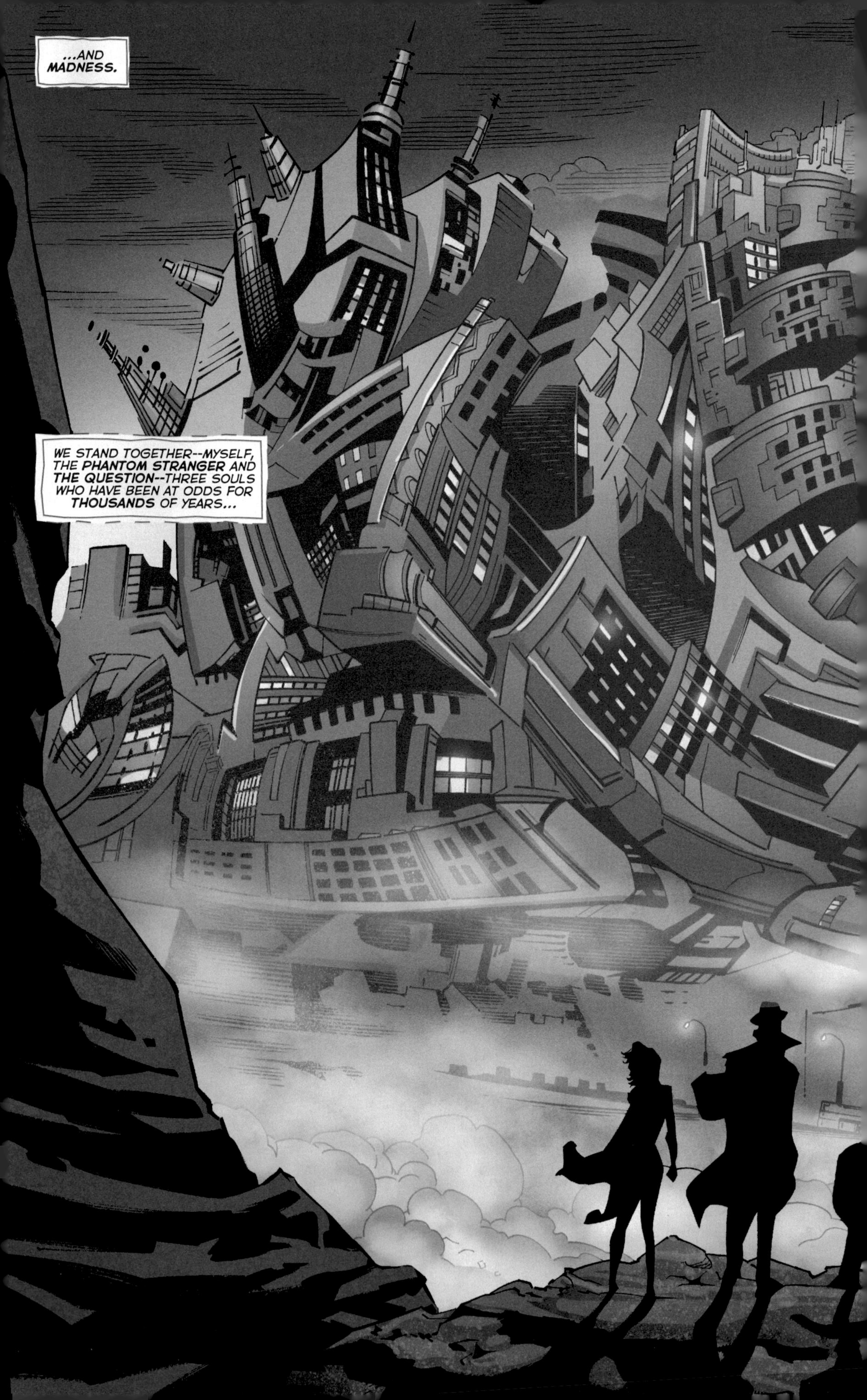
...AND MADNESS.
WE STAND TOGETHER--MYSELF, THE PHANTOM STRANGER AND THE QUESTION--THREE SOULS WHO HAVE BEEN AT ODDS FOR THOUSANDS OF YEARS...

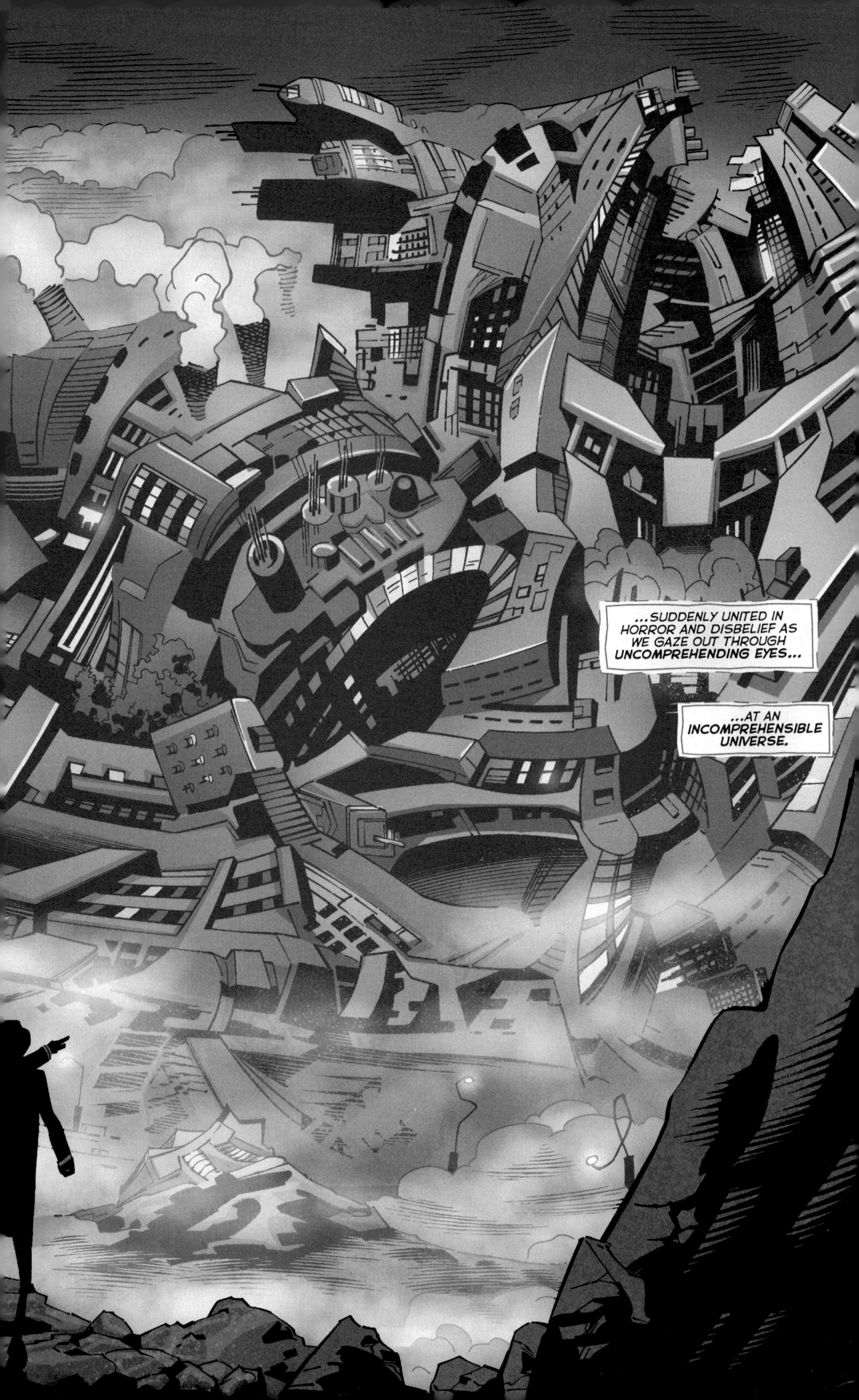
...SUDDENLY UNITED IN HORROR AND DISBELIEF AS WE GAZE OUT THROUGH UNCOMPREHENDING EYES...
...AT AN INCOMPREHENSIBLE UNIVERSE.

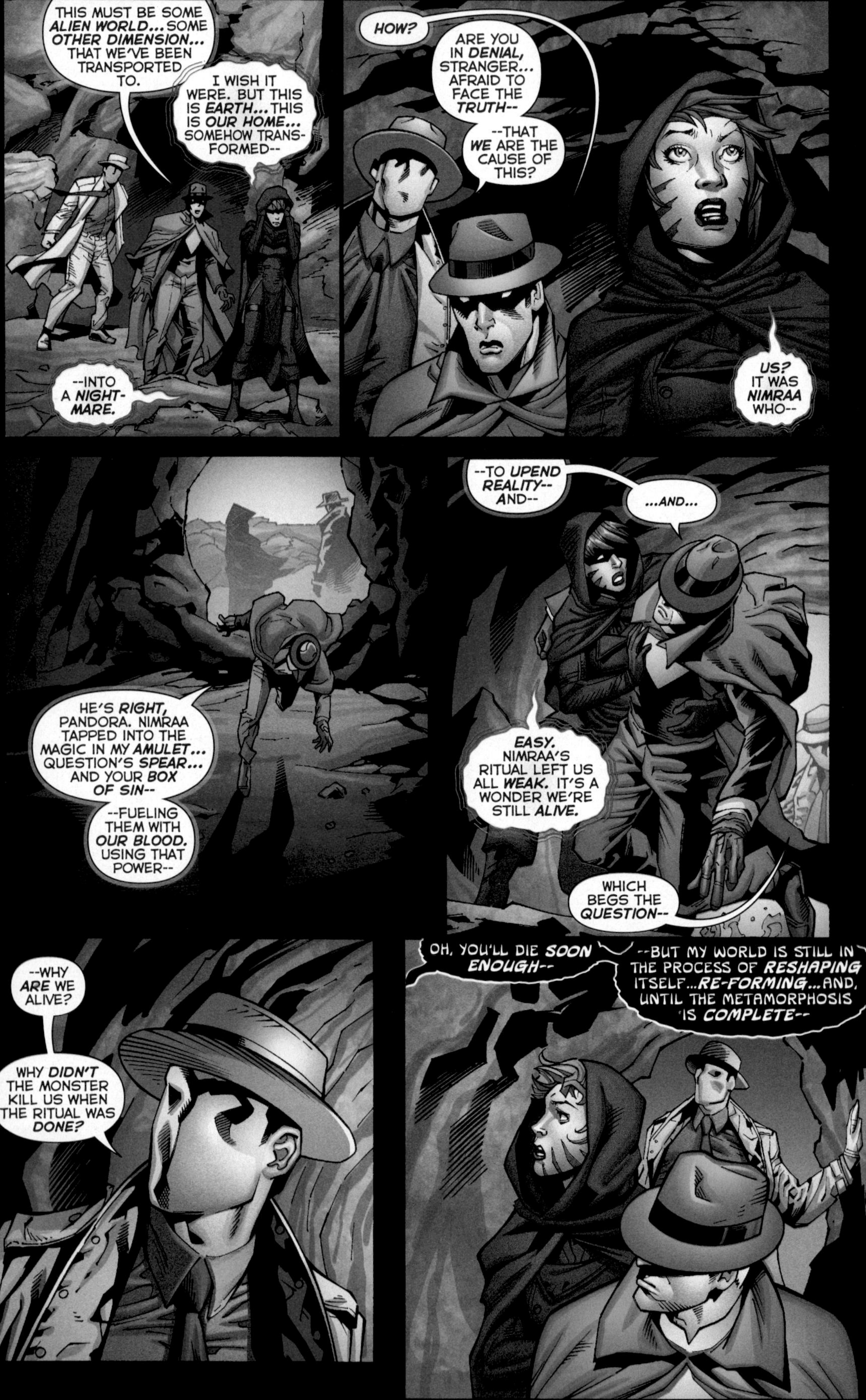
THIS MUST BE SOME ALIEN WORLD... SOME OTHER DIMENSION... THAT WE'VE BEEN TRANSPORTED TO.
I WISH IT WERE. BUT THIS IS EARTH... THIS IS OUR HOME... SOMEHOW TRANSFORMED--
--INTO A NIGHTMARE.
HOW?
ARE YOU IN DENIAL, STRANGER... AFRAID TO FACE THE TRUTH--
--THAT WE ARE THE CAUSE OF THIS?
US? IT WAS NIMRAA WHO--
HE'S RIGHT, PANDORA. NIMRAA TAPPED INTO THE MAGIC IN MY AMULET... QUESTION'S SPEAR... AND YOUR BOX OF SIN--
--FUELING THEM WITH OUR BLOOD. USING THAT POWER--
--TO UPEND REALITY--AND--
...AND...
EASY. NIMRAA'S RITUAL LEFT US ALL WEAK. IT'S A WONDER WE'RE STILL ALIVE.
WHICH BEGS THE QUESTION--
--WHY ARE WE ALIVE?
WHY DIDN'T THE MONSTER KILL US WHEN THE RITUAL WAS DONE?
OH, YOU'LL DIE SOON ENOUGH--
--BUT MY WORLD IS STILL IN THE PROCESS OF RESHAPING ITSELF...RE-FORMING...AND, UNTIL THE METAMORPHOSIS IS COMPLETE--

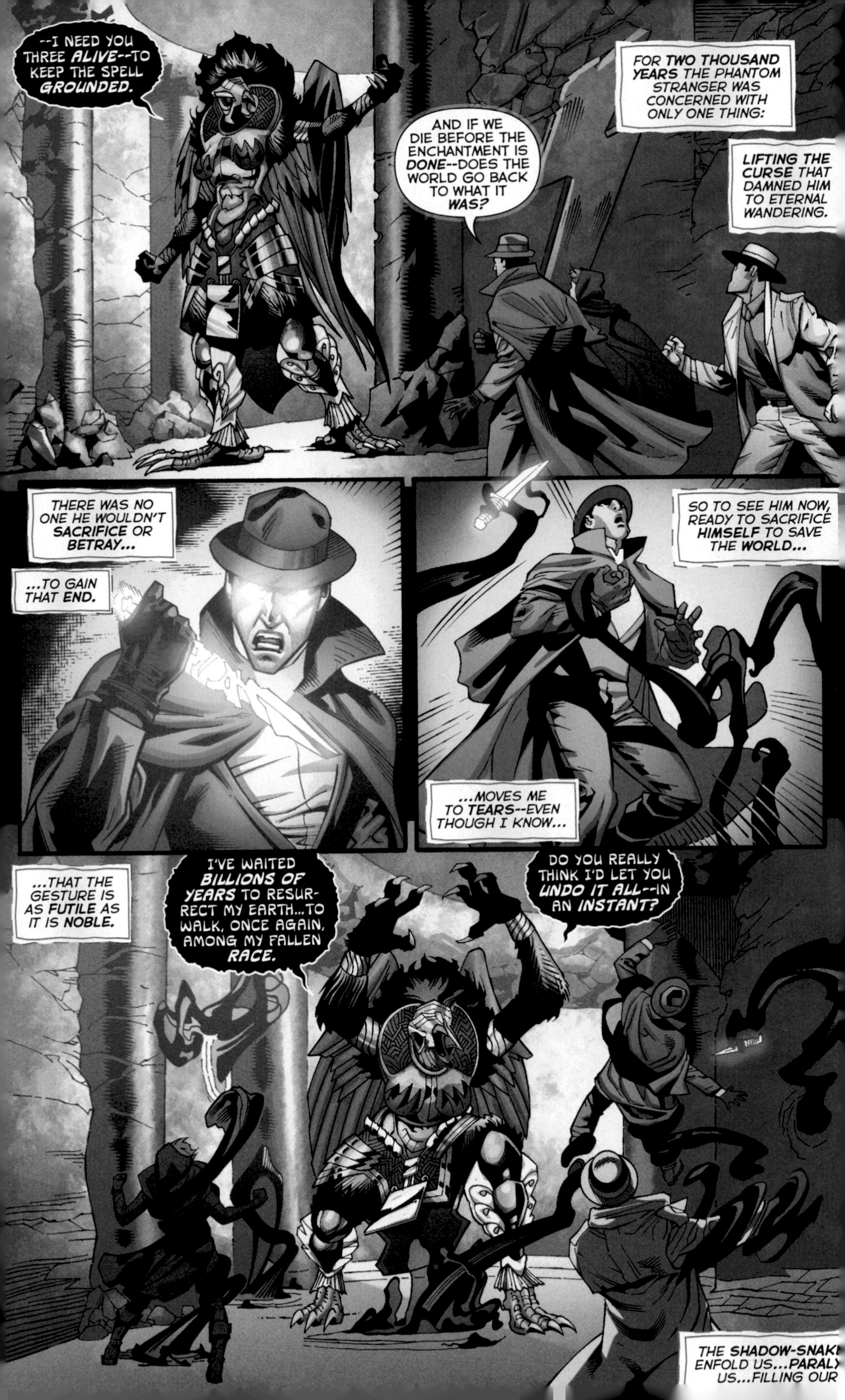
--I NEED YOU THREE ALIVE--TO KEEP THE SPELL GROUNDED.
AND IF WE DIE BEFORE THE ENCHANTMENT IS DONE--DOES THE WORLD GO BACK TO WHAT IT WAS?
FOR TWO THOUSAND YEARS THE PHANTOM STRANGER WAS CONCERNED WITH ONLY ONE THING:
LIFTING THE CURSE THAT DAMNED HIM TO ETERNAL WANDERING.
THERE WAS NO ONE HE WOULDN'T SACRIFICE OR BETRAY...
...TO GAIN THAT END.
SO TO SEE HIM NOW, READY TO SACRIFICE HIMSELF TO SAVE THE WORLD...
...MOVES ME TO TEARS--EVEN THOUGH I KNOW...
...THAT THE GESTURE IS AS FUTILE AS IT IS NOBLE.
I'VE WAITED BILLIONS OF YEARS TO RESURRECT MY EARTH...TO WALK, ONCE AGAIN, AMONG MY FALLEN RACE.
DO YOU REALLY THINK I'D LET YOU UNDO IT ALL--IN AN INSTANT?
THE SHADOW-SNAKE
ENFOLD US...PARALY
US...FILLING OUR

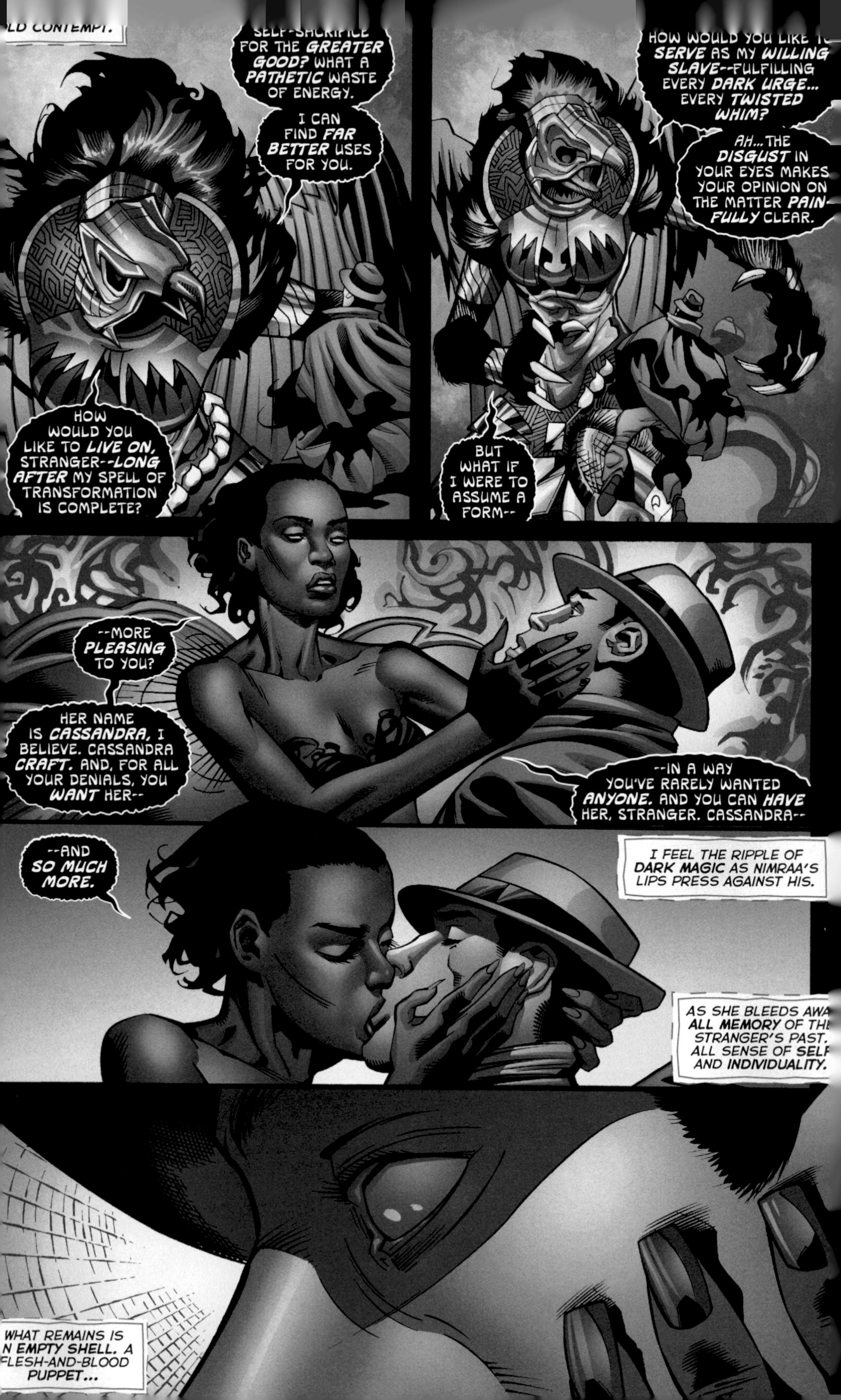
LD CONTEMPT.
SELF-SACRIFICE FOR THE GREATER GOOD? WHAT A PATHETIC WASTE OF ENERGY.
I CAN FIND FAR BETTER USES FOR YOU.
HOW WOULD YOU LIKE TO LIVE ON, STRANGER--LONG AFTER MY SPELL OF TRANSFORMATION IS COMPLETE?
HOW WOULD YOU LIKE TO SERVE AS MY WILLING SLAVE--FULFILLING EVERY DARK URGE... EVERY TWISTED WHIM?
AH...THE DISGUST IN YOUR EYES MAKES YOUR OPINION ON THE MATTER PAINFULLY CLEAR.
BUT WHAT IF I WERE TO ASSUME A FORM--
--MORE PLEASING TO YOU?
HER NAME IS CASSANDRA, I BELIEVE. CASSANDRA CRAFT. AND, FOR ALL YOUR DENIALS, YOU WANT HER--
--IN A WAY YOU'VE RARELY WANTED ANYONE. AND YOU CAN HAVE HER, STRANGER. CASSANDRA--
--AND SO MUCH MORE.
I FEEL THE RIPPLE OF DARK MAGIC AS NIMRAA'S LIPS PRESS AGAINST HIS.
AS SHE BLEEDS AWA ALL MEMORY OF THE STRANGER'S PAST. ALL SENSE OF SEL AND INDIVIDUALITY.
WHAT REMAINS IS N EMPTY SHELL. A FLESH-AND-BLOOD PUPPET...

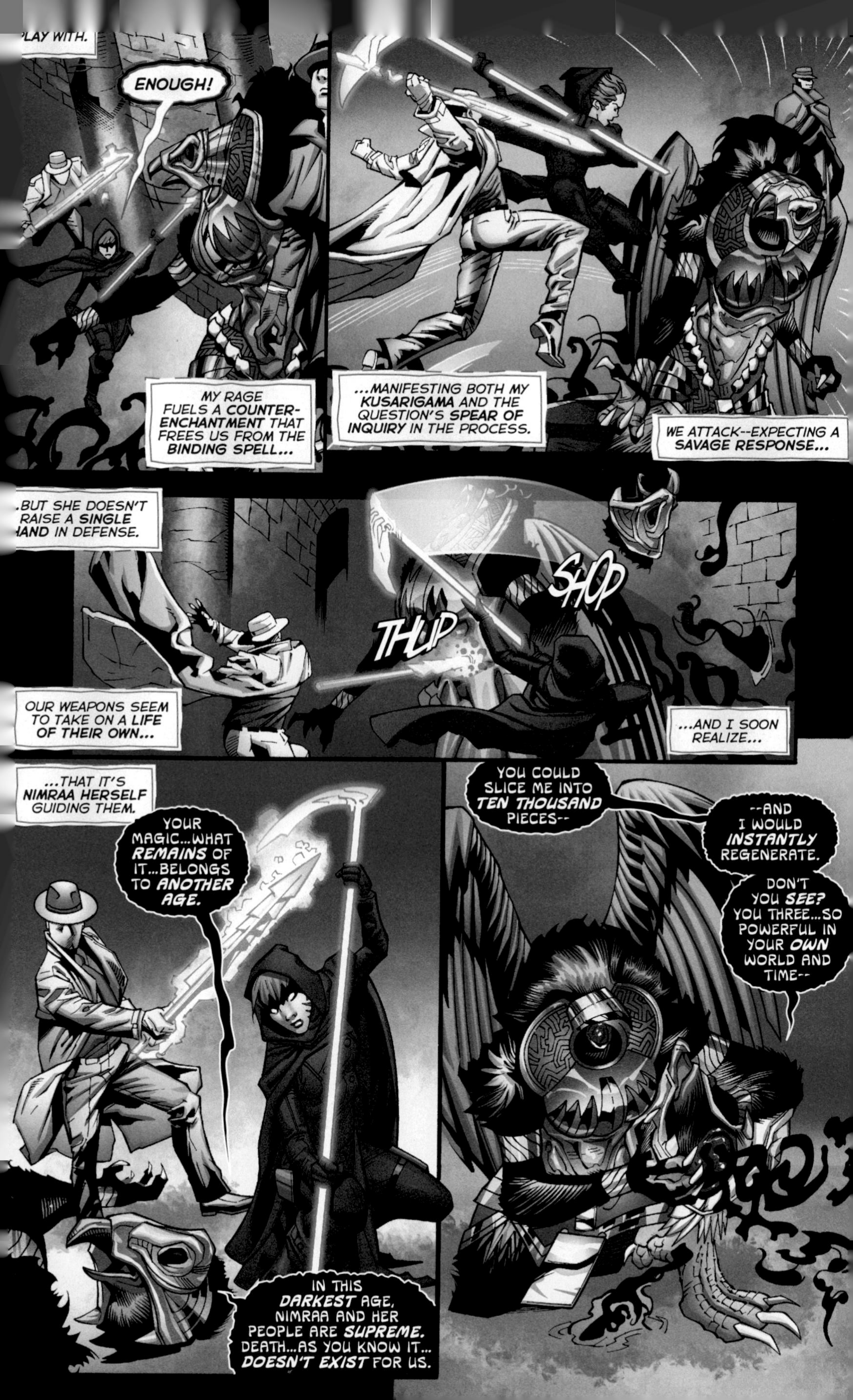
PLAY WITH.
ENOUGH!
MY RAGE FUELS A COUNTER-ENCHANTMENT THAT FREES US FROM THE BINDING SPELL...
...MANIFESTING BOTH MY KUSARIGAMA AND THE QUESTION'S SPEAR OF INQUIRY IN THE PROCESS.
WE ATTACK--EXPECTING A SAVAGE RESPONSE...
.BUT SHE DOESN'T RAISE A SINGLE HAND IN DEFENSE.
SHOP
THUP
OUR WEAPONS SEEM TO TAKE ON A LIFE OF THEIR OWN...
...AND I SOON REALIZE...
...THAT IT'S NIMRAA HERSELF GUIDING THEM.
YOUR MAGIC...WHAT REMAINS OF IT...BELONGS TO ANOTHER AGE.
IN THIS DARKEST AGE, NIMRAA AND HER PEOPLE ARE SUPREME. DEATH...AS YOU KNOW IT... DOESN'T EXIST FOR US.
YOU COULD SLICE ME INTO TEN THOUSAND PIECES--
--AND I WOULD INSTANTLY REGENERATE.
DON'T YOU SEE? YOU THREE...SO POWERFUL IN YOUR OWN WORLD AND TIME--

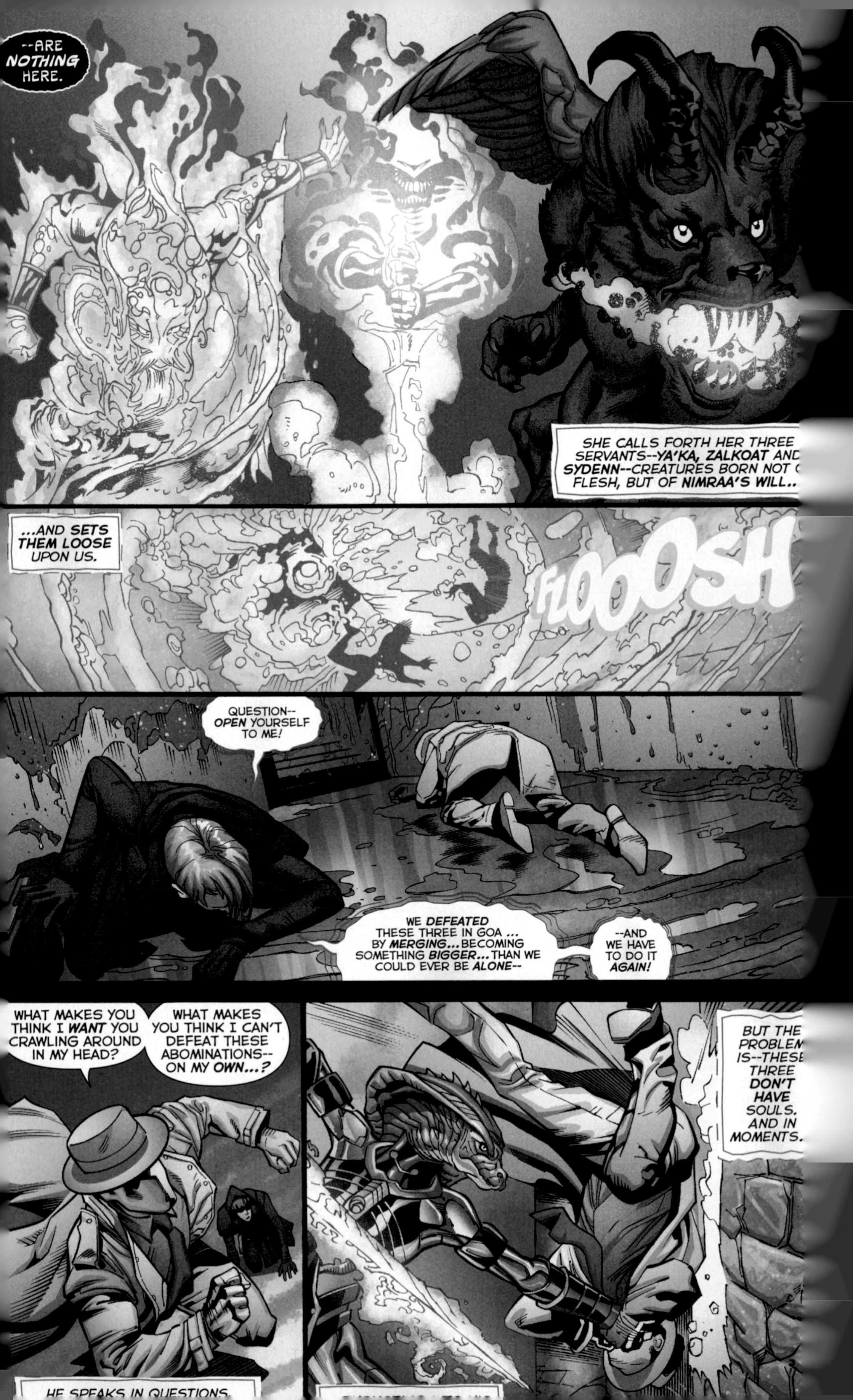
--ARE NOTHING HERE.
SHE CALLS FORTH HER THREE SERVANTS--YA'KA, ZALKOAT AND SYDENN--CREATURES BORN NOT OF FLESH, BUT OF NIMRAA'S WILL...
...AND SETS THEM LOOSE UPON US.
FLOOOSH
QUESTION-- OPEN YOURSELF TO ME!
WE DEFEATED THESE THREE IN GOA ... BY MERGING... BECOMING SOMETHING BIGGER... THAN WE COULD EVER BE ALONE--
--AND WE HAVE TO DO IT AGAIN!
WHAT MAKES YOU THINK I WANT YOU CRAWLING AROUND IN MY HEAD?
WHAT MAKES YOU THINK I CAN'T DEFEAT THESE ABOMINATIONS-- ON MY OWN...?
BUT THE PROBLEM IS--THESE THREE DON'T HAVE SOULS. AND IN MOMENTS...
HE SPEAKS IN QUESTIONS.

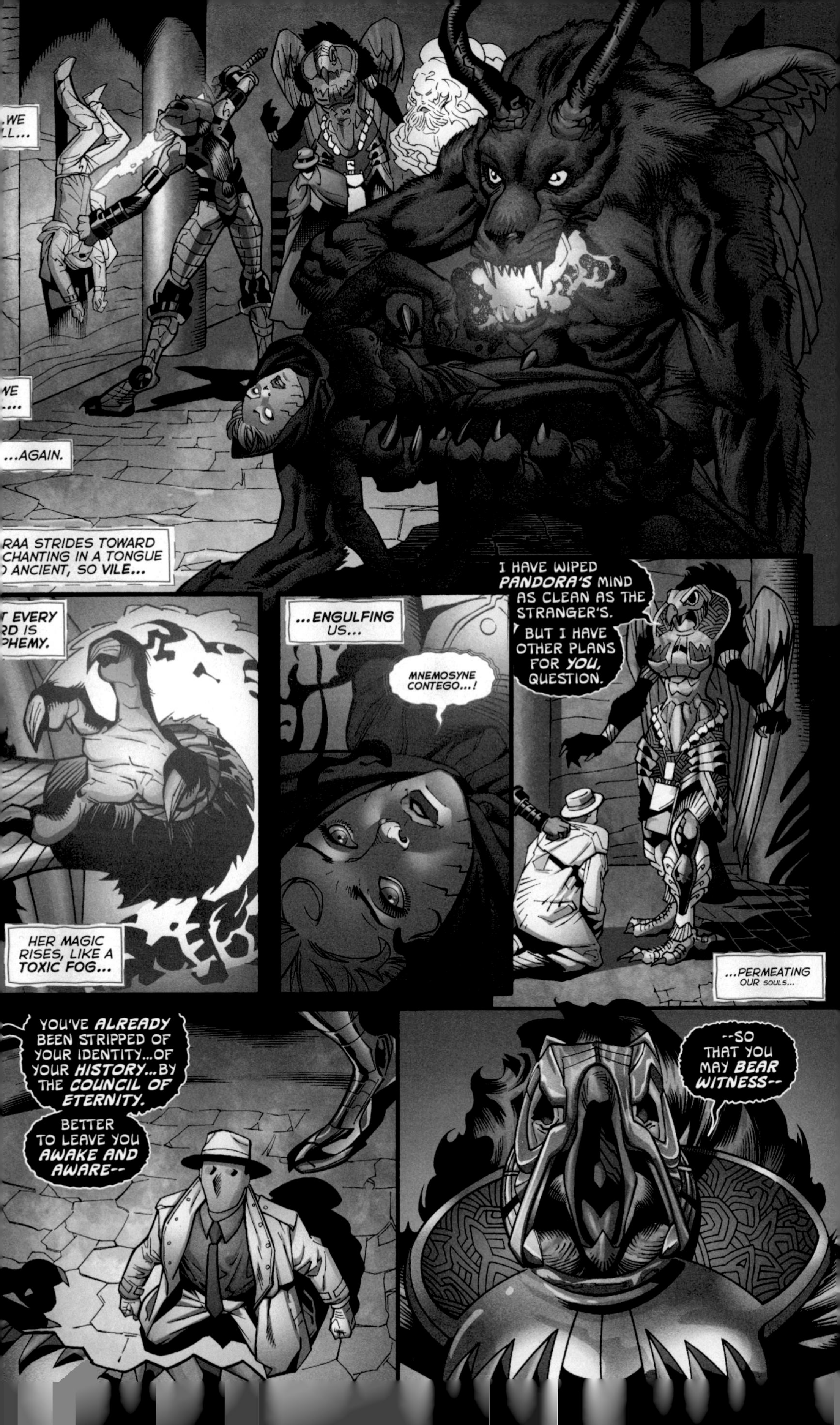

...WE
...LL...
WE
...
...AGAIN.
...RAA STRIDES TOWARD ...CHANTING IN A TONGUE ...O ANCIENT, SO VILE...
...T EVERY ...RD IS ...PHEMY.
HER MAGIC RISES, LIKE A TOXIC FOG...
...ENGULFING US...
MNEMOSYNE CONTEGO...!
I HAVE WIPED PANDORA'S MIND AS CLEAN AS THE STRANGER'S.
BUT I HAVE OTHER PLANS FOR YOU, QUESTION.
...PERMEATING OUR SOULS...
YOU'VE ALREADY BEEN STRIPPED OF YOUR IDENTITY...OF YOUR HISTORY...BY THE COUNCIL OF ETERNITY.
BETTER TO LEAVE YOU AWAKE AND AWARE--
--SO THAT YOU MAY BEAR WITNESS--

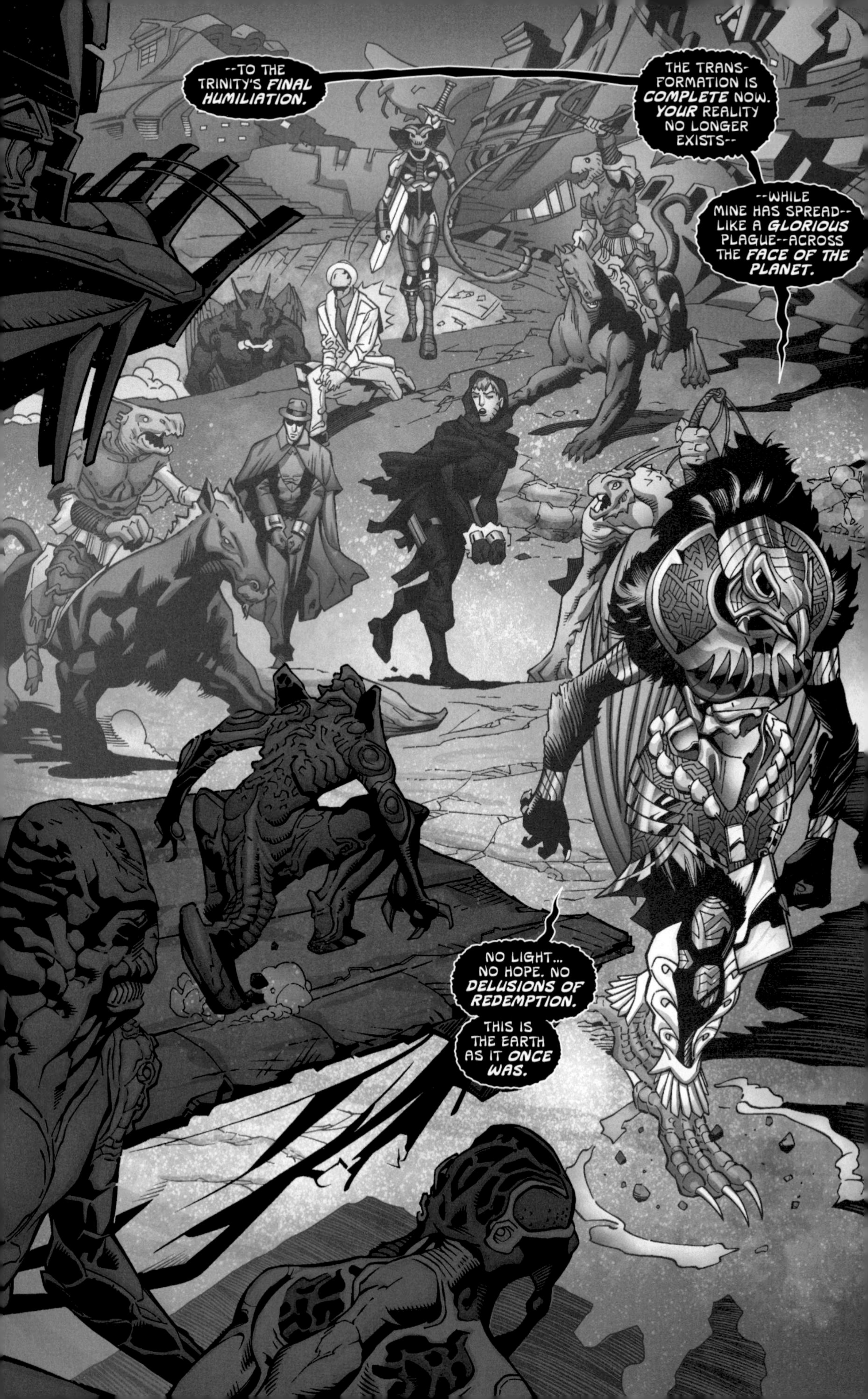
--TO THE TRINITY'S *FINAL HUMILIATION.*
THE TRANS-FORMATION IS *COMPLETE* NOW. *YOUR* REALITY NO LONGER EXISTS--
--WHILE MINE HAS SPREAD--LIKE A *GLORIOUS* PLAGUE--ACROSS THE *FACE OF THE PLANET.*
NO LIGHT... NO HOPE. NO *DELUSIONS OF REDEMPTION.*
THIS IS THE EARTH AS IT *ONCE WAS.*

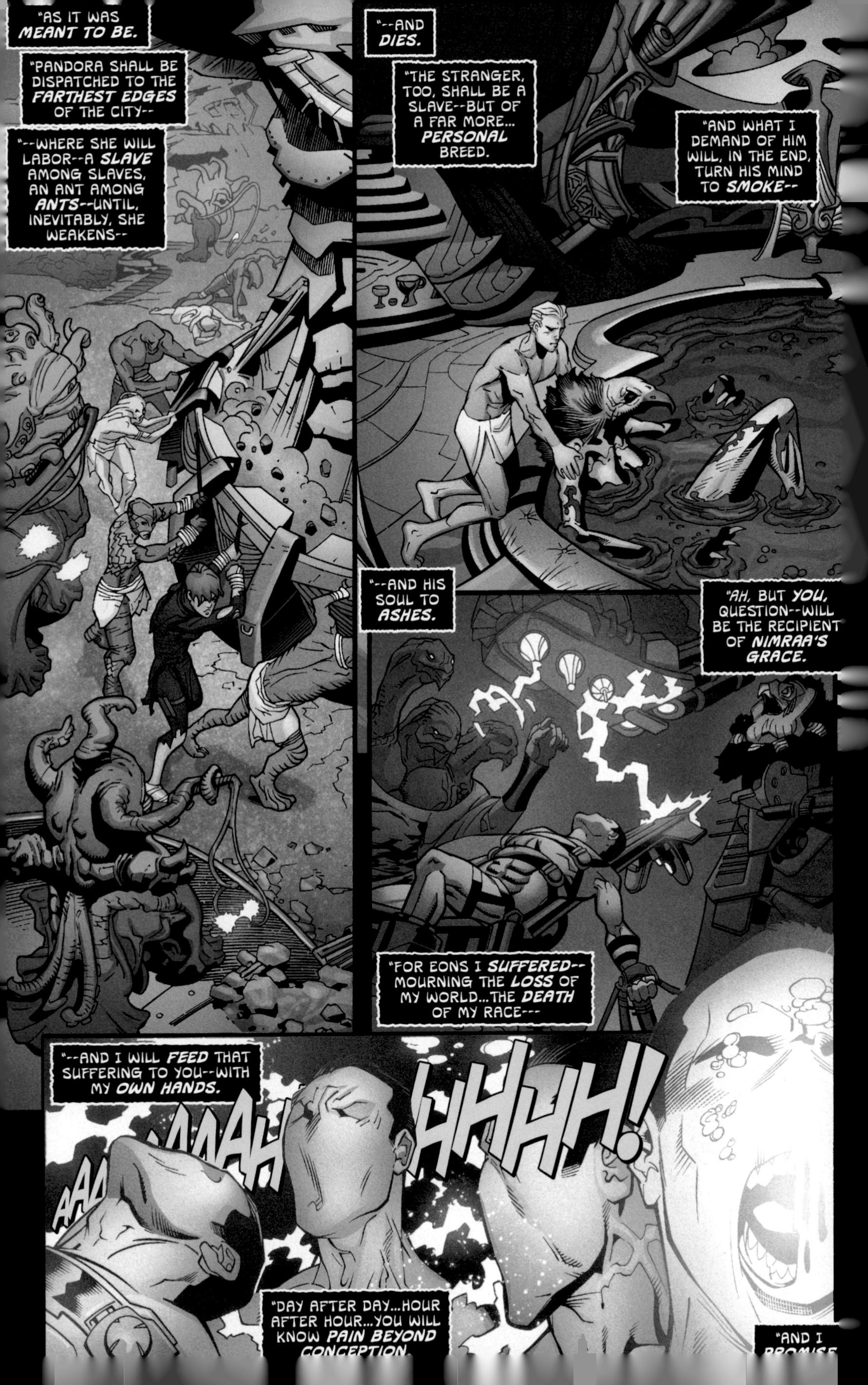
"AS IT WAS MEANT TO BE.
"PANDORA SHALL BE DISPATCHED TO THE FARTHEST EDGES OF THE CITY--
"--WHERE SHE WILL LABOR--A SLAVE AMONG SLAVES, AN ANT AMONG ANTS--UNTIL, INEVITABLY, SHE WEAKENS--
"--AND DIES.
"THE STRANGER, TOO, SHALL BE A SLAVE--BUT OF A FAR MORE... PERSONAL BREED.
"AND WHAT I DEMAND OF HIM WILL, IN THE END, TURN HIS MIND TO SMOKE--
"--AND HIS SOUL TO ASHES.
"AH, BUT YOU, QUESTION--WILL BE THE RECIPIENT OF NIMRAA'S GRACE.
"FOR EONS I SUFFERED--MOURNING THE LOSS OF MY WORLD...THE DEATH OF MY RACE---
"--AND I WILL FEED THAT SUFFERING TO YOU--WITH MY OWN HANDS.
AAAAAHHHHHH!
"DAY AFTER DAY...HOUR AFTER HOUR...YOU WILL KNOW PAIN BEYOND CONCEPTION.
"AND I

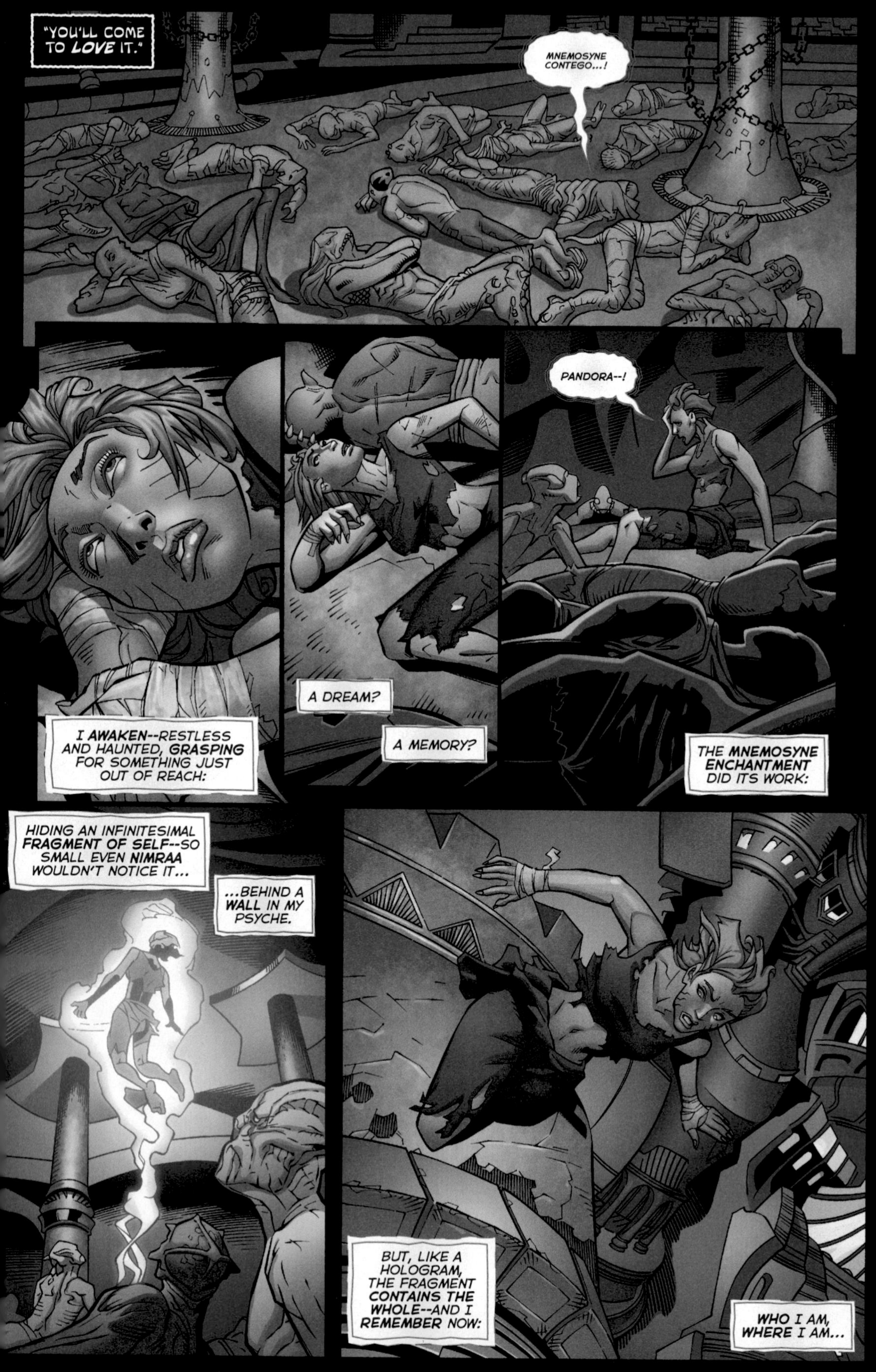
"YOU'LL COME TO LOVE IT."
MNEMOSYNE CONTEGO...!
I AWAKEN--RESTLESS AND HAUNTED, GRASPING FOR SOMETHING JUST OUT OF REACH:
A DREAM?
A MEMORY?
PANDORA--!
THE MNEMOSYNE ENCHANTMENT DID ITS WORK:
HIDING AN INFINITESIMAL FRAGMENT OF SELF--SO SMALL EVEN NIMRAA WOULDN'T NOTICE IT...
...BEHIND A WALL IN MY PSYCHE.
BUT, LIKE A HOLOGRAM, THE FRAGMENT CONTAINS THE WHOLE--AND I REMEMBER NOW:
WHO I AM, WHERE I AM...

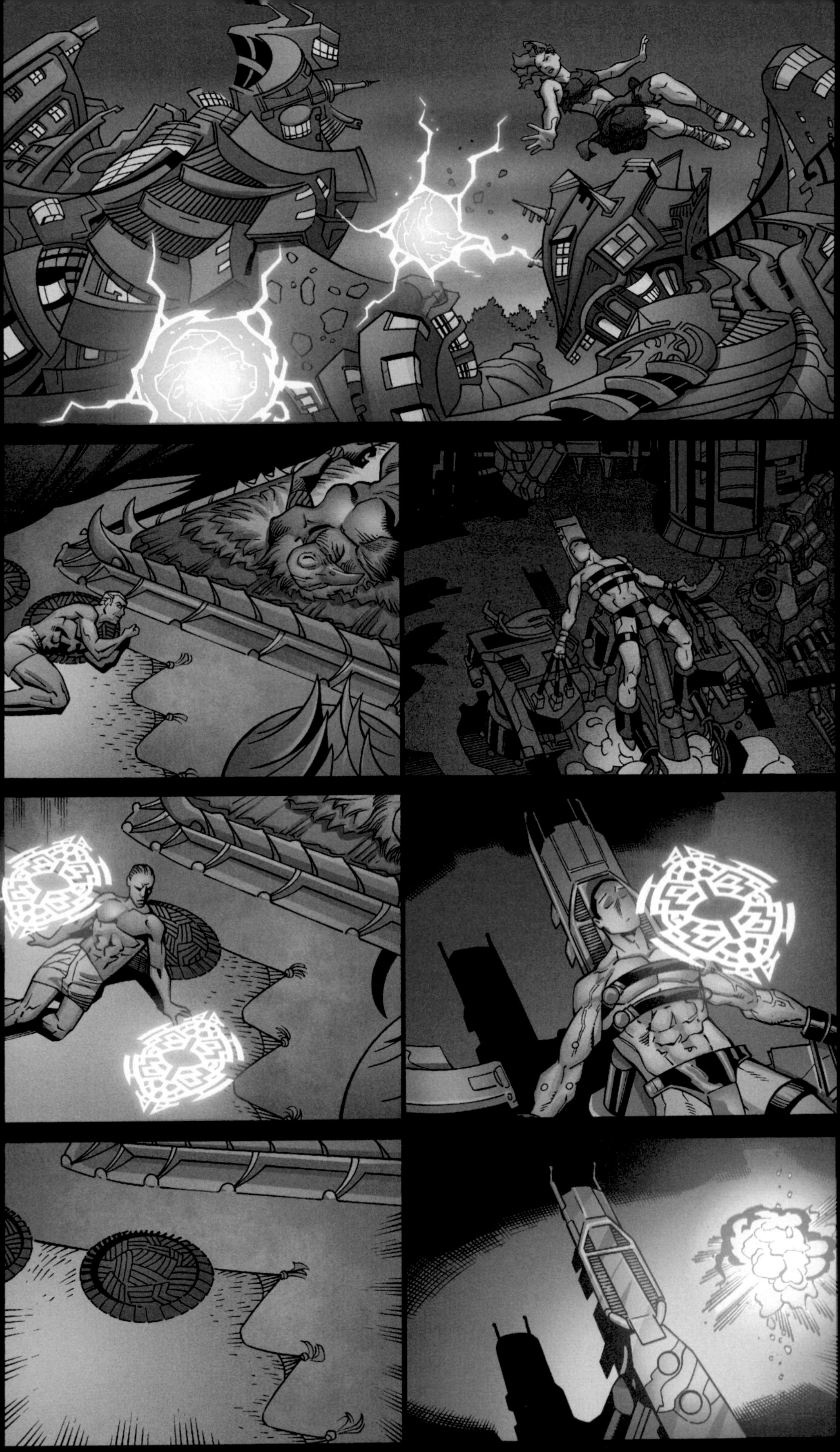

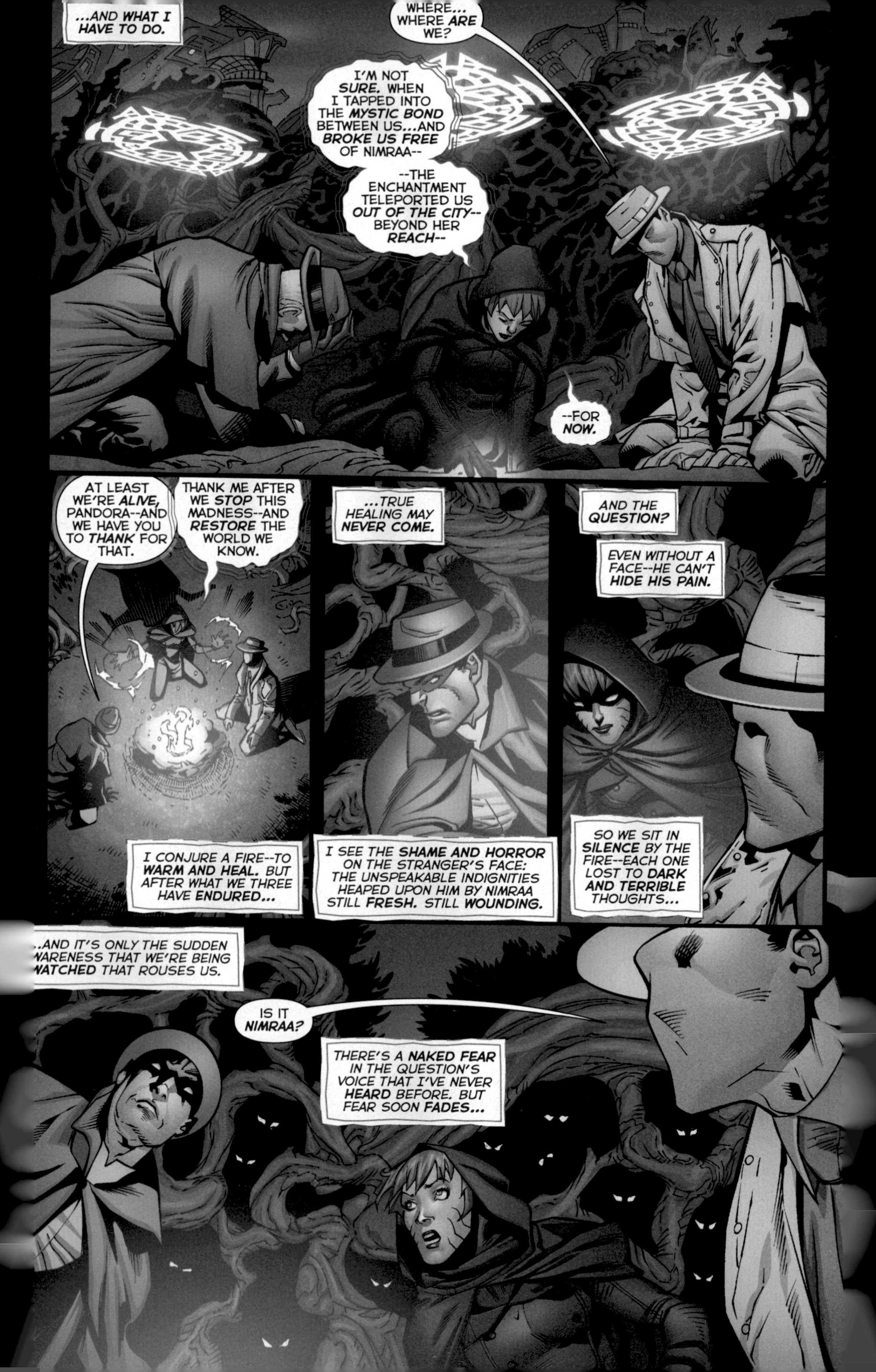
...AND WHAT I HAVE TO DO.
WHERE... WHERE ARE WE?
I'M NOT SURE. WHEN I TAPPED INTO THE MYSTIC BOND BETWEEN US...AND BROKE US FREE OF NIMRAA--
--THE ENCHANTMENT TELEPORTED US OUT OF THE CITY-- BEYOND HER REACH--
--FOR NOW.
AT LEAST WE'RE ALIVE, PANDORA--AND WE HAVE YOU TO THANK FOR THAT.
THANK ME AFTER WE STOP THIS MADNESS--AND RESTORE THE WORLD WE KNOW.
I CONJURE A FIRE--TO WARM AND HEAL. BUT AFTER WHAT WE THREE HAVE ENDURED...
...TRUE HEALING MAY NEVER COME.
I SEE THE SHAME AND HORROR ON THE STRANGER'S FACE: THE UNSPEAKABLE INDIGNITIES HEAPED UPON HIM BY NIMRAA STILL FRESH. STILL WOUNDING.
AND THE QUESTION?
EVEN WITHOUT A FACE--HE CAN'T HIDE HIS PAIN.
SO WE SIT IN SILENCE BY THE FIRE--EACH ONE LOST TO DARK AND TERRIBLE THOUGHTS...
..AND IT'S ONLY THE SUDDEN WARENESS THAT WE'RE BEING WATCHED THAT ROUSES US.
IS IT NIMRAA?
THERE'S A NAKED FEAR IN THE QUESTION'S VOICE THAT I'VE NEVER HEARD BEFORE. BUT FEAR SOON FADES...

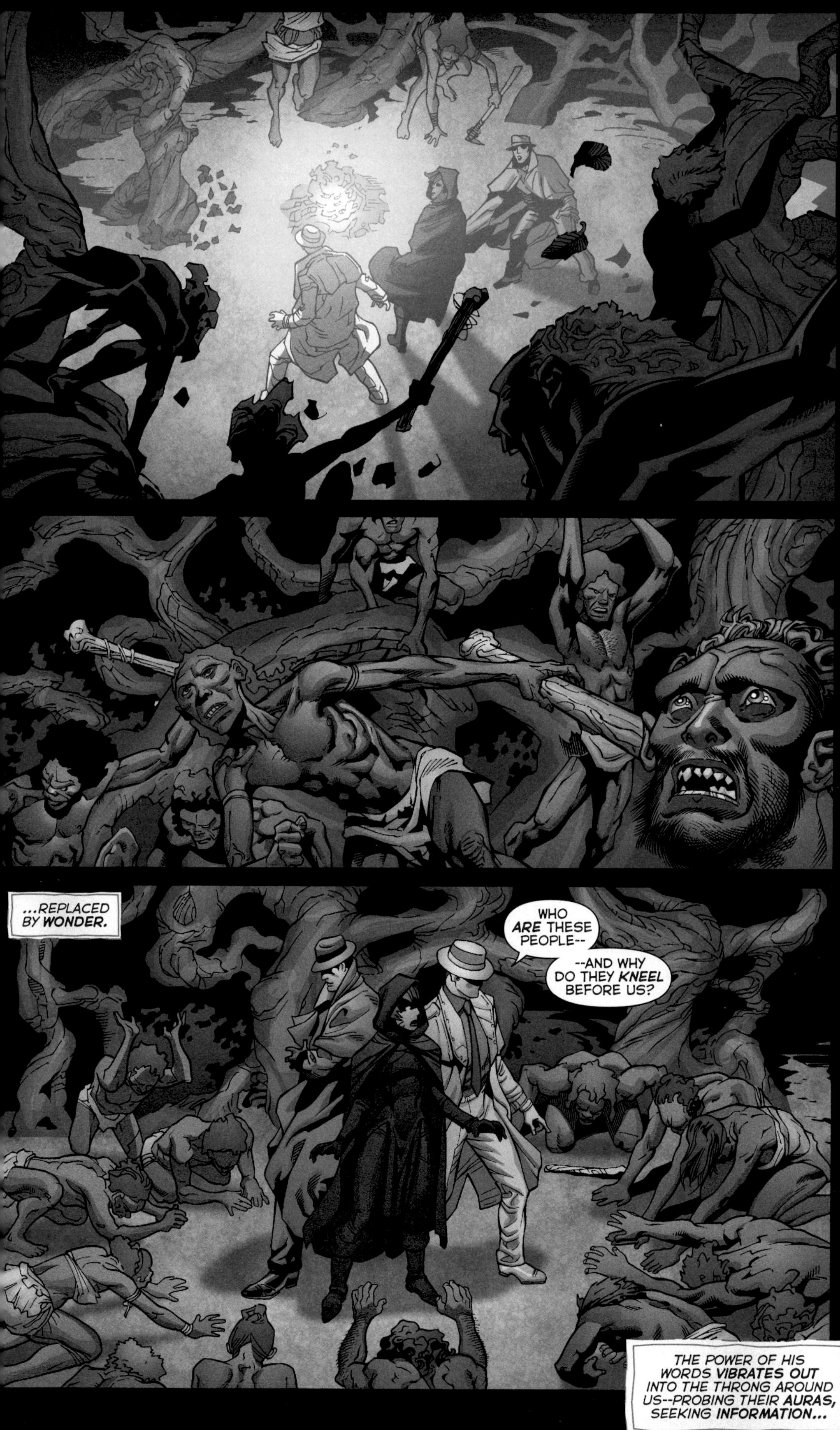
...REPLACED BY WONDER.
WHO ARE THESE PEOPLE--
--AND WHY DO THEY KNEEL BEFORE US?
THE POWER OF HIS WORDS VIBRATES OUT INTO THE THRONG AROUND US--PROBING THEIR AURAS, SEEKING INFORMATION...

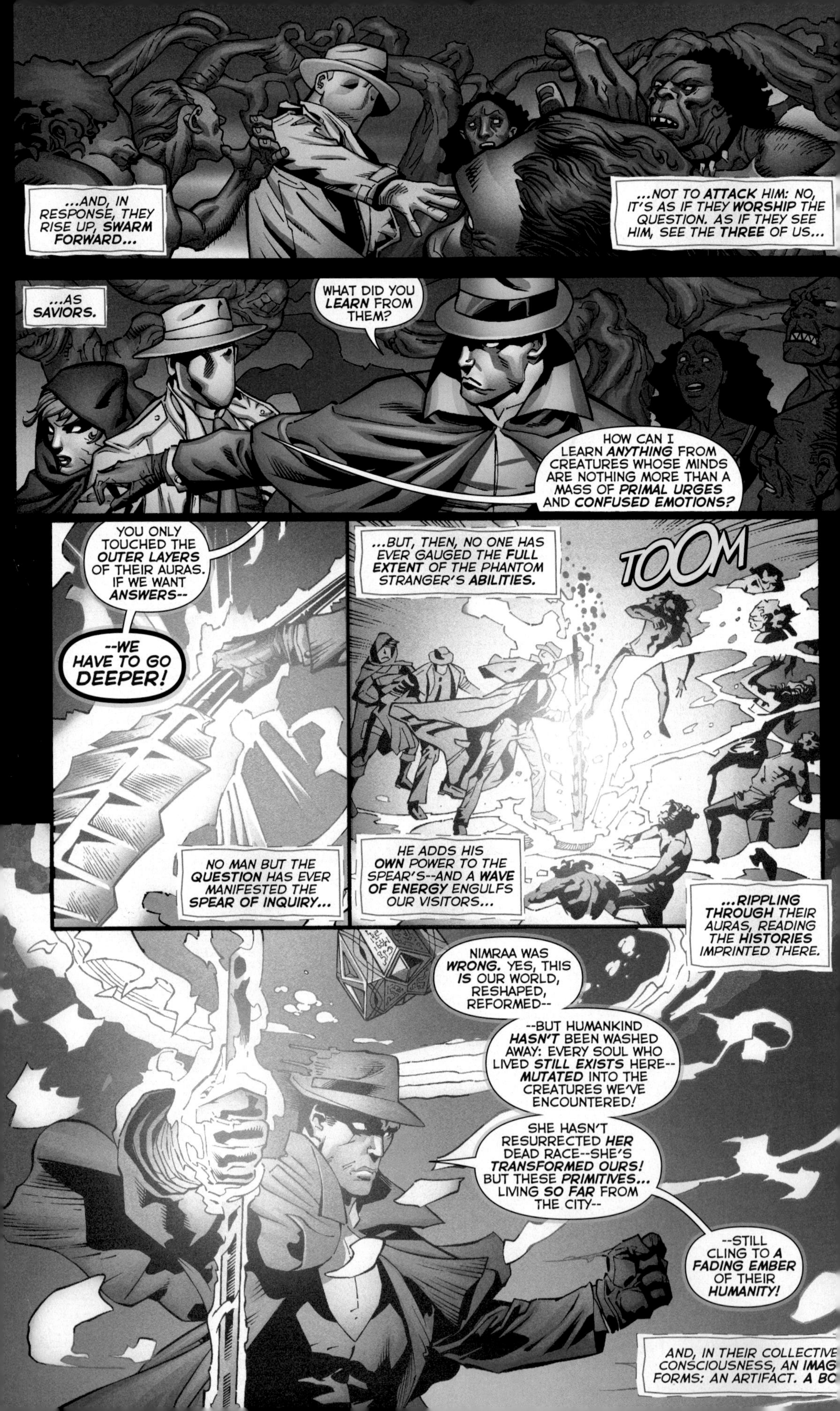
...AND, IN RESPONSE, THEY RISE UP, SWARM FORWARD...
...NOT TO ATTACK HIM: NO, IT'S AS IF THEY WORSHIP THE QUESTION. AS IF THEY SEE HIM, SEE THE THREE OF US...
...AS SAVIORS.
WHAT DID YOU LEARN FROM THEM?
HOW CAN I LEARN ANYTHING FROM CREATURES WHOSE MINDS ARE NOTHING MORE THAN A MASS OF PRIMAL URGES AND CONFUSED EMOTIONS?
YOU ONLY TOUCHED THE OUTER LAYERS OF THEIR AURAS. IF WE WANT ANSWERS--
--WE HAVE TO GO DEEPER!
NO MAN BUT THE QUESTION HAS EVER MANIFESTED THE SPEAR OF INQUIRY...
...BUT, THEN, NO ONE HAS EVER GAUGED THE FULL EXTENT OF THE PHANTOM STRANGER'S ABILITIES.
TOOM
HE ADDS HIS OWN POWER TO THE SPEAR'S--AND A WAVE OF ENERGY ENGULFS OUR VISITORS...
...RIPPLING THROUGH THEIR AURAS, READING THE HISTORIES IMPRINTED THERE.
NIMRAA WAS WRONG. YES, THIS IS OUR WORLD, RESHAPED, REFORMED--
--BUT HUMANKIND HASN'T BEEN WASHED AWAY: EVERY SOUL WHO LIVED STILL EXISTS HERE--MUTATED INTO THE CREATURES WE'VE ENCOUNTERED!
SHE HASN'T RESURRECTED HER DEAD RACE--SHE'S TRANSFORMED OURS! BUT THESE PRIMITIVES... LIVING SO FAR FROM THE CITY--
--STILL CLING TO A FADING EMBER OF THEIR HUMANITY!
AND, IN THEIR COLLECTIVE CONSCIOUSNESS, AN IMAG
FORMS: AN ARTIFACT. A BO

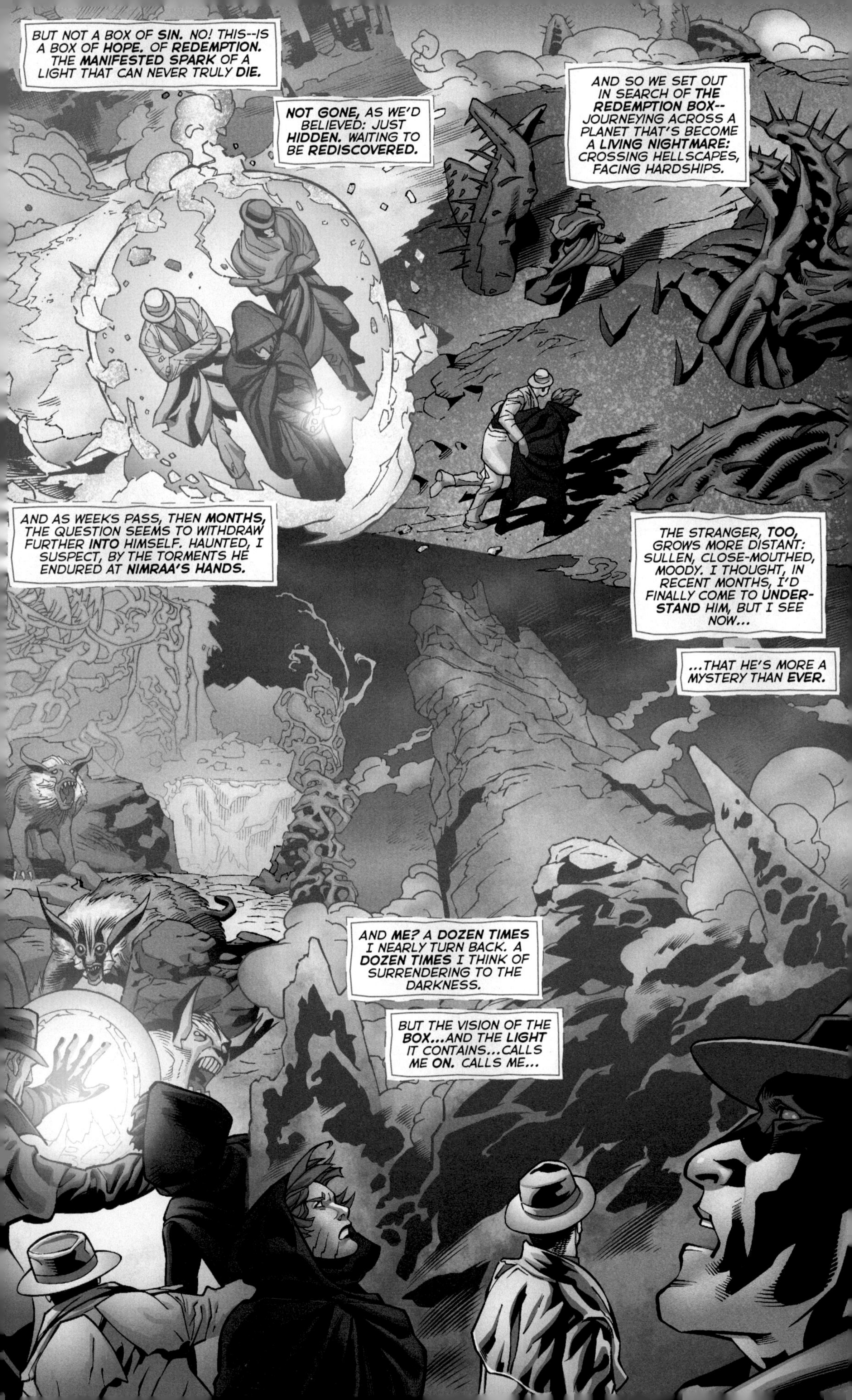
BUT NOT A BOX OF SIN. NO! THIS--IS A BOX OF HOPE. OF REDEMPTION. THE MANIFESTED SPARK OF A LIGHT THAT CAN NEVER TRULY DIE.
NOT GONE, AS WE'D BELIEVED: JUST HIDDEN. WAITING TO BE REDISCOVERED.
AND SO WE SET OUT IN SEARCH OF THE REDEMPTION BOX--JOURNEYING ACROSS A PLANET THAT'S BECOME A LIVING NIGHTMARE: CROSSING HELLSCAPES, FACING HARDSHIPS.
AND AS WEEKS PASS, THEN MONTHS, THE QUESTION SEEMS TO WITHDRAW FURTHER INTO HIMSELF. HAUNTED, I SUSPECT, BY THE TORMENTS HE ENDURED AT NIMRAA'S HANDS.
THE STRANGER, TOO, GROWS MORE DISTANT: SULLEN, CLOSE-MOUTHED, MOODY. I THOUGHT, IN RECENT MONTHS, I'D FINALLY COME TO UNDER-STAND HIM, BUT I SEE NOW...
...THAT HE'S MORE A MYSTERY THAN EVER.
AND ME? A DOZEN TIMES I NEARLY TURN BACK. A DOZEN TIMES I THINK OF SURRENDERING TO THE DARKNESS.
BUT THE VISION OF THE BOX...AND THE LIGHT IT CONTAINS...CALLS ME ON. CALLS ME...

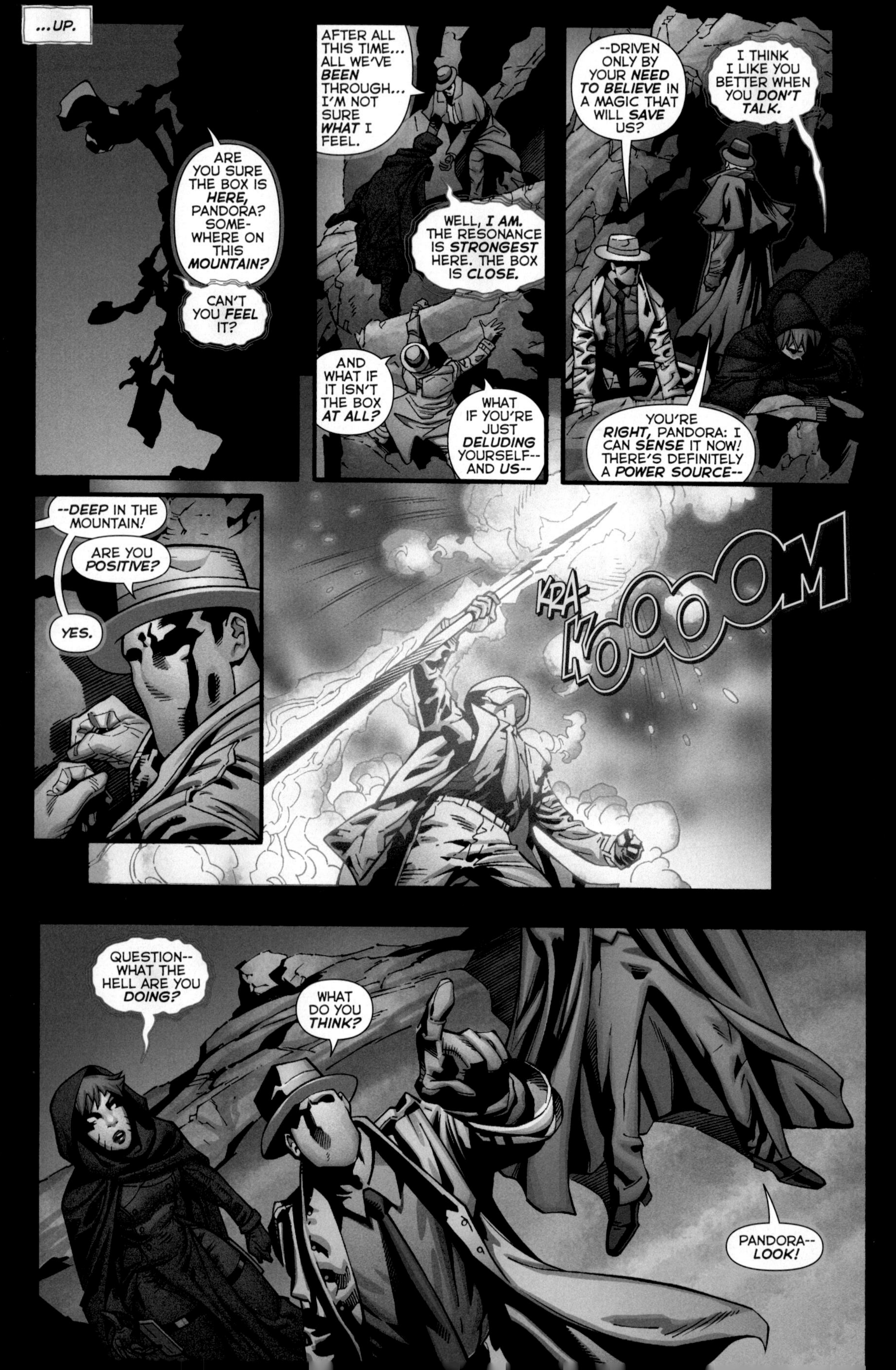
...UP.
ARE YOU SURE THE BOX IS HERE, PANDORA? SOMEWHERE ON THIS MOUNTAIN?
CAN'T YOU FEEL IT?
AFTER ALL THIS TIME... ALL WE'VE BEEN THROUGH... I'M NOT SURE WHAT I FEEL.
WELL, I AM. THE RESONANCE IS STRONGEST HERE. THE BOX IS CLOSE.
AND WHAT IF IT ISN'T THE BOX AT ALL?
WHAT IF YOU'RE JUST DELUDING YOURSELF--AND US--
--DRIVEN ONLY BY YOUR NEED TO BELIEVE IN A MAGIC THAT WILL SAVE US?
I THINK I LIKE YOU BETTER WHEN YOU DON'T TALK.
YOU'RE RIGHT, PANDORA: I CAN SENSE IT NOW! THERE'S DEFINITELY A POWER SOURCE--
--DEEP IN THE MOUNTAIN!
ARE YOU POSITIVE?
YES.
KRA-KOOOOOM
QUESTION--WHAT THE HELL ARE YOU DOING?
WHAT DO YOU THINK?
PANDORA--LOOK!

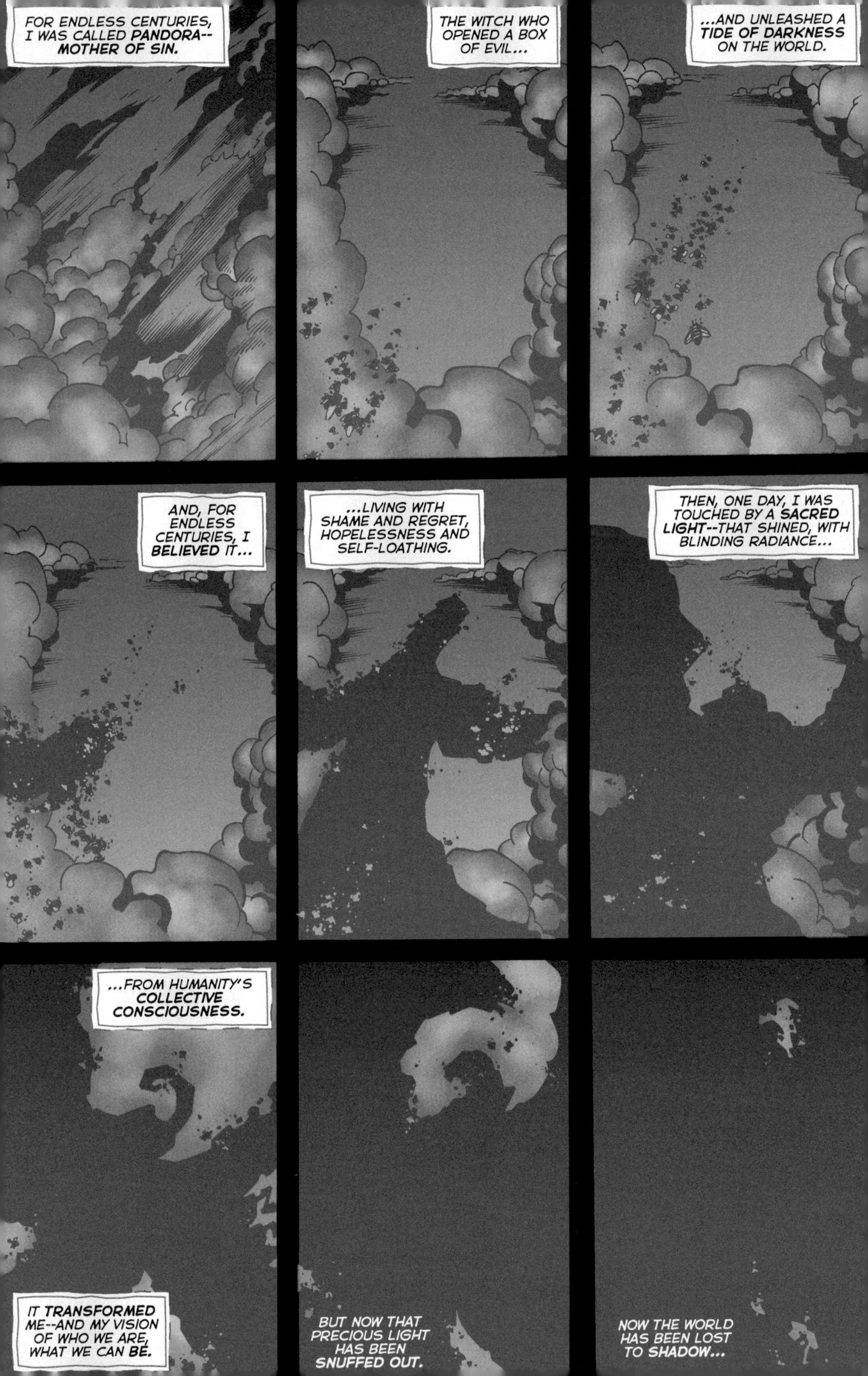
FOR ENDLESS CENTURIES, I WAS CALLED PANDORA-- MOTHER OF SIN.
THE WITCH WHO OPENED A BOX OF EVIL...
...AND UNLEASHED A TIDE OF DARKNESS ON THE WORLD.
AND, FOR ENDLESS CENTURIES, I BELIEVED IT...
...LIVING WITH SHAME AND REGRET, HOPELESSNESS AND SELF-LOATHING.
THEN, ONE DAY, I WAS TOUCHED BY A SACRED LIGHT--THAT SHINED, WITH BLINDING RADIANCE...
...FROM HUMANITY'S COLLECTIVE CONSCIOUSNESS.
IT TRANSFORMED ME--AND MY VISION OF WHO WE ARE, WHAT WE CAN BE.
BUT NOW THAT PRECIOUS LIGHT HAS BEEN SNUFFED OUT.
NOW THE WORLD HAS BEEN LOST TO SHADOW...

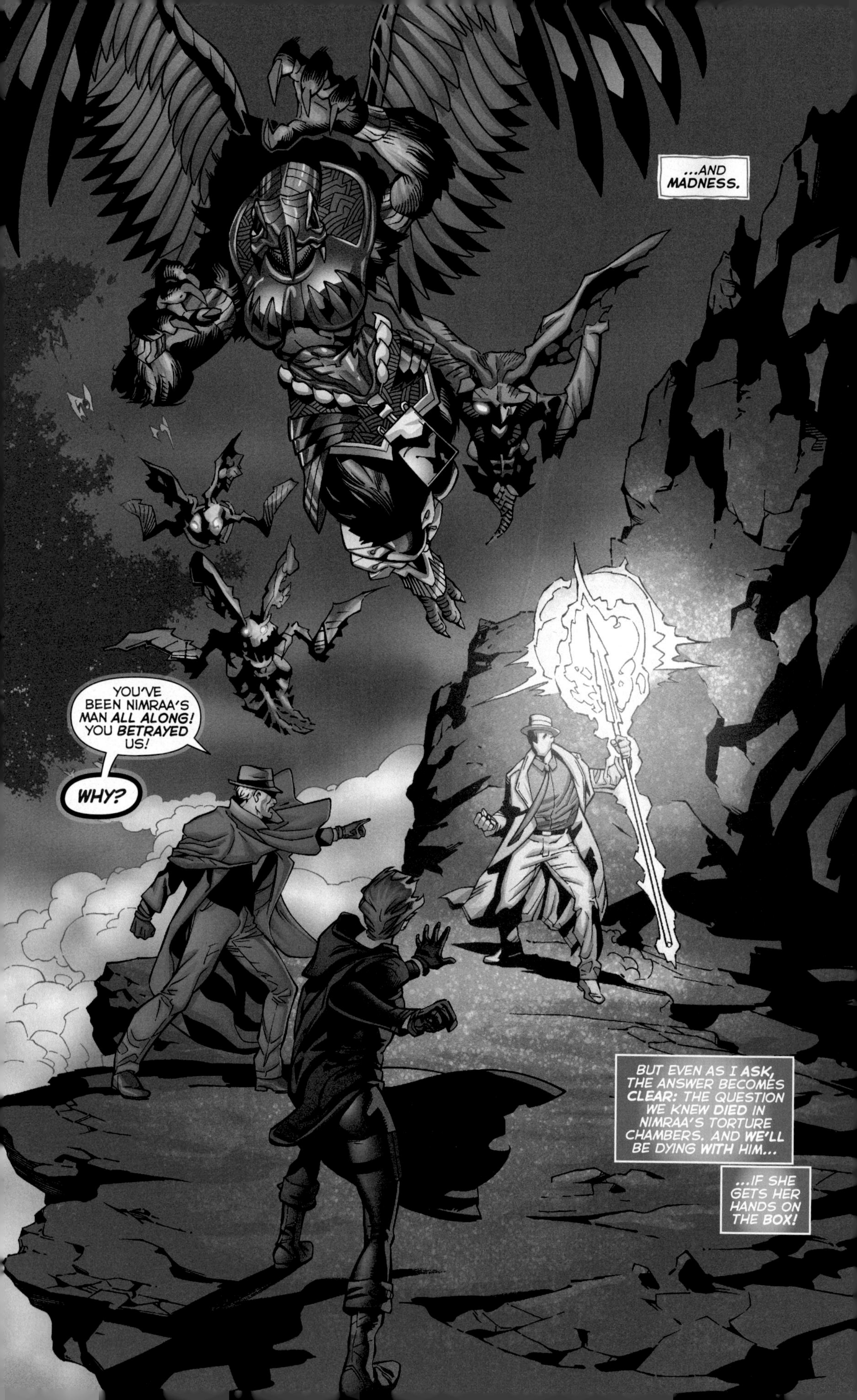
...AND MADNESS.
YOU'VE BEEN NIMRAA'S MAN ALL ALONG! YOU BETRAYED US!
WHY?
BUT EVEN AS I ASK, THE ANSWER BECOMES CLEAR: THE QUESTION WE KNEW DIED IN NIMRAA'S TORTURE CHAMBERS. AND WE'LL BE DYING WITH HIM...
...IF SHE GETS HER HANDS ON THE BOX!

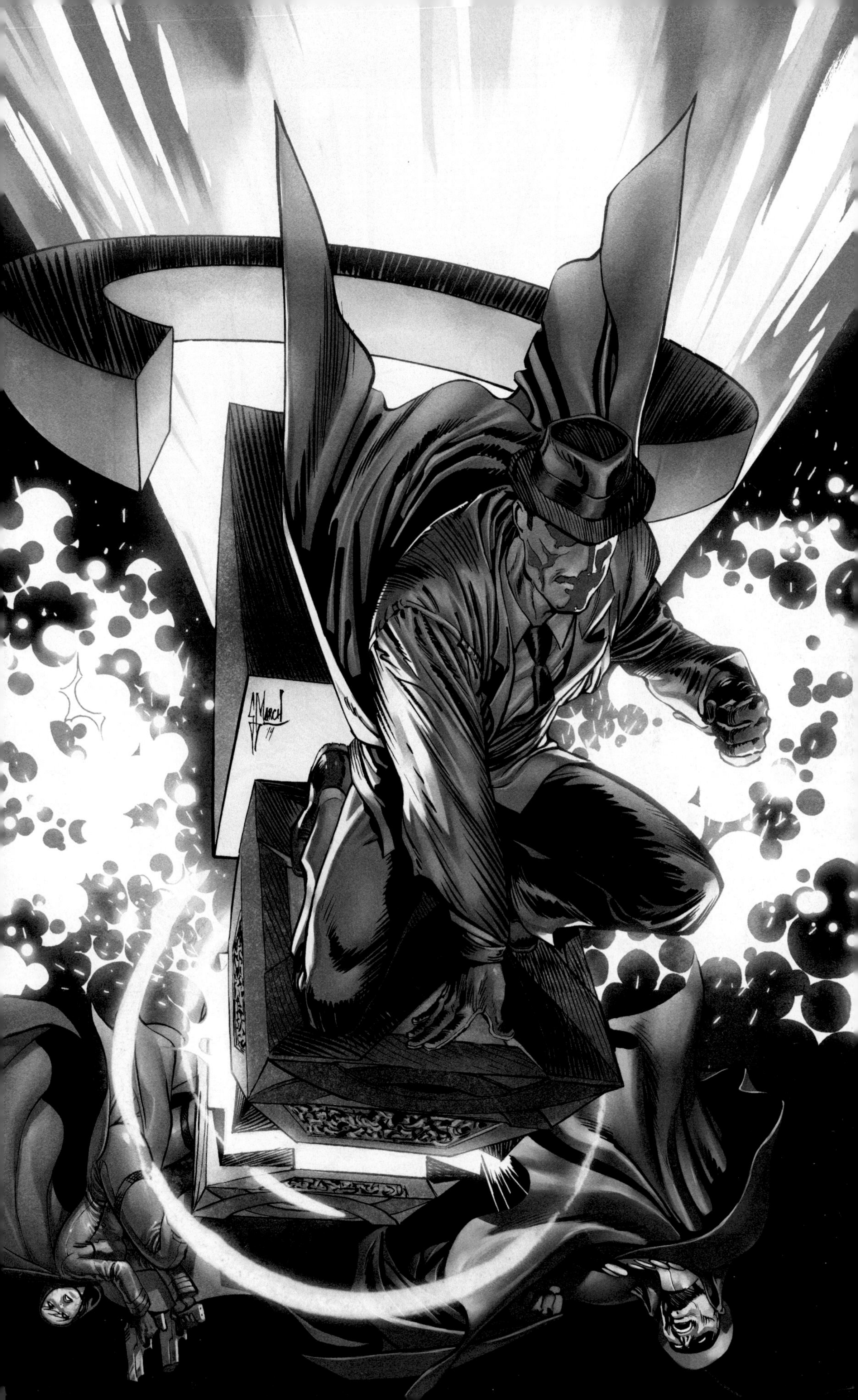

PART FOUR: FIRE ON THE MOUNTAIN

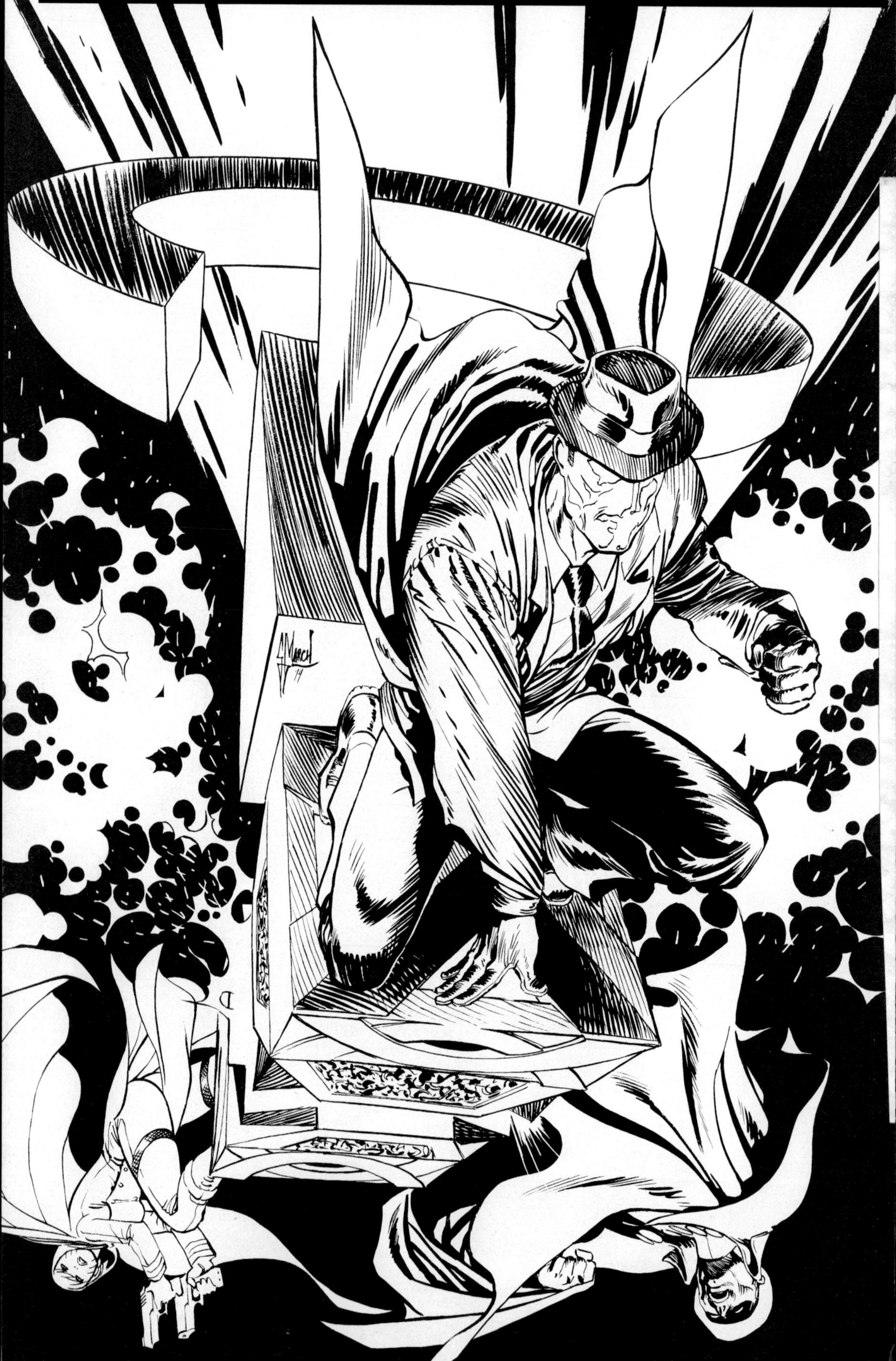

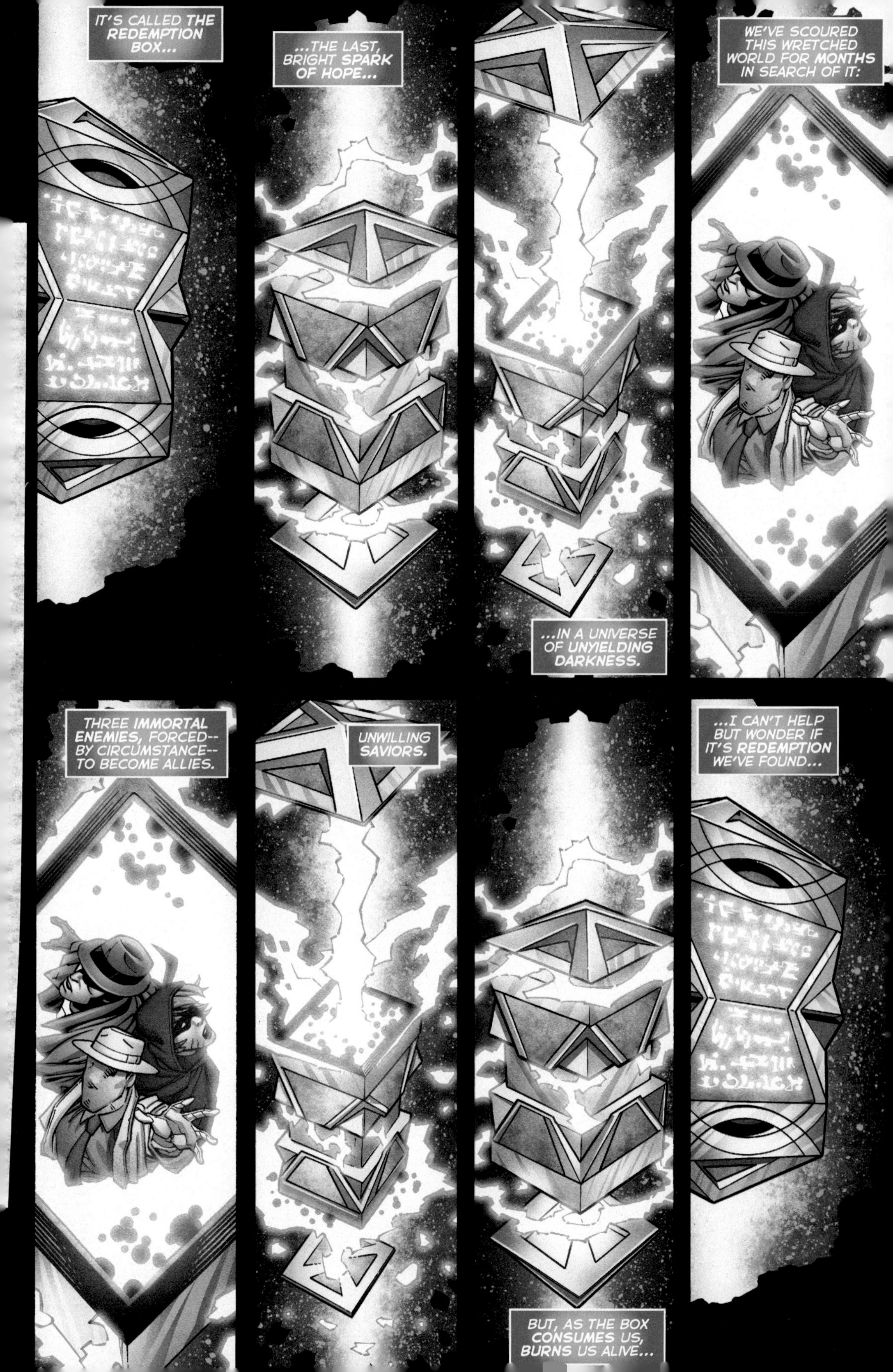

IT'S CALLED THE REDEMPTION BOX...
...THE LAST, BRIGHT SPARK OF HOPE...
...IN A UNIVERSE OF UNYIELDING DARKNESS.
WE'VE SCOURED THIS WRETCHED WORLD FOR MONTHS IN SEARCH OF IT:
THREE IMMORTAL ENEMIES, FORCED--BY CIRCUMSTANCE--TO BECOME ALLIES.
UNWILLING SAVIORS.
BUT, AS THE BOX CONSUMES US, BURNS US ALIVE...
...I CAN'T HELP BUT WONDER IF IT'S REDEMPTION WE'VE FOUND...

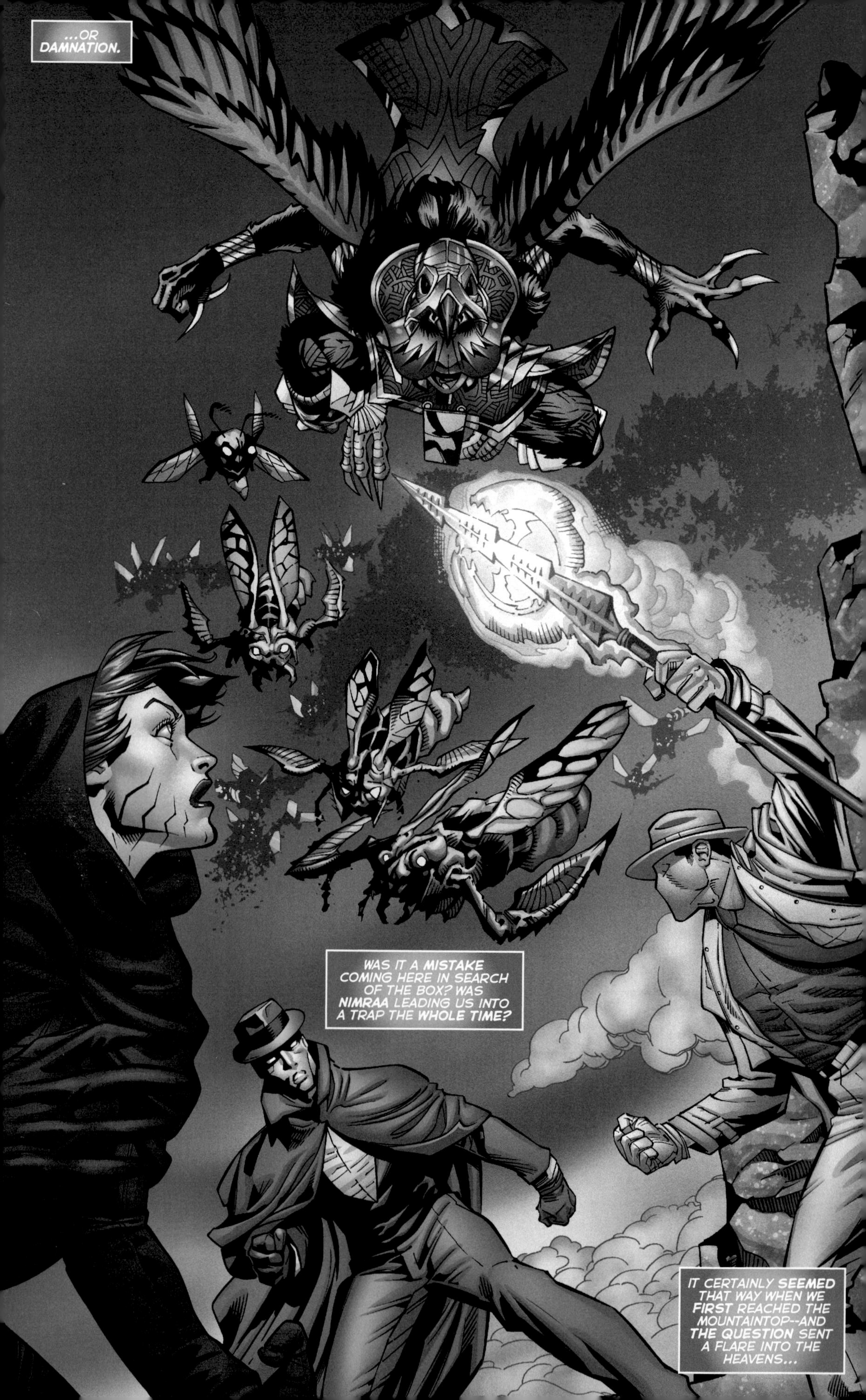
...OR DAMNATION.
WAS IT A MISTAKE COMING HERE IN SEARCH OF THE BOX? WAS NIMRAA LEADING US INTO A TRAP THE WHOLE TIME?
IT CERTAINLY SEEMED THAT WAY WHEN WE FIRST REACHED THE MOUNTAINTOP--AND THE QUESTION SENT A FLARE INTO THE HEAVENS...

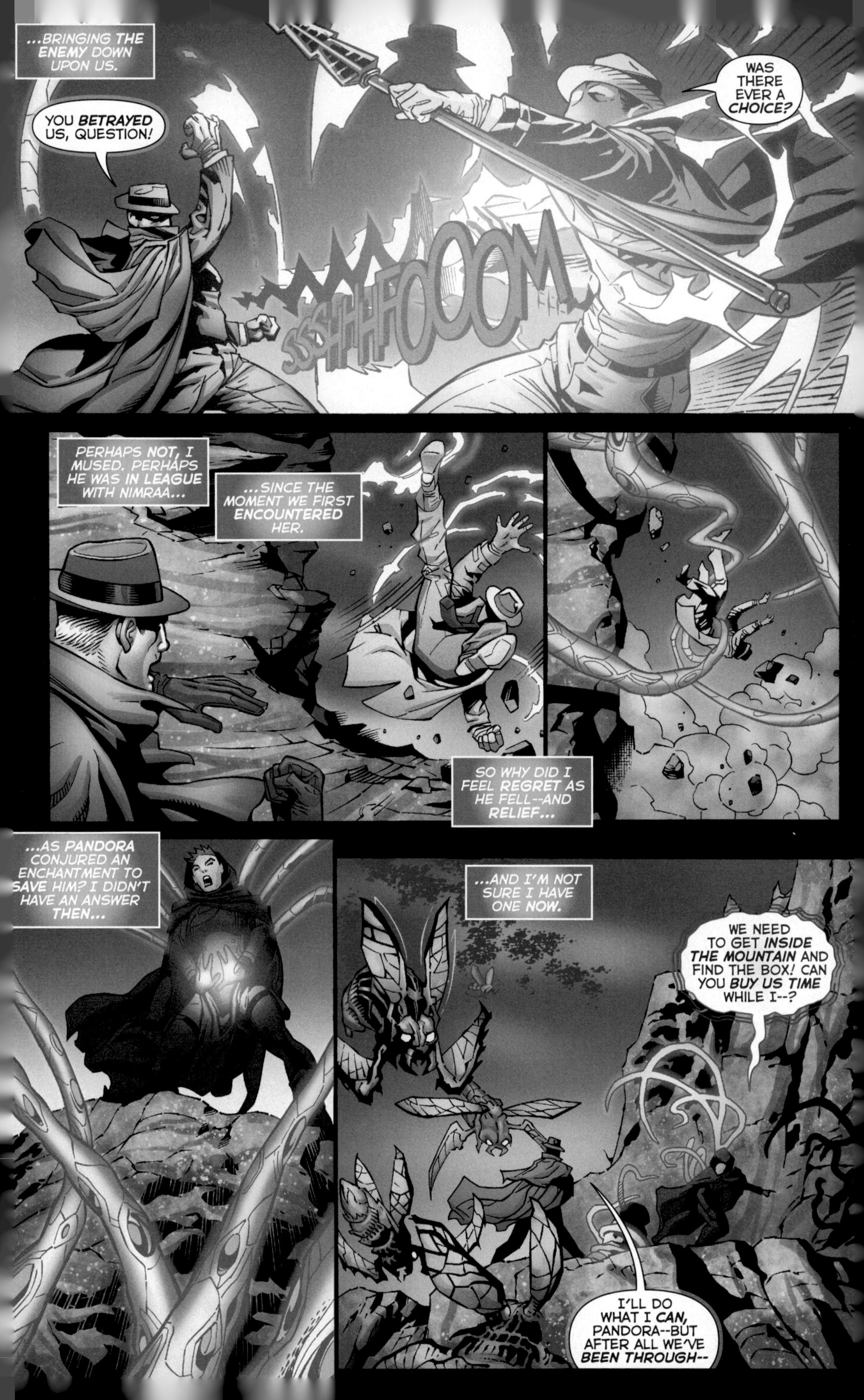
...BRINGING THE ENEMY DOWN UPON US.
YOU BETRAYED US, QUESTION!
WAS THERE EVER A CHOICE?
SSSHHHFOOOM
PERHAPS NOT, I MUSED. PERHAPS HE WAS IN LEAGUE WITH NIMRAA...
...SINCE THE MOMENT WE FIRST ENCOUNTERED HER.
SO WHY DID I FEEL REGRET AS HE FELL--AND RELIEF...
...AS PANDORA CONJURED AN ENCHANTMENT TO SAVE HIM? I DIDN'T HAVE AN ANSWER THEN...
...AND I'M NOT SURE I HAVE ONE NOW.
WE NEED TO GET INSIDE THE MOUNTAIN AND FIND THE BOX! CAN YOU BUY US TIME WHILE I--?
I'LL DO WHAT I CAN, PANDORA--BUT AFTER ALL WE'VE BEEN THROUGH--

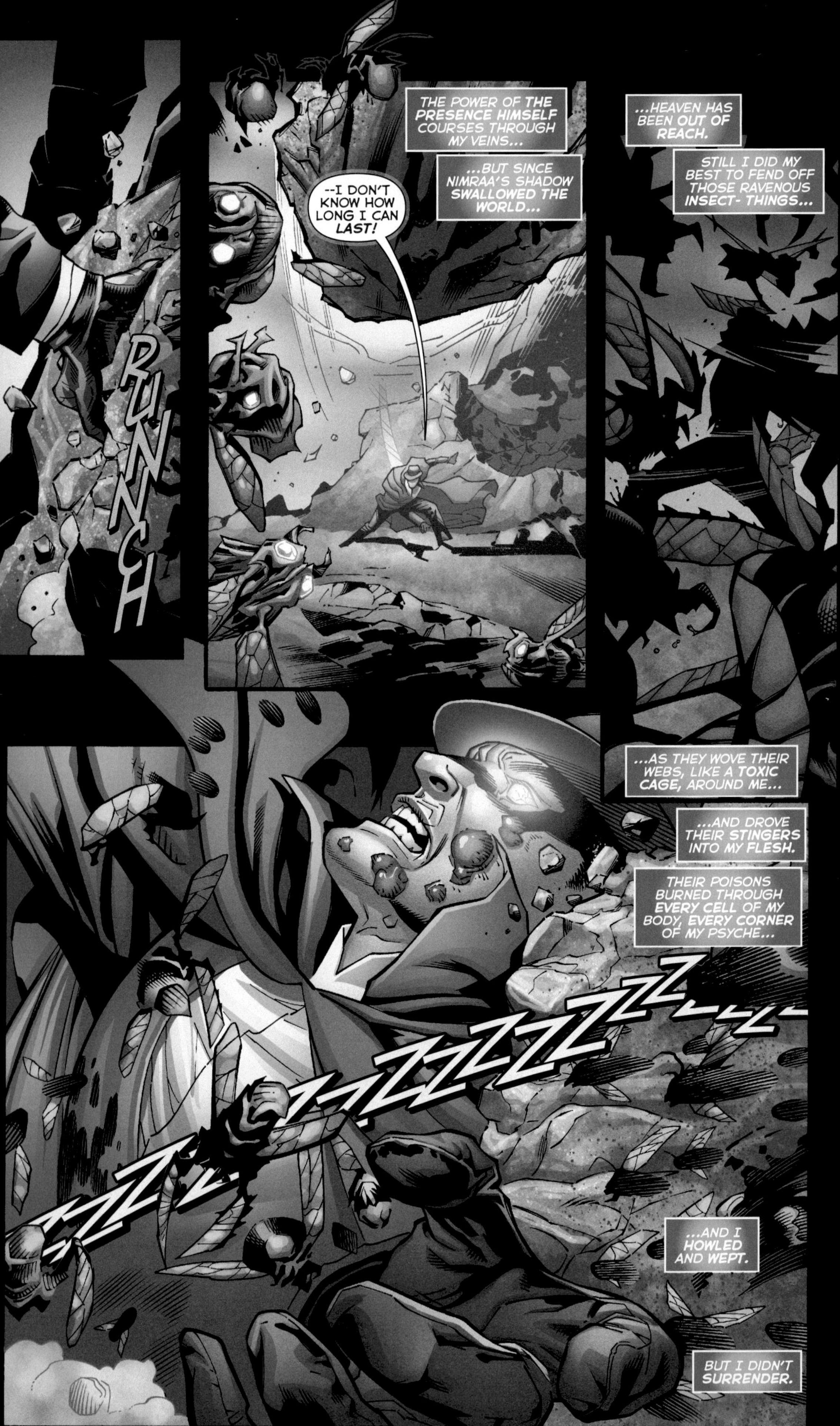
KRUNCH
THE POWER OF THE PRESENCE HIMSELF COURSES THROUGH MY VEINS...
...BUT SINCE NIMRAA'S SHADOW SWALLOWED THE WORLD...
--I DON'T KNOW HOW LONG I CAN LAST!
...HEAVEN HAS BEEN OUT OF REACH.
STILL I DID MY BEST TO FEND OFF THOSE RAVENOUS INSECT- THINGS...
...AS THEY WOVE THEIR WEBS, LIKE A TOXIC CAGE, AROUND ME...
...AND DROVE THEIR STINGERS INTO MY FLESH.
THEIR POISONS BURNED THROUGH EVERY CELL OF MY BODY, EVERY CORNER OF MY PSYCHE...
ZZZZZZZZZZZZZZZZ
...AND I HOWLED AND WEPT.
BUT I DIDN'T SURRENDER.

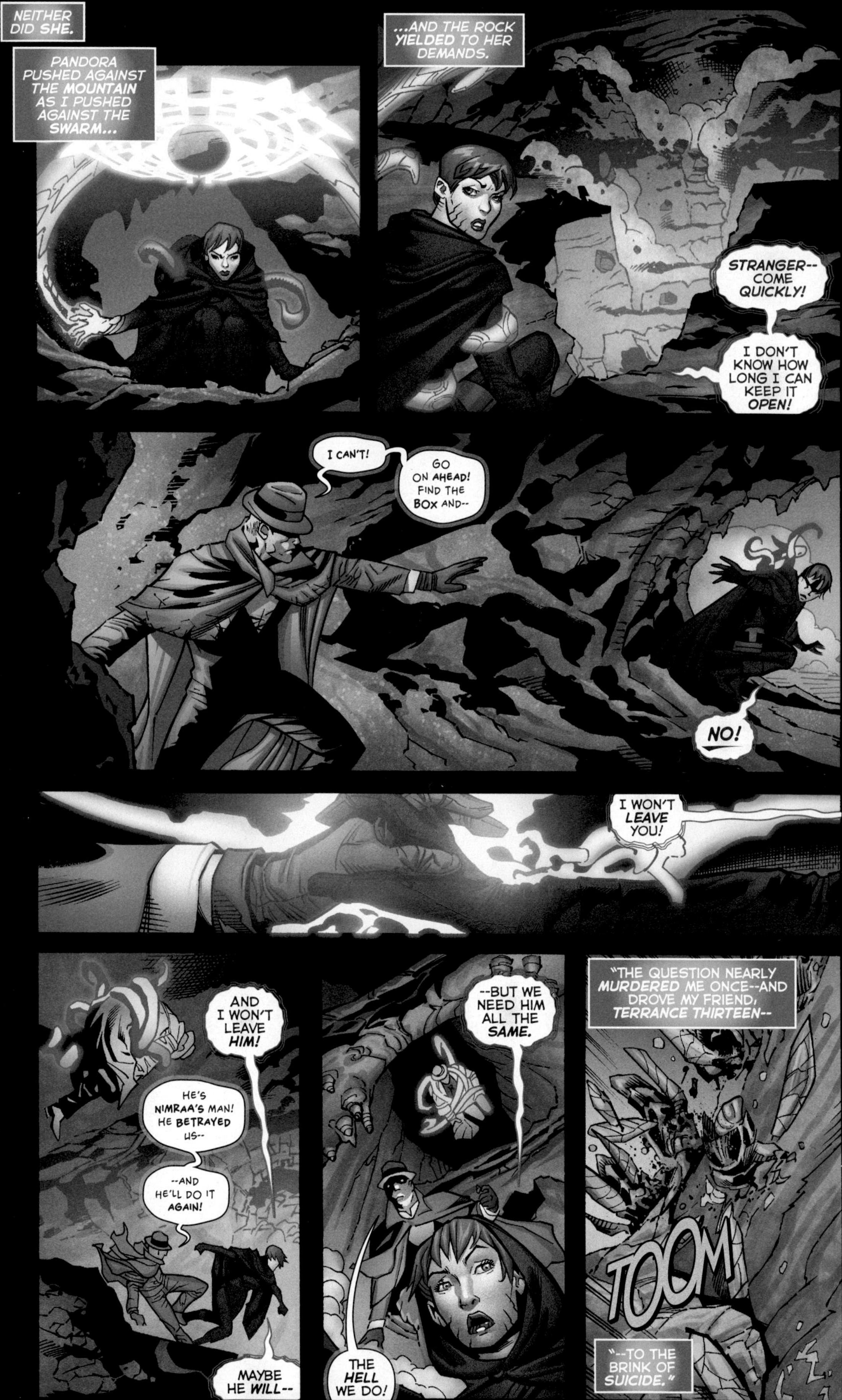
NEITHER DID SHE.
PANDORA PUSHED AGAINST THE MOUNTAIN AS I PUSHED AGAINST THE SWARM...
...AND THE ROCK YIELDED TO HER DEMANDS.
STRANGER--COME QUICKLY!
I DON'T KNOW HOW LONG I CAN KEEP IT OPEN!
I CAN'T!
GO ON AHEAD! FIND THE BOX AND--
NO!
I WON'T LEAVE YOU!
AND I WON'T LEAVE HIM!
HE'S NIMRAA'S MAN! HE BETRAYED US--
--AND HE'LL DO IT AGAIN!
MAYBE HE WILL--
--BUT WE NEED HIM ALL THE SAME.
THE HELL WE DO!
"THE QUESTION NEARLY MURDERED ME ONCE--AND DROVE MY FRIEND, TERRANCE THIRTEEN--
TOOM
"--TO THE BRINK OF SUICIDE."

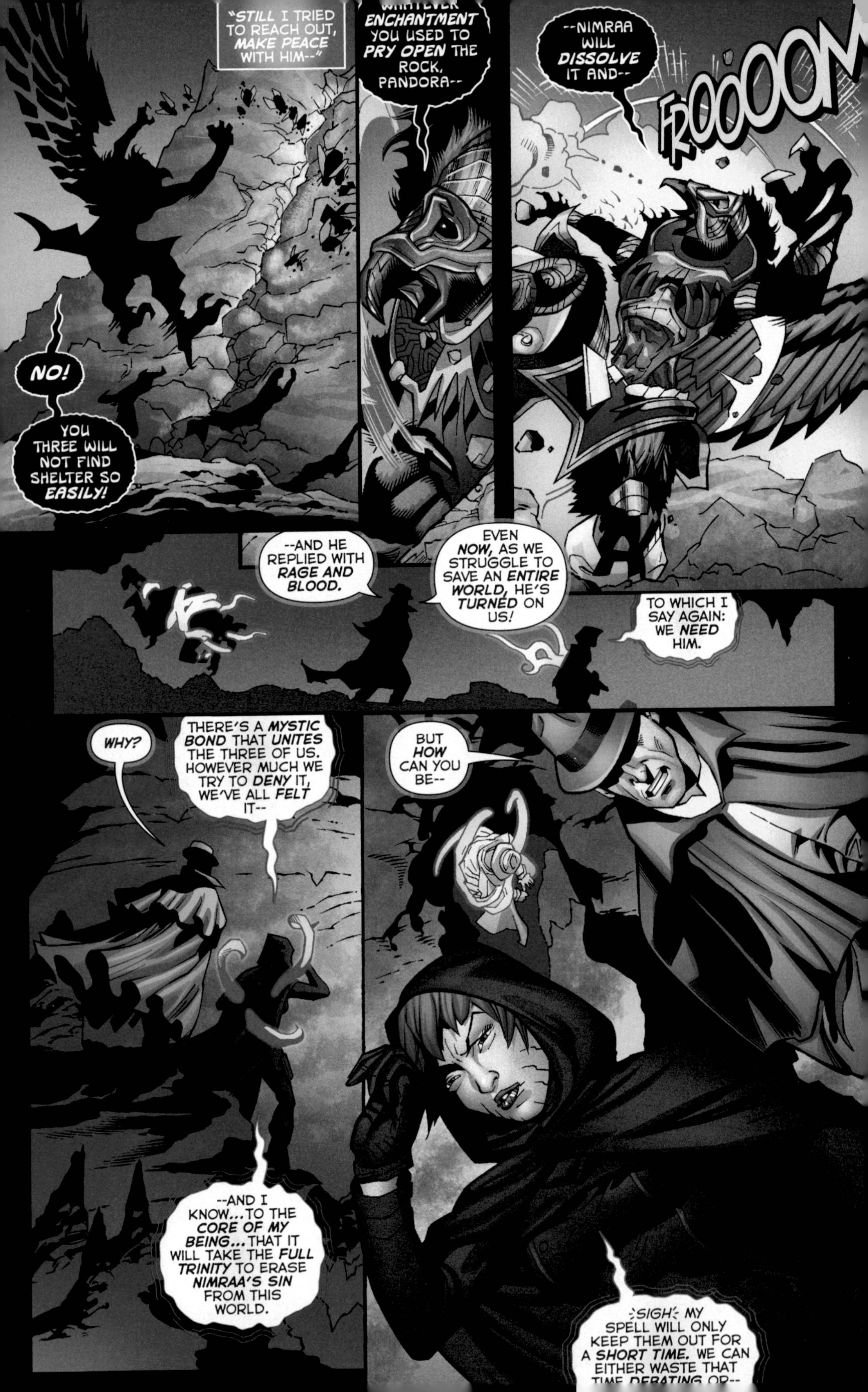

"STILL I TRIED TO REACH OUT, MAKE PEACE WITH HIM--"
NO!
YOU THREE WILL NOT FIND SHELTER SO EASILY!
ENCHANTMENT YOU USED TO PRY OPEN THE ROCK, PANDORA--
--NIMRAA WILL DISSOLVE IT AND--
FROOOOOM
--AND HE REPLIED WITH RAGE AND BLOOD.
EVEN NOW, AS WE STRUGGLE TO SAVE AN ENTIRE WORLD, HE'S TURNED ON US!
TO WHICH I SAY AGAIN: WE NEED HIM.
WHY?
THERE'S A MYSTIC BOND THAT UNITES THE THREE OF US. HOWEVER MUCH WE TRY TO DENY IT, WE'VE ALL FELT IT--
--AND I KNOW...TO THE CORE OF MY BEING...THAT IT WILL TAKE THE FULL TRINITY TO ERASE NIMRAA'S SIN FROM THIS WORLD.
BUT HOW CAN YOU BE--
SIGH MY SPELL WILL ONLY KEEP THEM OUT FOR A SHORT TIME. WE CAN EITHER WASTE THAT TIME DEBATING OR--

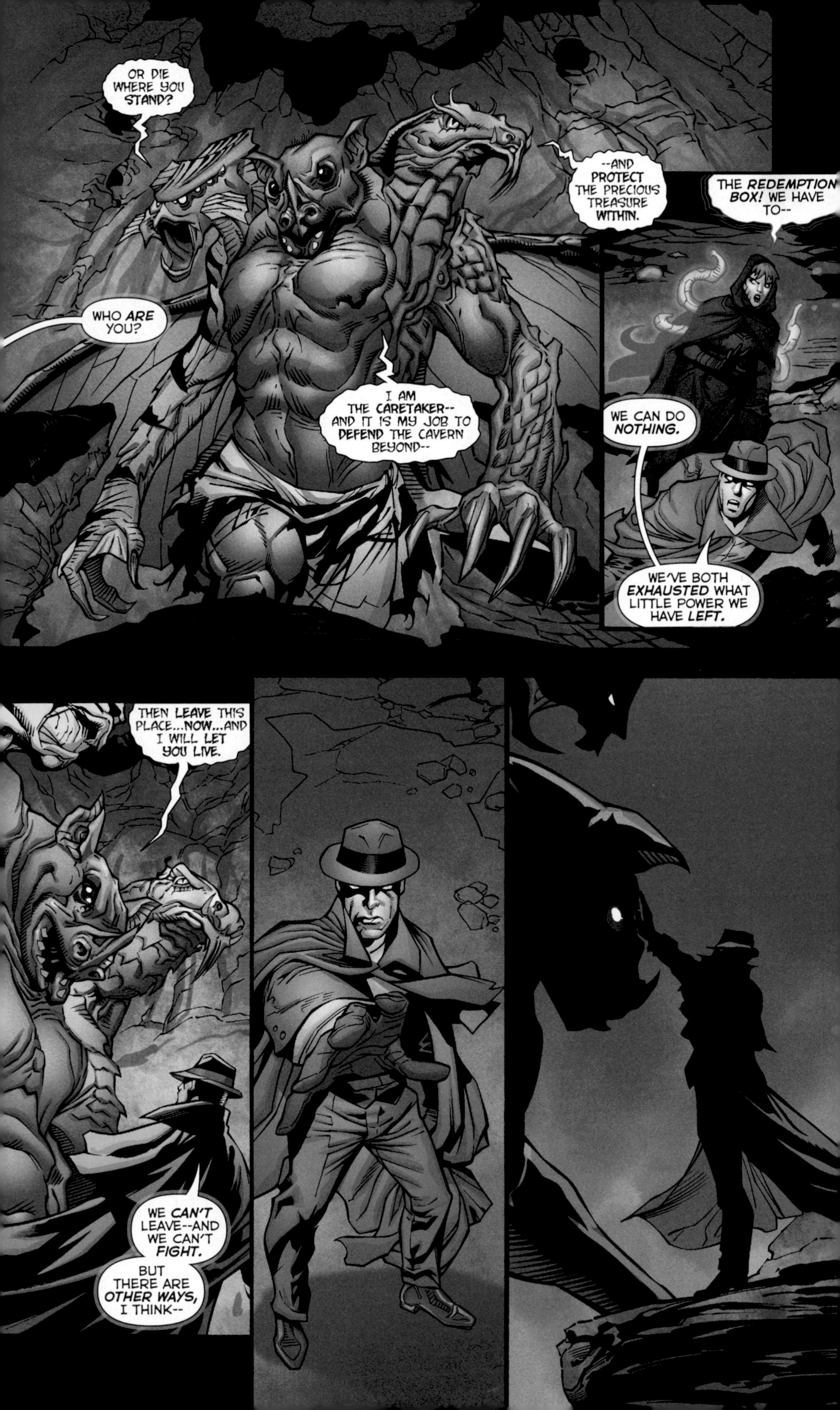
OR DIE WHERE YOU STAND?
WHO ARE YOU?
I AM THE CARETAKER--AND IT IS MY JOB TO DEFEND THE CAVERN BEYOND--
--AND PROTECT THE PRECIOUS TREASURE WITHIN.
THE REDEMPTION BOX! WE HAVE TO--
WE CAN DO NOTHING.
WE'VE BOTH EXHAUSTED WHAT LITTLE POWER WE HAVE LEFT.
THEN LEAVE THIS PLACE...NOW...AND I WILL LET YOU LIVE.
WE CAN'T LEAVE--AND WE CAN'T FIGHT.
BUT THERE ARE OTHER WAYS, I THINK--

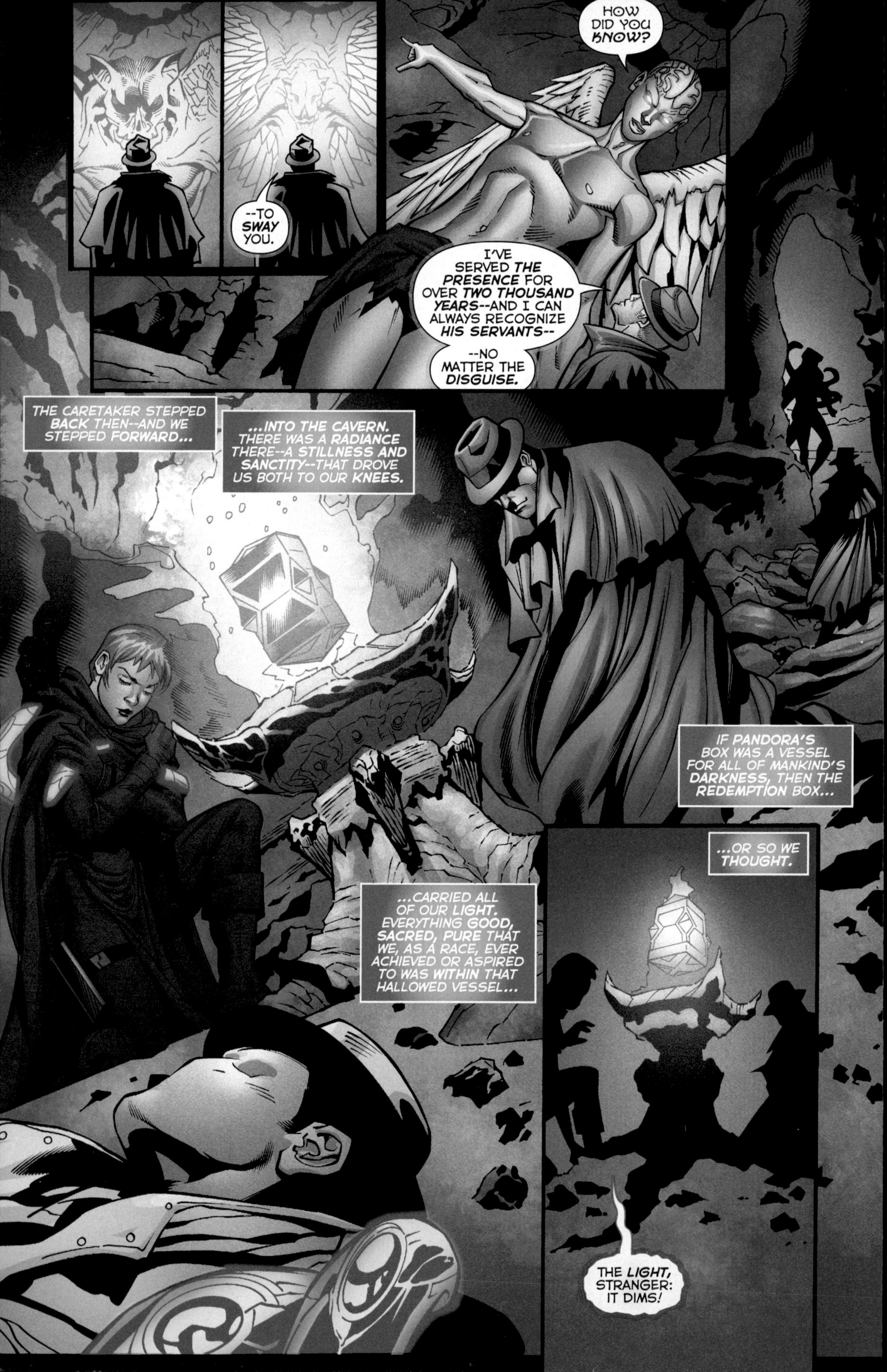
--TO SWAY YOU.
HOW DID YOU KNOW?
I'VE SERVED THE PRESENCE FOR OVER TWO THOUSAND YEARS--AND I CAN ALWAYS RECOGNIZE HIS SERVANTS--
--NO MATTER THE DISGUISE.
THE CARETAKER STEPPED BACK THEN--AND WE STEPPED FORWARD...
...INTO THE CAVERN. THERE WAS A RADIANCE THERE--A STILLNESS AND SANCTITY--THAT DROVE US BOTH TO OUR KNEES.
IF PANDORA'S BOX WAS A VESSEL FOR ALL OF MANKIND'S DARKNESS, THEN THE REDEMPTION BOX...
...CARRIED ALL OF OUR LIGHT. EVERYTHING GOOD, SACRED, PURE THAT WE, AS A RACE, EVER ACHIEVED OR ASPIRED TO WAS WITHIN THAT HALLOWED VESSEL...
...OR SO WE THOUGHT.
THE LIGHT, STRANGER: IT DIMS!

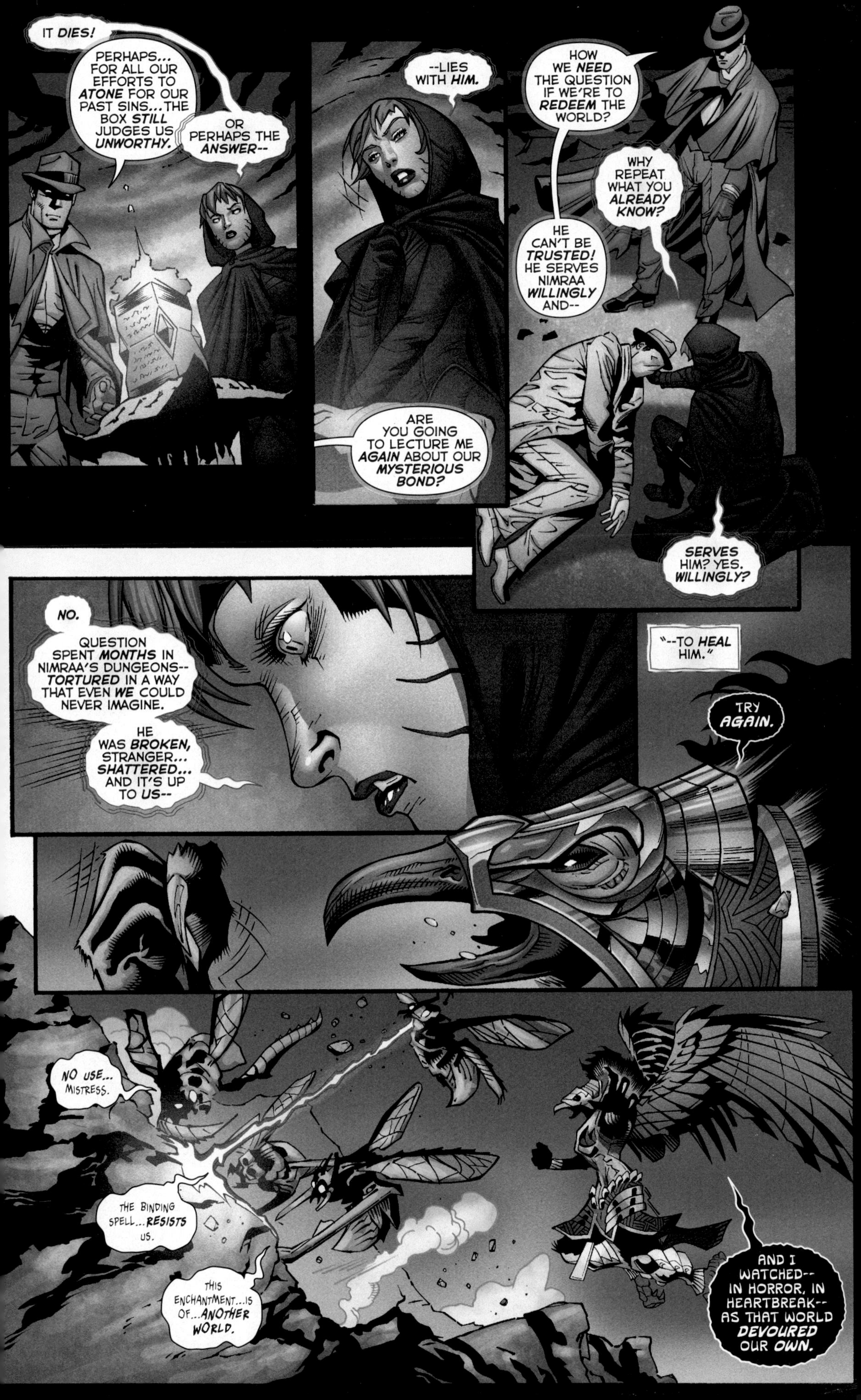
IT DIES!
PERHAPS... FOR ALL OUR EFFORTS TO ATONE FOR OUR PAST SINS... THE BOX STILL JUDGES US UNWORTHY.
OR PERHAPS THE ANSWER--
--LIES WITH HIM.
ARE YOU GOING TO LECTURE ME AGAIN ABOUT OUR MYSTERIOUS BOND?
HOW WE NEED THE QUESTION IF WE'RE TO REDEEM THE WORLD?
WHY REPEAT WHAT YOU ALREADY KNOW?
HE CAN'T BE TRUSTED! HE SERVES NIMRAA WILLINGLY AND--
SERVES HIM? YES. WILLINGLY?
NO.
QUESTION SPENT MONTHS IN NIMRAA'S DUNGEONS-- TORTURED IN A WAY THAT EVEN WE COULD NEVER IMAGINE.
HE WAS BROKEN, STRANGER... SHATTERED... AND IT'S UP TO US--
"--TO HEAL HIM."
TRY AGAIN.
NO USE... MISTRESS.
THE BINDING SPELL... RESISTS US.
THIS ENCHANTMENT... IS OF... ANOTHER WORLD.
AND I WATCHED-- IN HORROR, IN HEARTBREAK-- AS THAT WORLD DEVOURED OUR OWN.

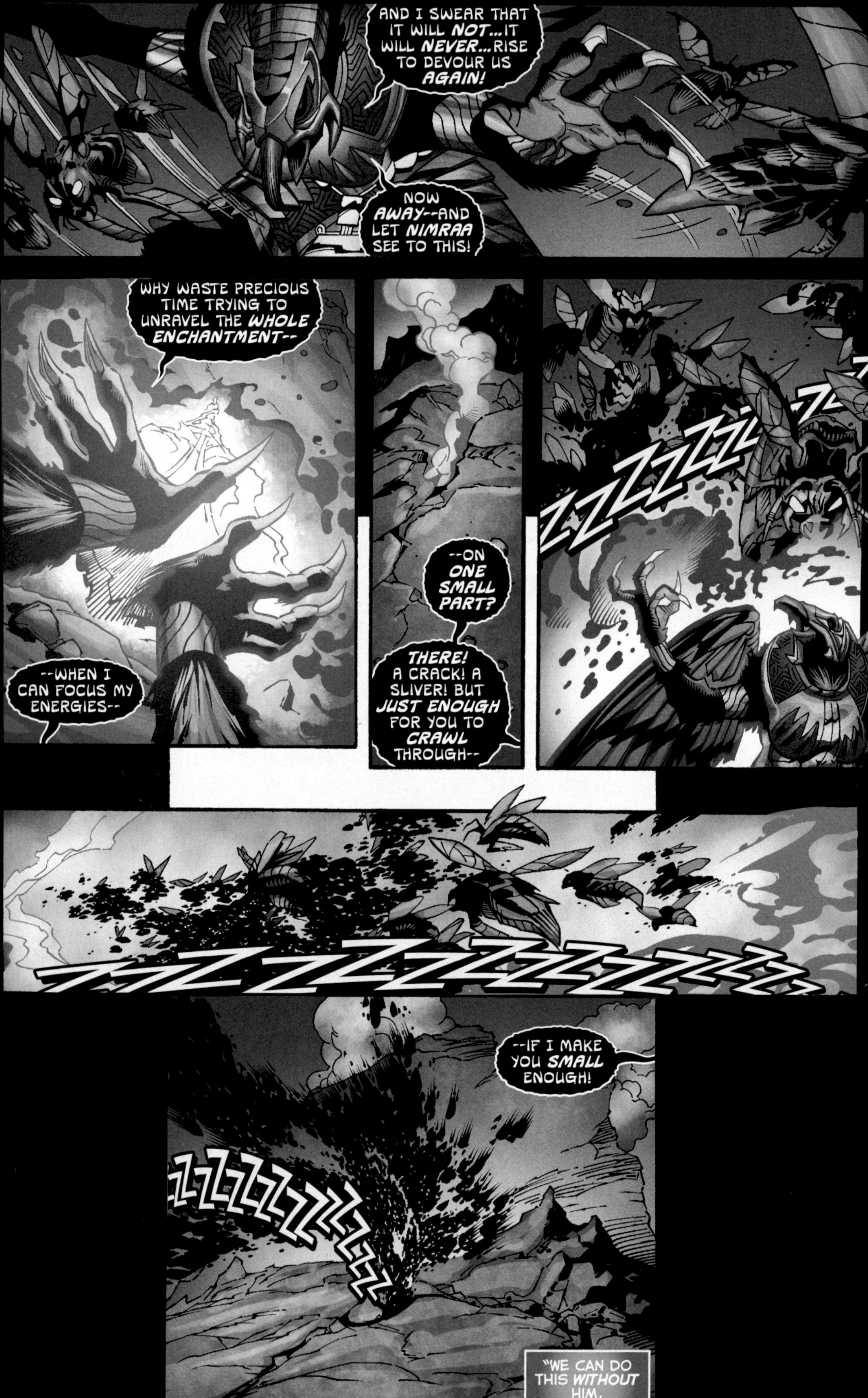
AND I SWEAR THAT IT WILL NOT...IT WILL NEVER...RISE TO DEVOUR US AGAIN!
NOW AWAY--AND LET NIMRAA SEE TO THIS!
WHY WASTE PRECIOUS TIME TRYING TO UNRAVEL THE WHOLE ENCHANTMENT--
--WHEN I CAN FOCUS MY ENERGIES--
--ON ONE SMALL PART?
THERE! A CRACK! A SLIVER! BUT JUST ENOUGH FOR YOU TO CRAWL THROUGH--
ZZZZZZZZZZZ
ZZZZZZZZZZZZZZZZZ
--IF I MAKE YOU SMALL ENOUGH!
ZZZZZZZZZZZZZZZZ
"WE CAN DO THIS WITHOUT HIM, PANDORA!"

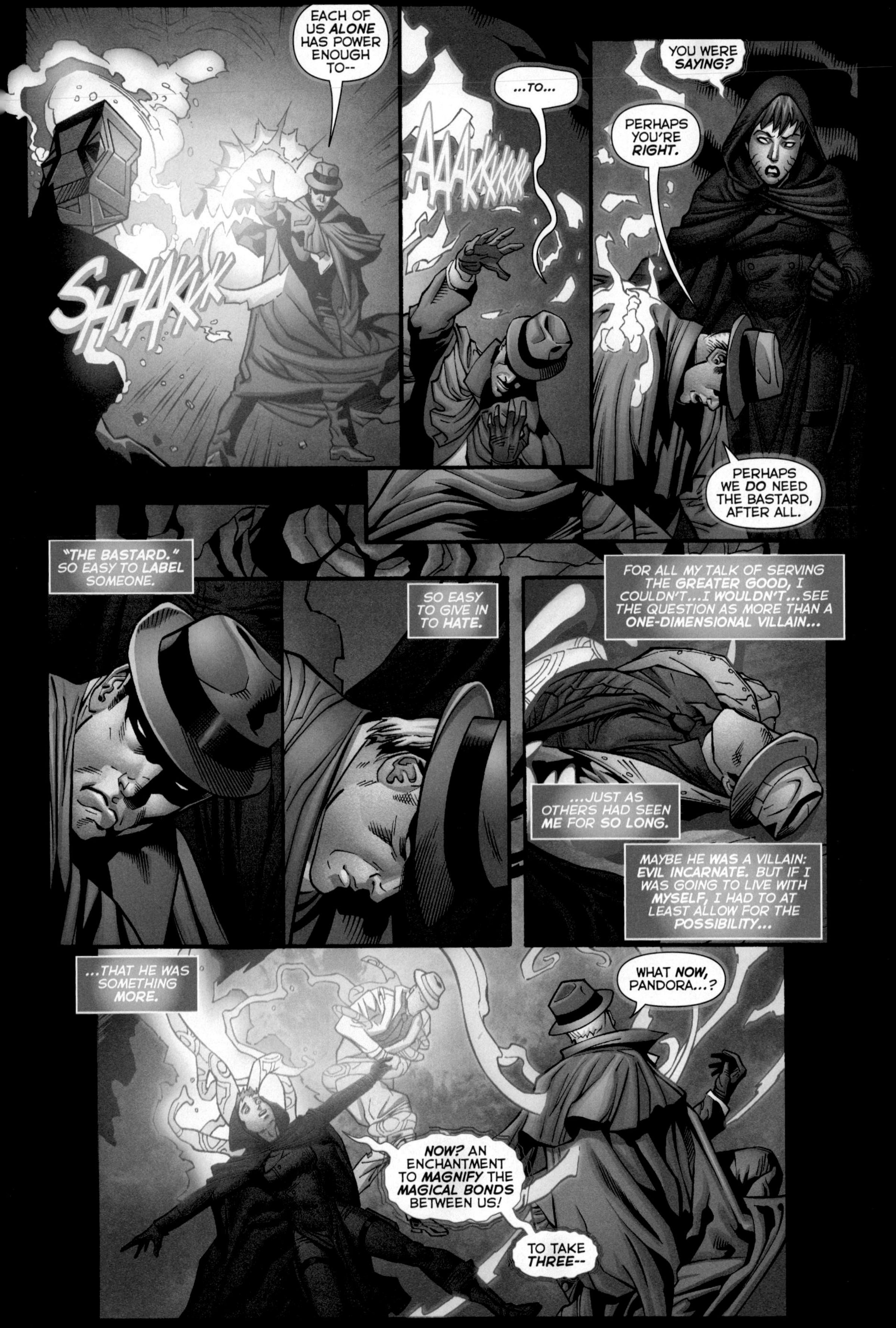
EACH OF US ALONE HAS POWER ENOUGH TO--
SHHAKKK
...TO...
AAAKKKKKK
YOU WERE SAYING?
PERHAPS YOU'RE RIGHT.
PERHAPS WE DO NEED THE BASTARD, AFTER ALL.
"THE BASTARD." SO EASY TO LABEL SOMEONE.
SO EASY TO GIVE IN TO HATE.
FOR ALL MY TALK OF SERVING THE GREATER GOOD, I COULDN'T...I WOULDN'T...SEE THE QUESTION AS MORE THAN A ONE-DIMENSIONAL VILLAIN...
...JUST AS OTHERS HAD SEEN ME FOR SO LONG.
MAYBE HE WAS A VILLAIN: EVIL INCARNATE. BUT IF I WAS GOING TO LIVE WITH MYSELF, I HAD TO AT LEAST ALLOW FOR THE POSSIBILITY...
...THAT HE WAS SOMETHING MORE.
WHAT NOW, PANDORA...?
NOW? AN ENCHANTMENT TO MAGNIFY THE MAGICAL BONDS BETWEEN US!
TO TAKE THREE--

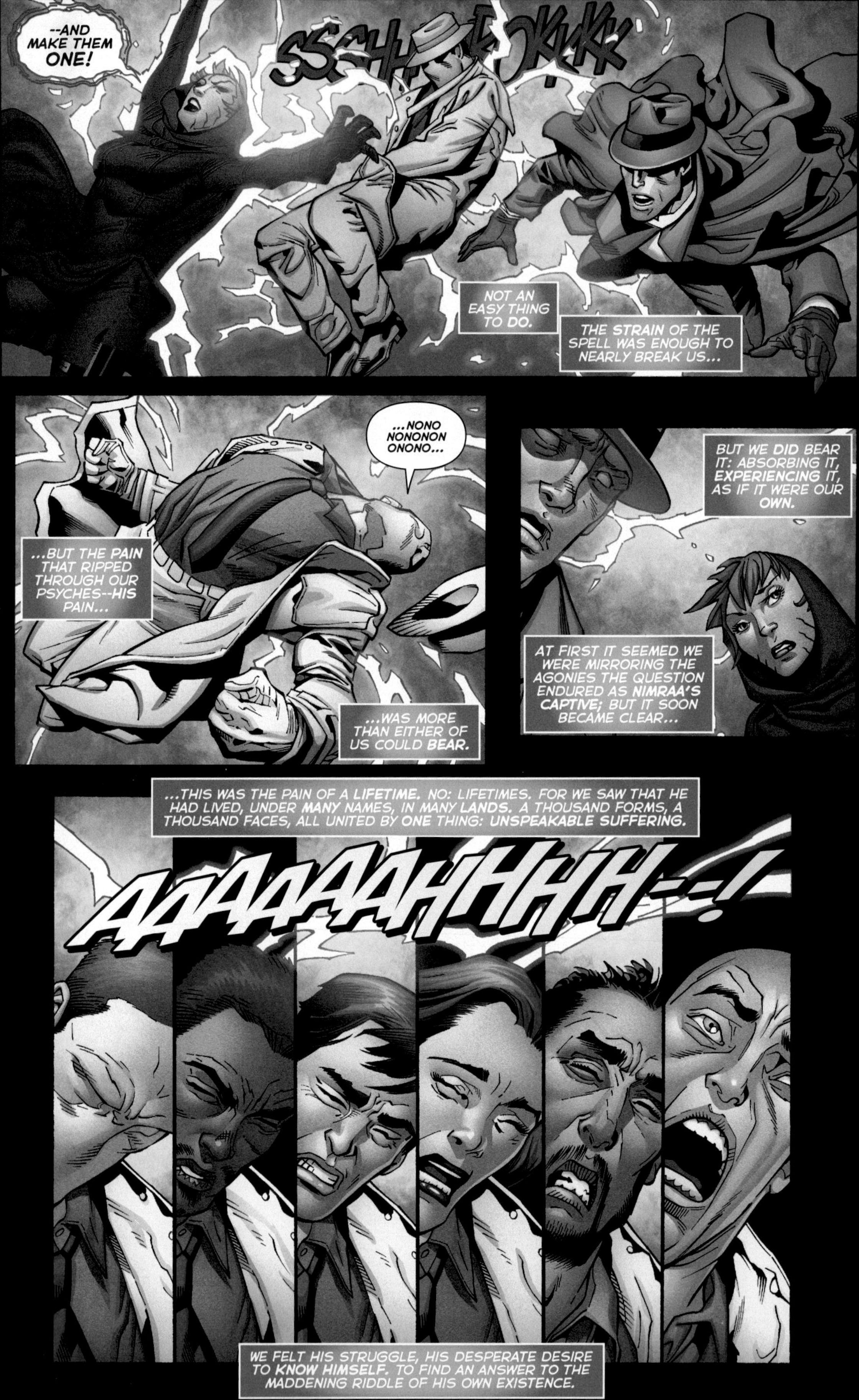
--AND MAKE THEM ONE!
NOT AN EASY THING TO DO.
THE STRAIN OF THE SPELL WAS ENOUGH TO NEARLY BREAK US...
...NONO NONONON ONONO...
...BUT THE PAIN THAT RIPPED THROUGH OUR PSYCHES--HIS PAIN...
...WAS MORE THAN EITHER OF US COULD BEAR.
BUT WE DID BEAR IT: ABSORBING IT, EXPERIENCING IT, AS IF IT WERE OUR OWN.
AT FIRST IT SEEMED WE WERE MIRRORING THE AGONIES THE QUESTION ENDURED AS NIMRAA'S CAPTIVE; BUT IT SOON BECAME CLEAR...
...THIS WAS THE PAIN OF A LIFETIME. NO: LIFETIMES. FOR WE SAW THAT HE HAD LIVED, UNDER MANY NAMES, IN MANY LANDS. A THOUSAND FORMS, A THOUSAND FACES, ALL UNITED BY ONE THING: UNSPEAKABLE SUFFERING.
AAAAAAHHHH--!
WE FELT HIS STRUGGLE, HIS DESPERATE DESIRE TO KNOW HIMSELF. TO FIND AN ANSWER TO THE MADDENING RIDDLE OF HIS OWN EXISTENCE.

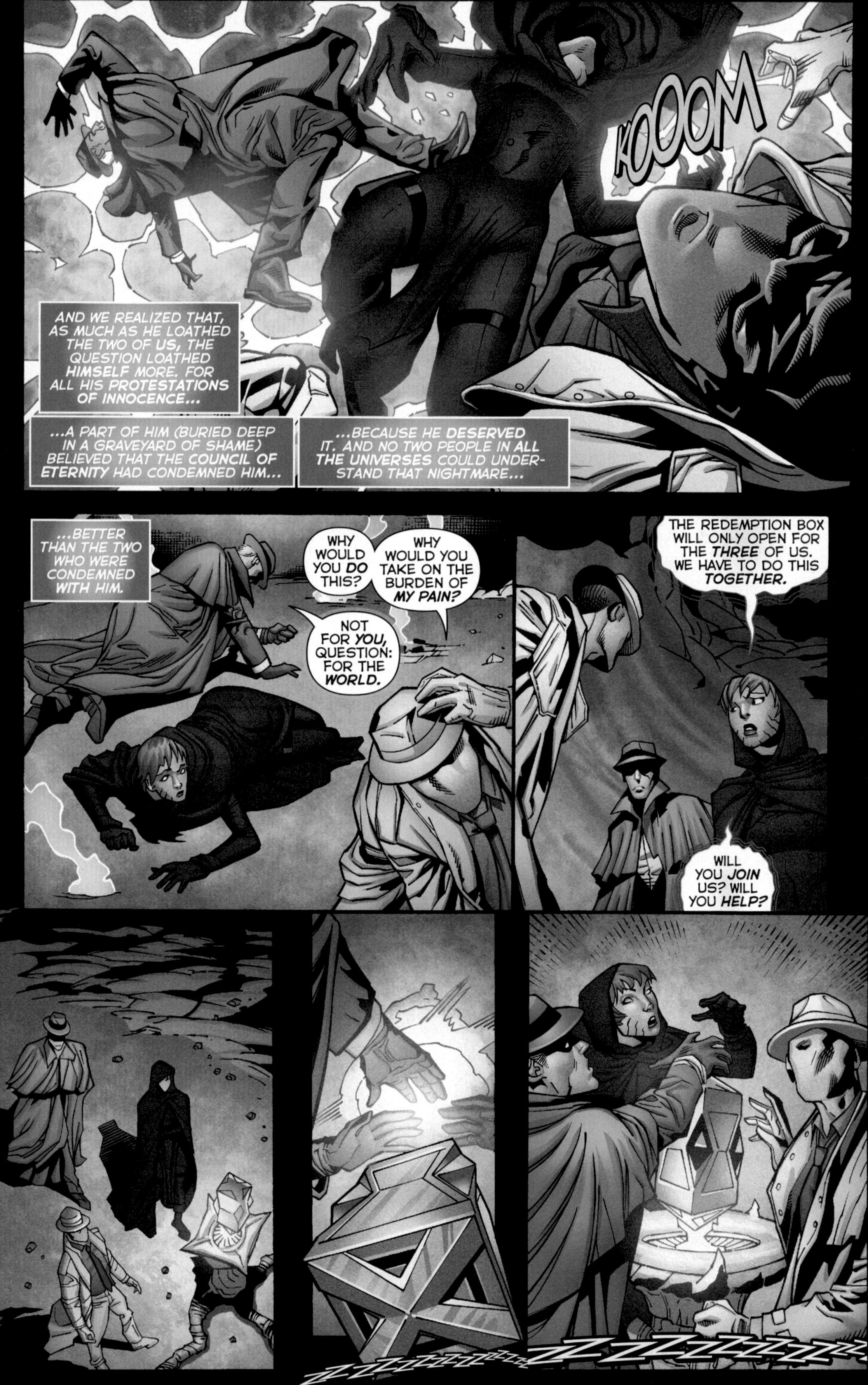
KOOOM
AND WE REALIZED THAT, AS MUCH AS HE LOATHED THE TWO OF US, THE QUESTION LOATHED HIMSELF MORE. FOR ALL HIS PROTESTATIONS OF INNOCENCE...
...A PART OF HIM (BURIED DEEP IN A GRAVEYARD OF SHAME) BELIEVED THAT THE COUNCIL OF ETERNITY HAD CONDEMNED HIM...
...BECAUSE HE DESERVED IT. AND NO TWO PEOPLE IN ALL THE UNIVERSES COULD UNDERSTAND THAT NIGHTMARE...
...BETTER THAN THE TWO WHO WERE CONDEMNED WITH HIM.
WHY WOULD YOU DO THIS?
WHY WOULD YOU TAKE ON THE BURDEN OF MY PAIN?
NOT FOR YOU, QUESTION: FOR THE WORLD.
THE REDEMPTION BOX WILL ONLY OPEN FOR THE THREE OF US. WE HAVE TO DO THIS TOGETHER.
WILL YOU JOIN US? WILL YOU HELP?
ZZZZZZZZZZZ

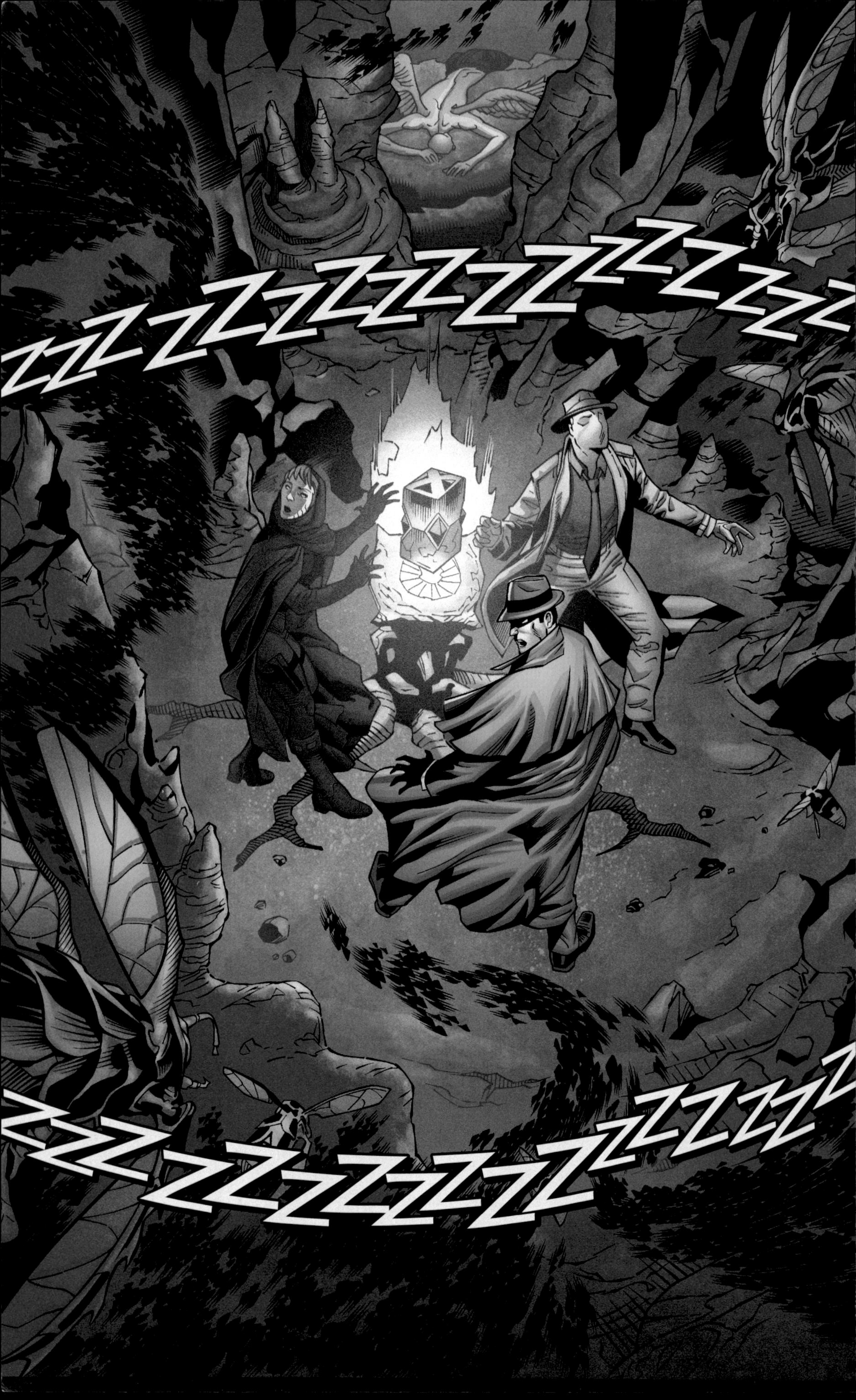
ZZZZZZZZZZZZZZZZZZZZ
ZZZZZZZZZZZZZZZZZZ

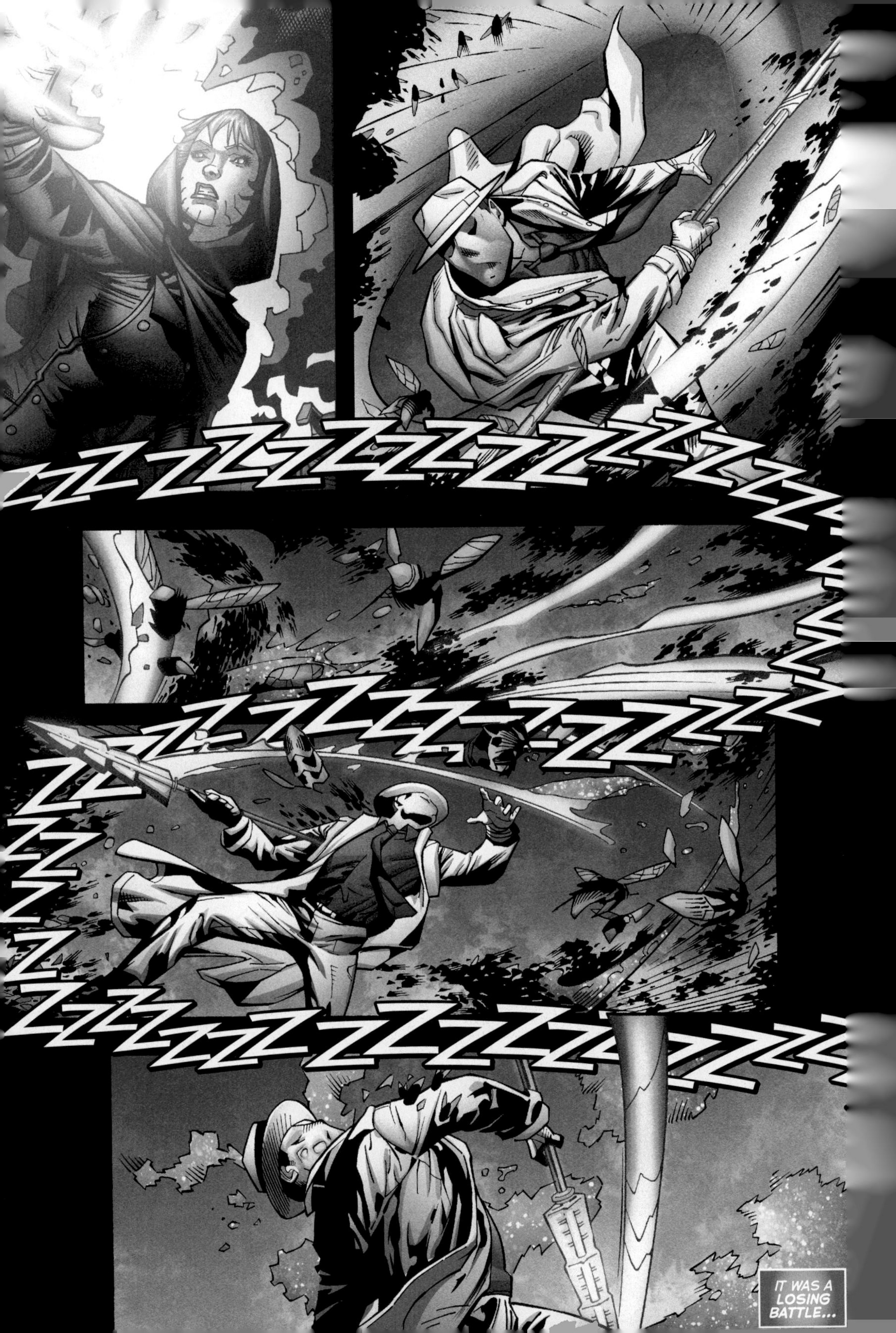
ZZZZZZZZZZZZZZ
ZZZZZZZZZZZZZZ
ZZZZZZZZZZZZZZ
IT WAS A LOSING BATTLE...

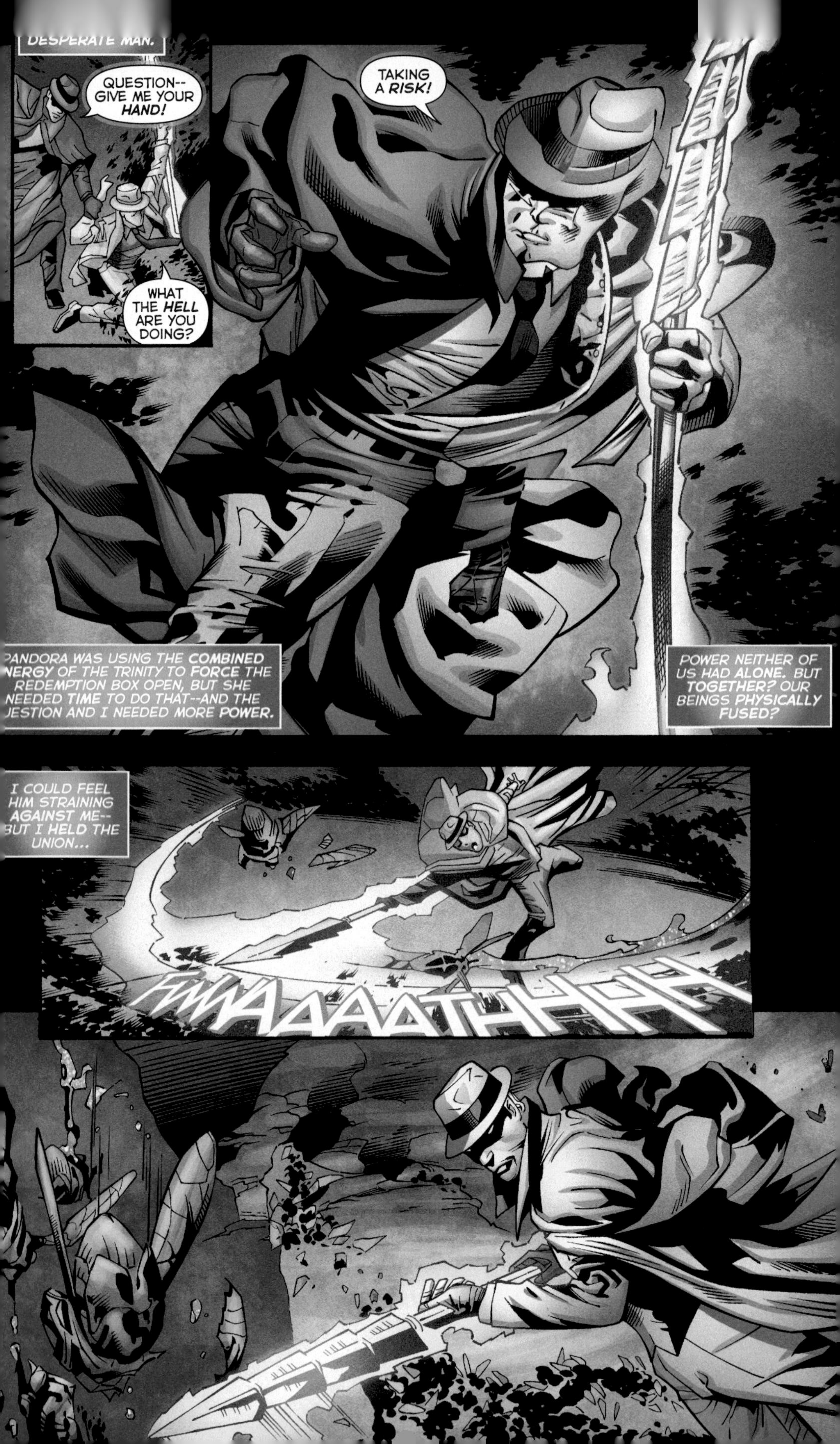
DESPERATE MAN.
QUESTION-- GIVE ME YOUR HAND!
WHAT THE HELL ARE YOU DOING?
TAKING A RISK!
PANDORA WAS USING THE COMBINED NERGY OF THE TRINITY TO FORCE THE REDEMPTION BOX OPEN, BUT SHE NEEDED TIME TO DO THAT--AND THE UESTION AND I NEEDED MORE POWER.
POWER NEITHER OF US HAD ALONE. BUT TOGETHER? OUR BEINGS PHYSICALLY FUSED?
I COULD FEEL HIM STRAINING AGAINST ME-- BUT I HELD THE UNION...
FWAAAAATHHHH

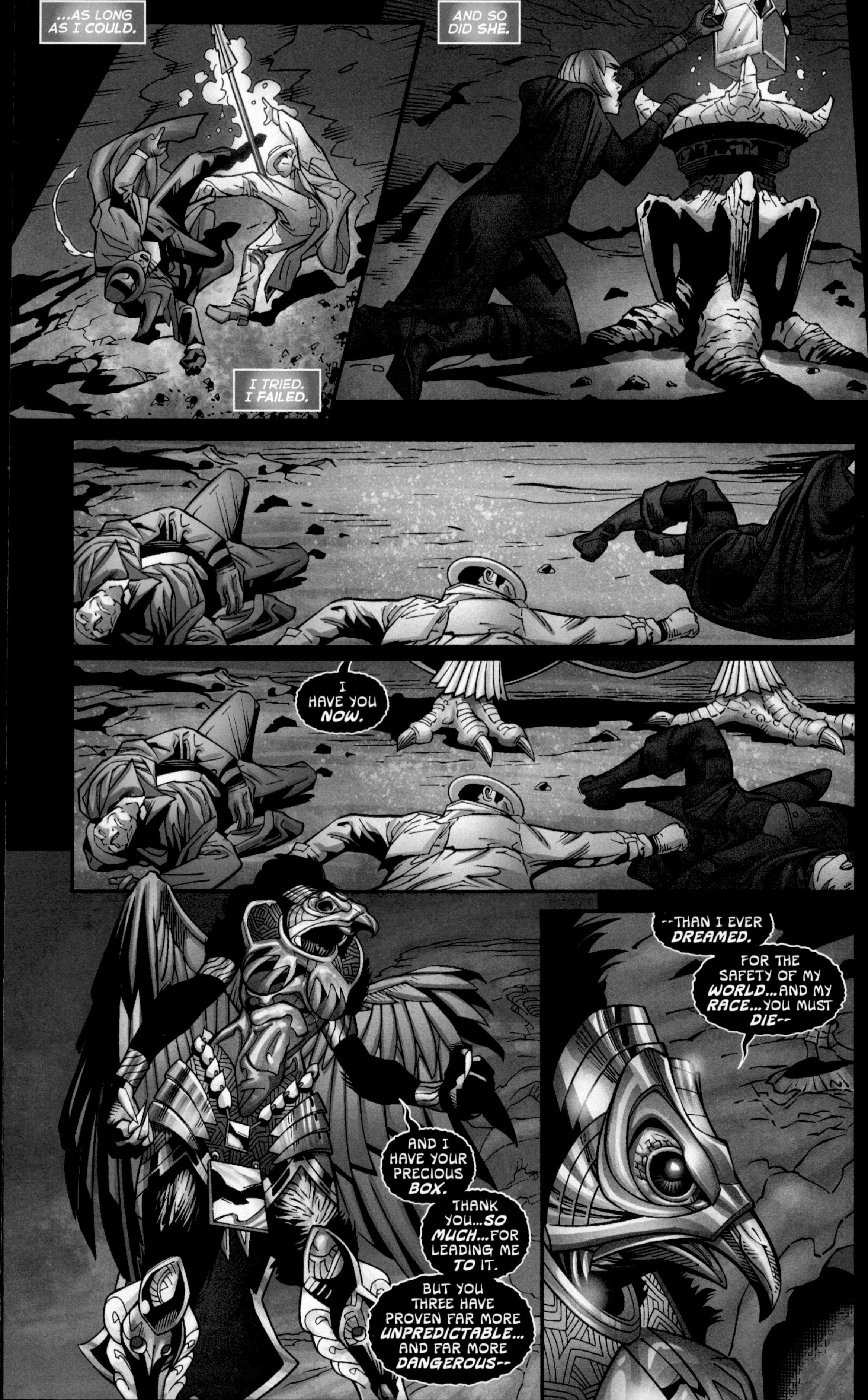
...AS LONG AS I COULD.
I TRIED. I FAILED.
AND SO DID SHE.
I HAVE YOU NOW.
AND I HAVE YOUR PRECIOUS BOX.
THANK YOU...SO MUCH...FOR LEADING ME TO IT.
BUT YOU THREE HAVE PROVEN FAR MORE UNPREDICTABLE... AND FAR MORE DANGEROUS--
--THAN I EVER DREAMED.
FOR THE SAFETY OF MY WORLD...AND MY RACE...YOU MUST DIE--

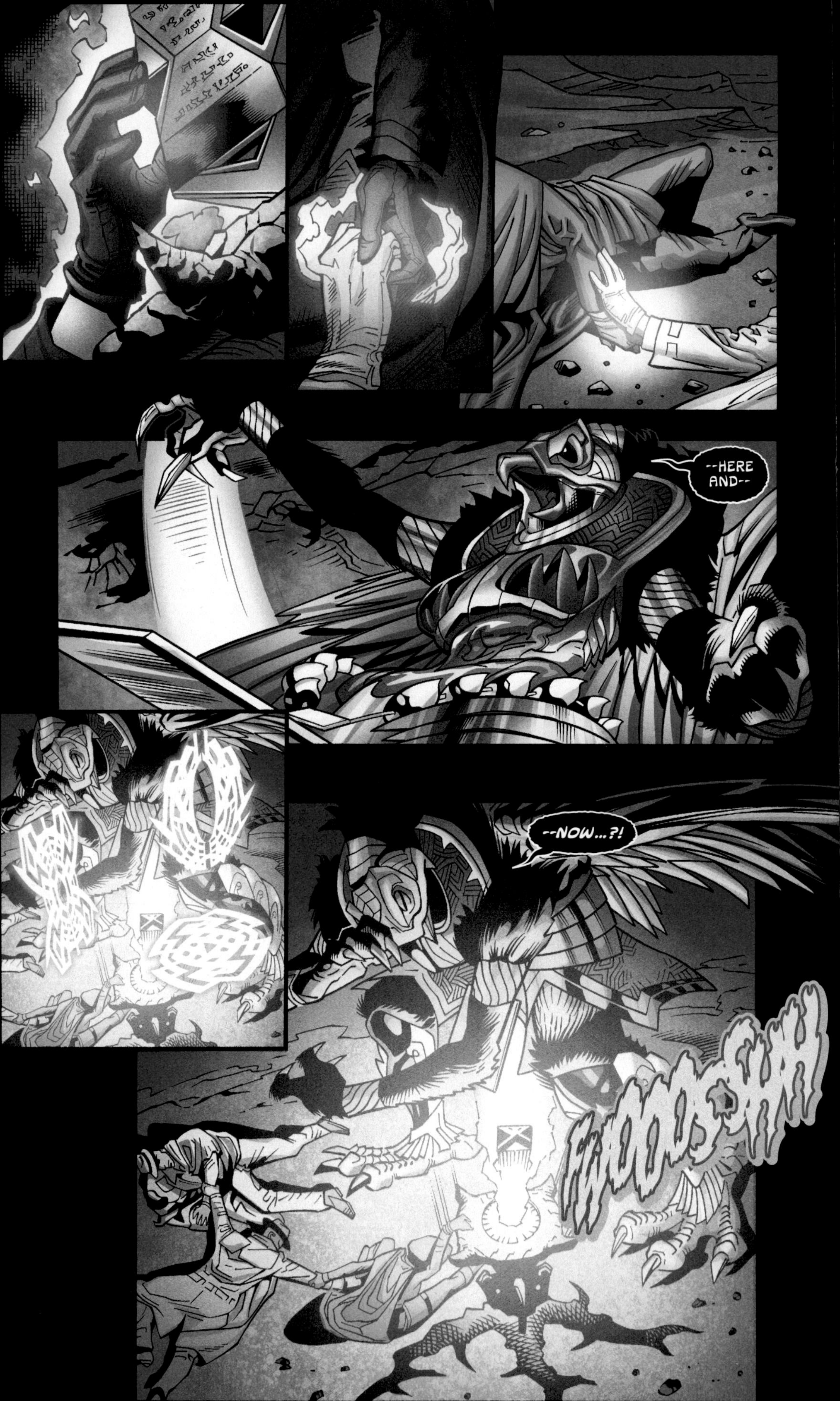
--HERE AND--
--NOW...?!
FWOOOSHHH

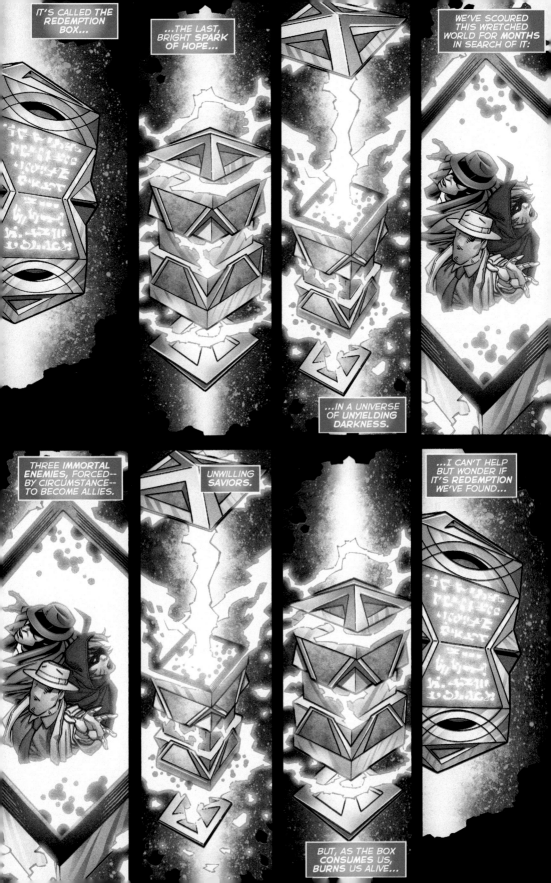

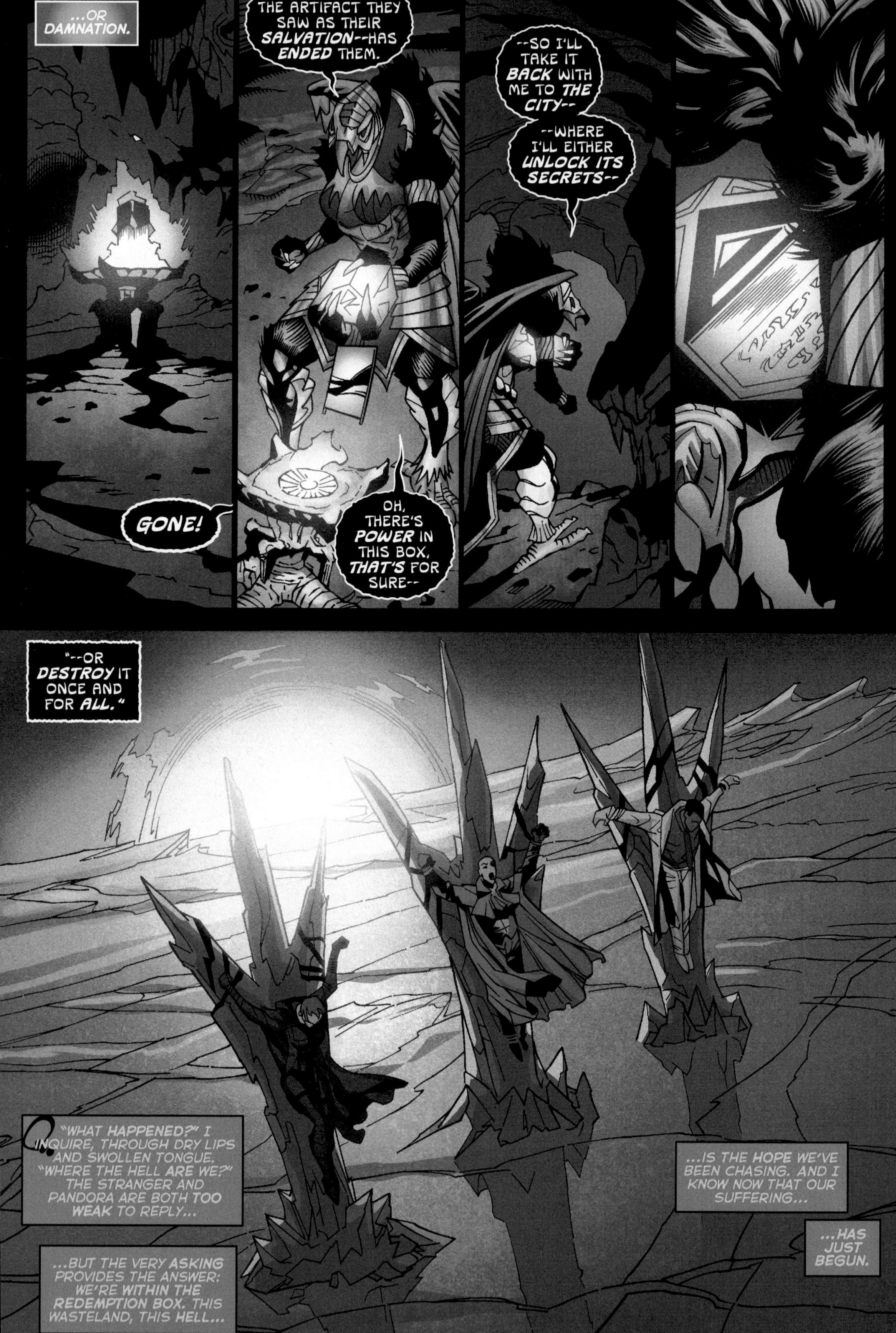
...OR DAMNATION.
GONE!
THE ARTIFACT THEY SAW AS THEIR SALVATION--HAS ENDED THEM.
OH, THERE'S POWER IN THIS BOX, THAT'S FOR SURE--
--SO I'LL TAKE IT BACK WITH ME TO THE CITY--
--WHERE I'LL EITHER UNLOCK ITS SECRETS--
"--OR DESTROY IT ONCE AND FOR ALL."
"WHAT HAPPENED?" I INQUIRE, THROUGH DRY LIPS AND SWOLLEN TONGUE. "WHERE THE HELL ARE WE?" THE STRANGER AND PANDORA ARE BOTH TOO WEAK TO REPLY...
...BUT THE VERY ASKING PROVIDES THE ANSWER: WE'RE WITHIN THE REDEMPTION BOX. THIS WASTELAND, THIS HELL...
...IS THE HOPE WE'VE BEEN CHASING. AND I KNOW NOW THAT OUR SUFFERING...
...HAS JUST BEGUN.

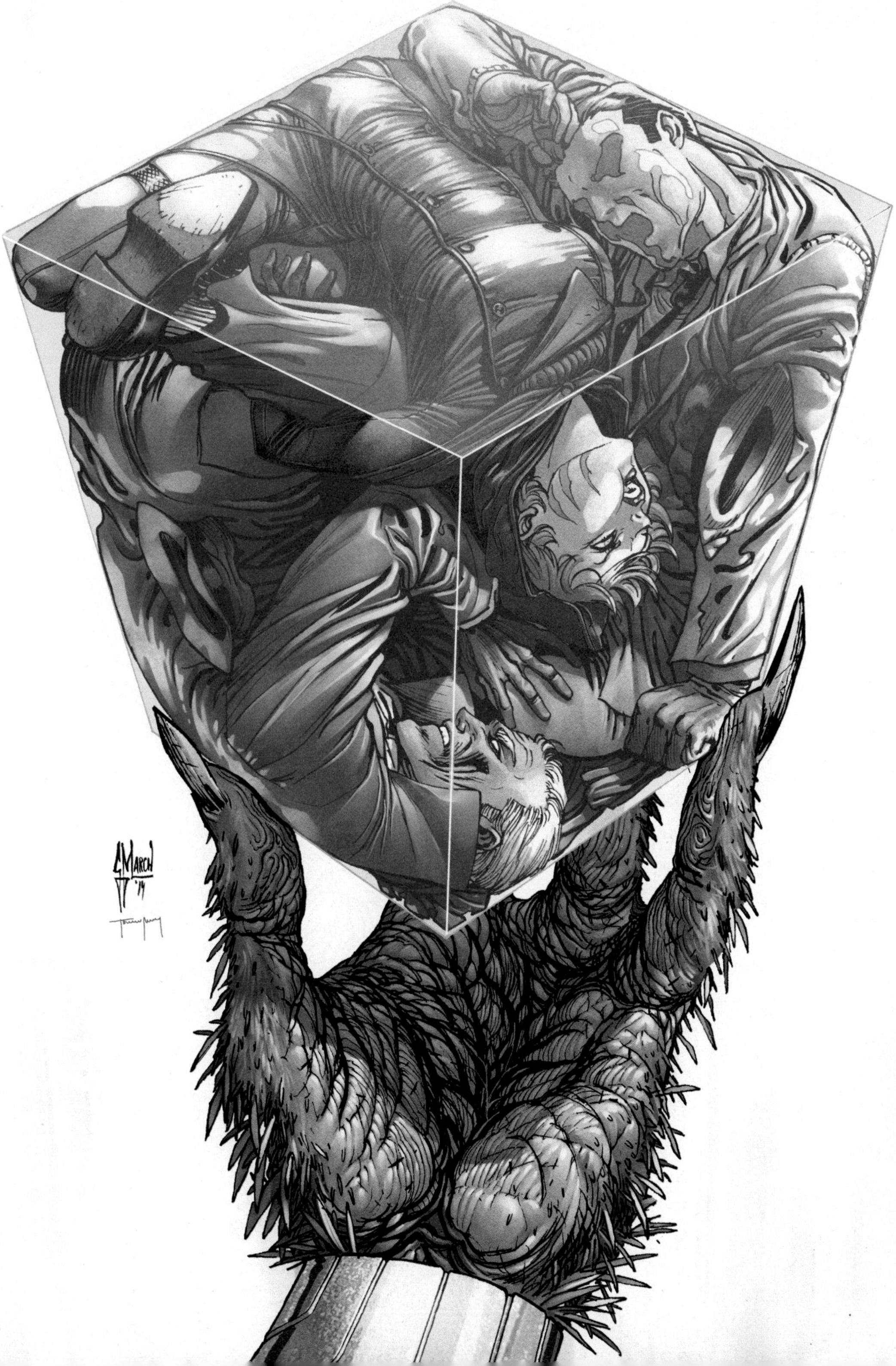

PART FIVE: THE CEREMONY OF INNOCENCE

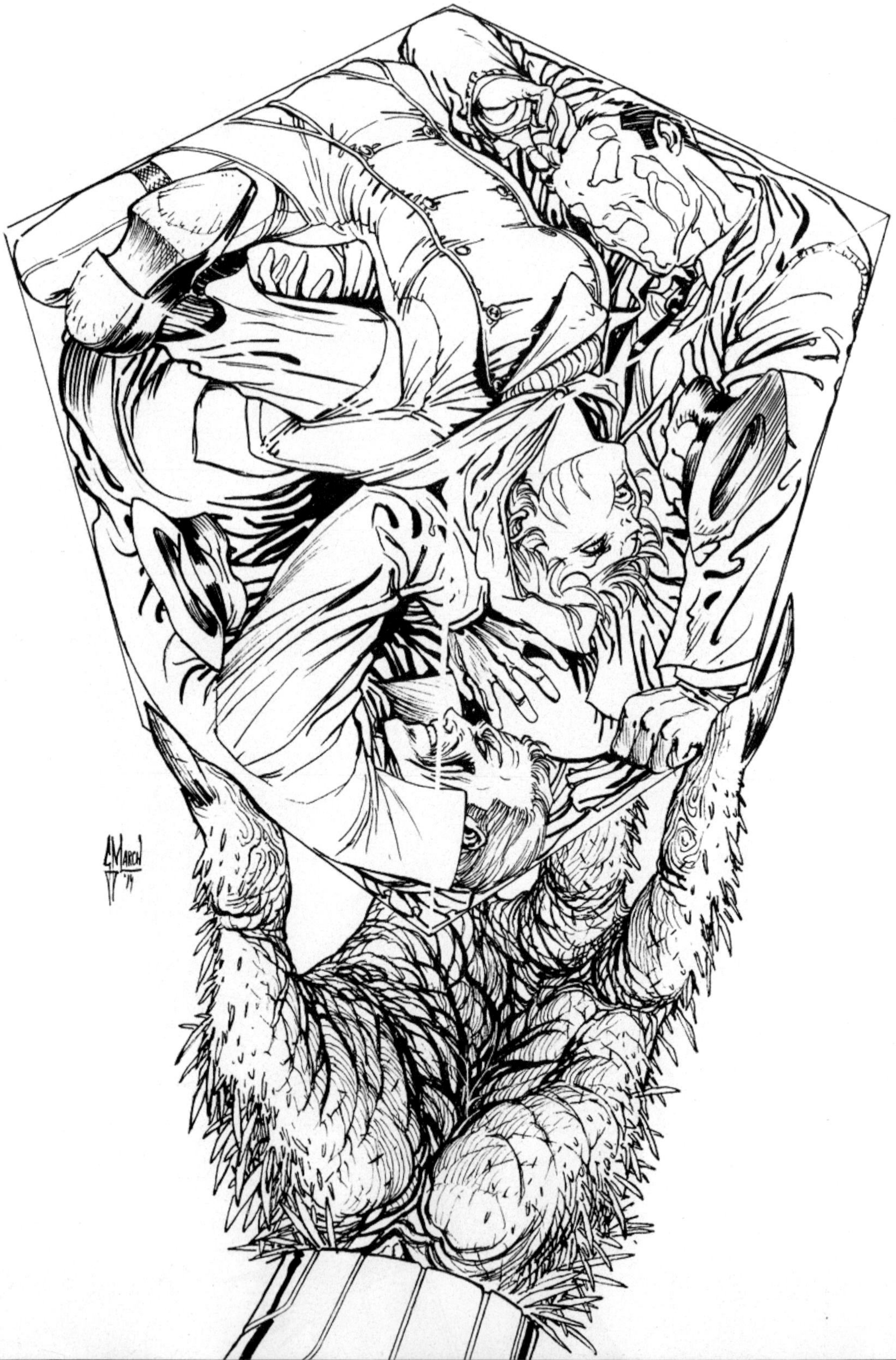

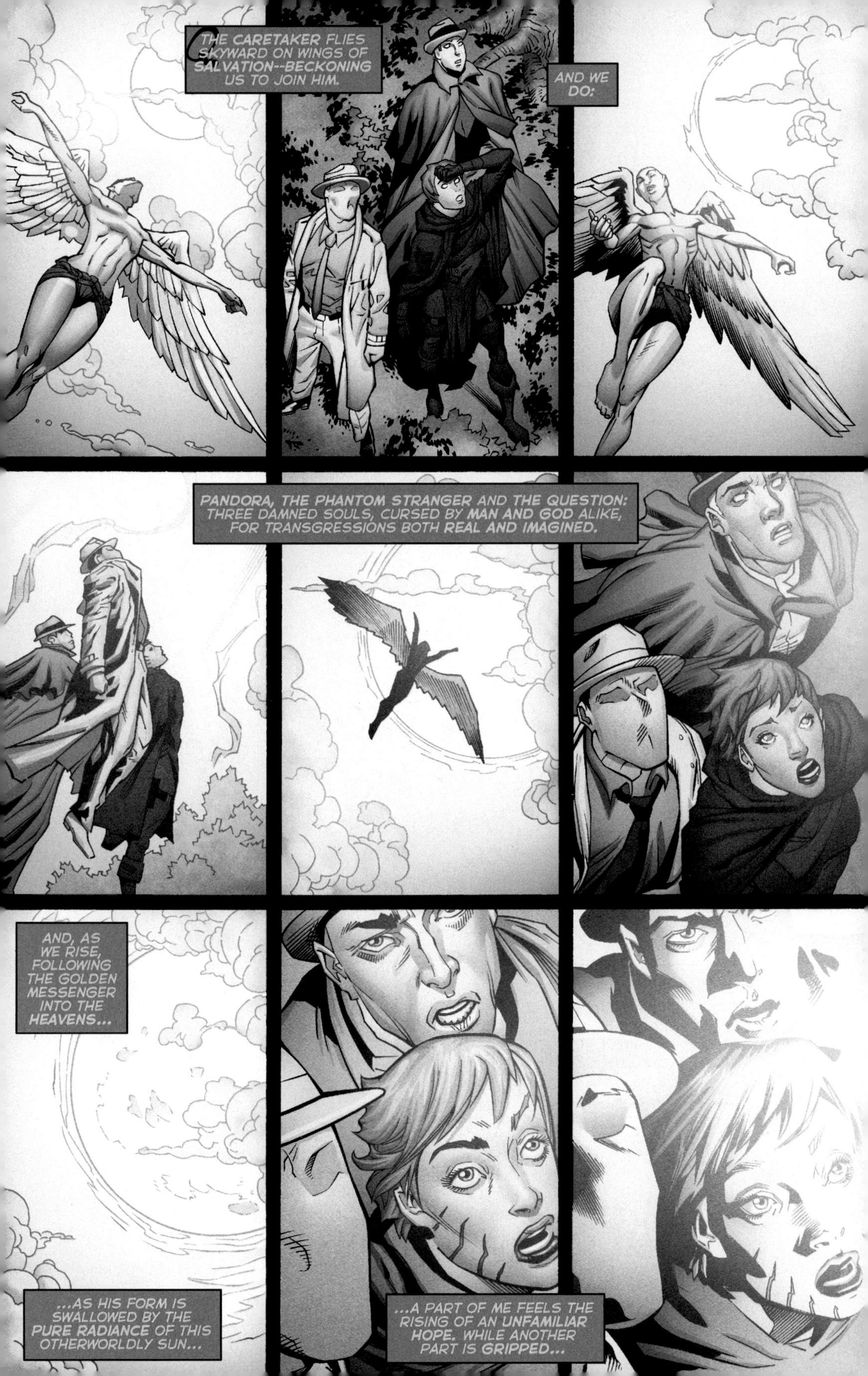
THE CARETAKER FLIES SKYWARD ON WINGS OF SALVATION--BECKONING US TO JOIN HIM.
AND WE DO:
PANDORA, THE PHANTOM STRANGER AND THE QUESTION: THREE DAMNED SOULS, CURSED BY MAN AND GOD ALIKE, FOR TRANSGRESSIONS BOTH REAL AND IMAGINED.
AND, AS WE RISE, FOLLOWING THE GOLDEN MESSENGER INTO THE HEAVENS...
...AS HIS FORM IS SWALLOWED BY THE PURE RADIANCE OF THIS OTHERWORLDLY SUN...
...A PART OF ME FEELS THE RISING OF AN UNFAMILIAR HOPE. WHILE ANOTHER PART IS GRIPPED...

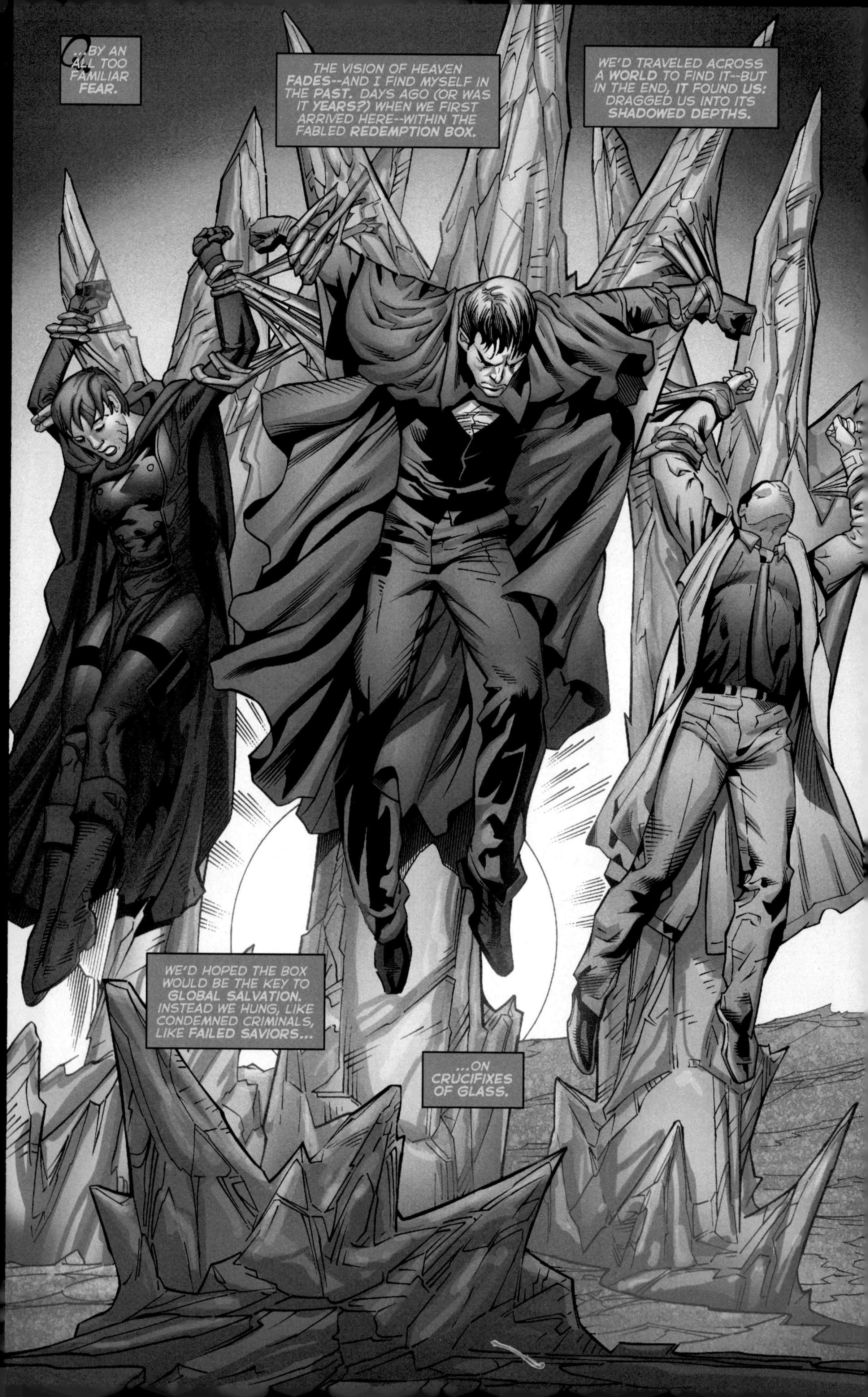
...BY AN ALL TOO FAMILIAR FEAR.
THE VISION OF HEAVEN FADES--AND I FIND MYSELF IN THE PAST. DAYS AGO (OR WAS IT YEARS?) WHEN WE FIRST ARRIVED HERE--WITHIN THE FABLED REDEMPTION BOX.
WE'D TRAVELED ACROSS A WORLD TO FIND IT--BUT IN THE END, IT FOUND US: DRAGGED US INTO ITS SHADOWED DEPTHS.
WE'D HOPED THE BOX WOULD BE THE KEY TO GLOBAL SALVATION. INSTEAD WE HUNG, LIKE CONDEMNED CRIMINALS, LIKE FAILED SAVIORS...
...ON CRUCIFIXES OF GLASS.

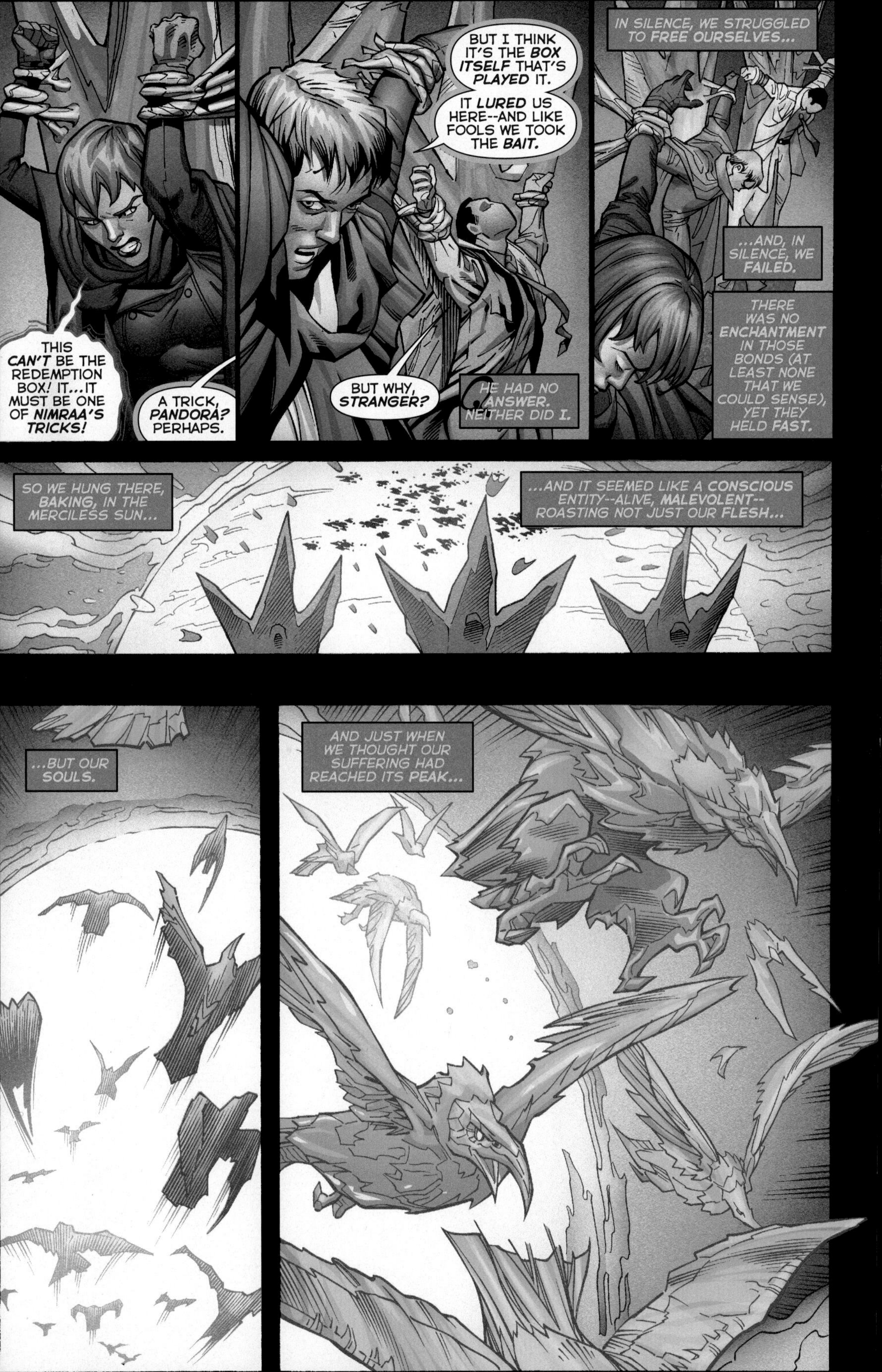
THIS CAN'T BE THE REDEMPTION BOX! IT...IT MUST BE ONE OF NIMRAA'S TRICKS!
A TRICK, PANDORA? PERHAPS.
BUT I THINK IT'S THE BOX ITSELF THAT'S PLAYED IT.
IT LURED US HERE--AND LIKE FOOLS WE TOOK THE BAIT.
BUT WHY, STRANGER?
HE HAD NO ANSWER. NEITHER DID I.
IN SILENCE, WE STRUGGLED TO FREE OURSELVES...
...AND, IN SILENCE, WE FAILED.
THERE WAS NO ENCHANTMENT IN THOSE BONDS (AT LEAST NONE THAT WE COULD SENSE), YET THEY HELD FAST.
SO WE HUNG THERE, BAKING, IN THE MERCILESS SUN...
...AND IT SEEMED LIKE A CONSCIOUS ENTITY--ALIVE, MALEVOLENT--ROASTING NOT JUST OUR FLESH--
...BUT OUR SOULS.
AND JUST WHEN WE THOUGHT OUR SUFFERING HAD REACHED ITS PEAK...

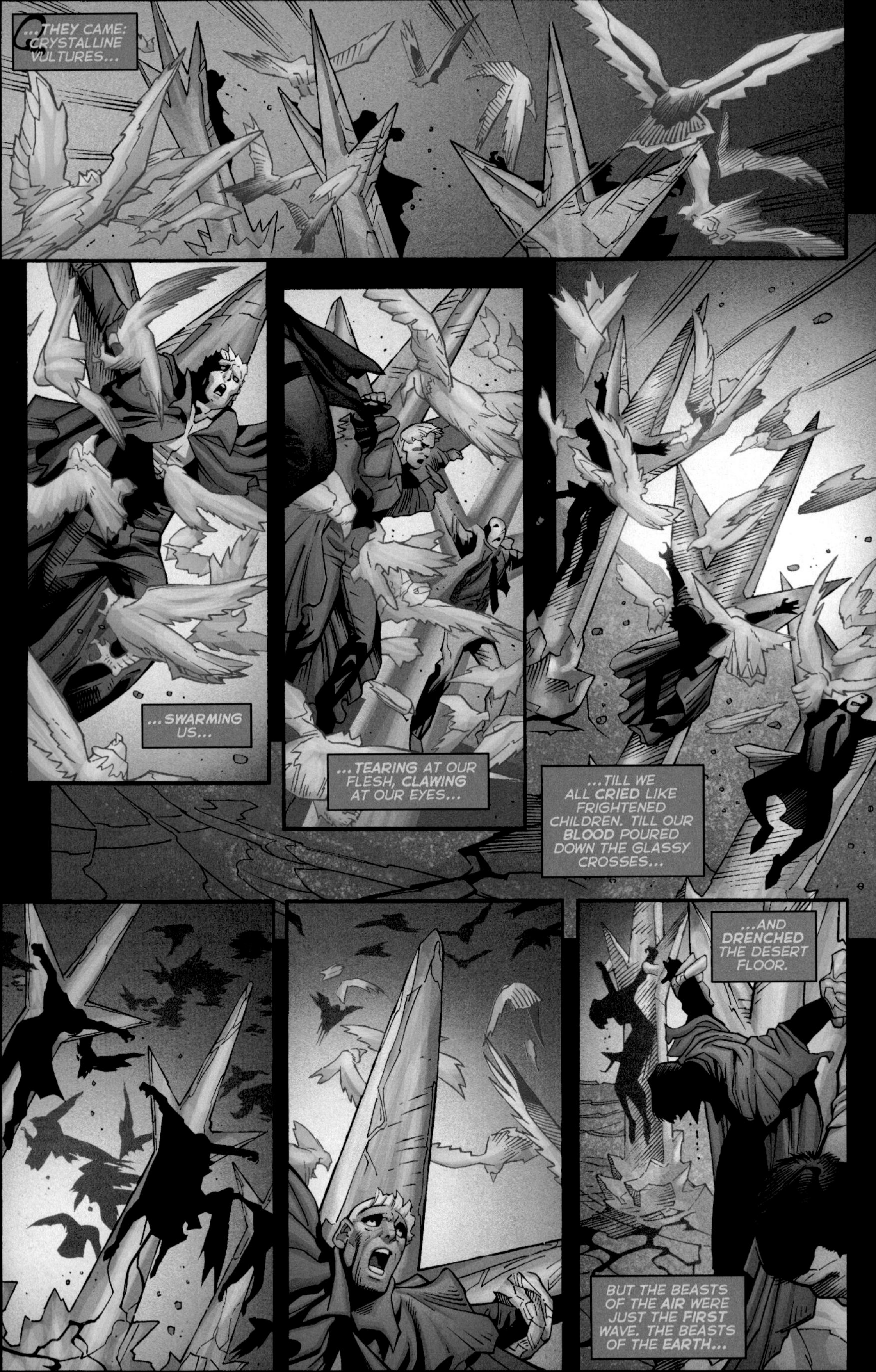
...THEY CAME: CRYSTALLINE VULTURES...
...SWARMING US...
...TEARING AT OUR FLESH, CLAWING AT OUR EYES...
...TILL WE ALL CRIED LIKE FRIGHTENED CHILDREN. TILL OUR BLOOD POURED DOWN THE GLASSY CROSSES...
...AND DRENCHED THE DESERT FLOOR.
BUT THE BEASTS OF THE AIR WERE JUST THE FIRST WAVE. THE BEASTS OF THE EARTH...

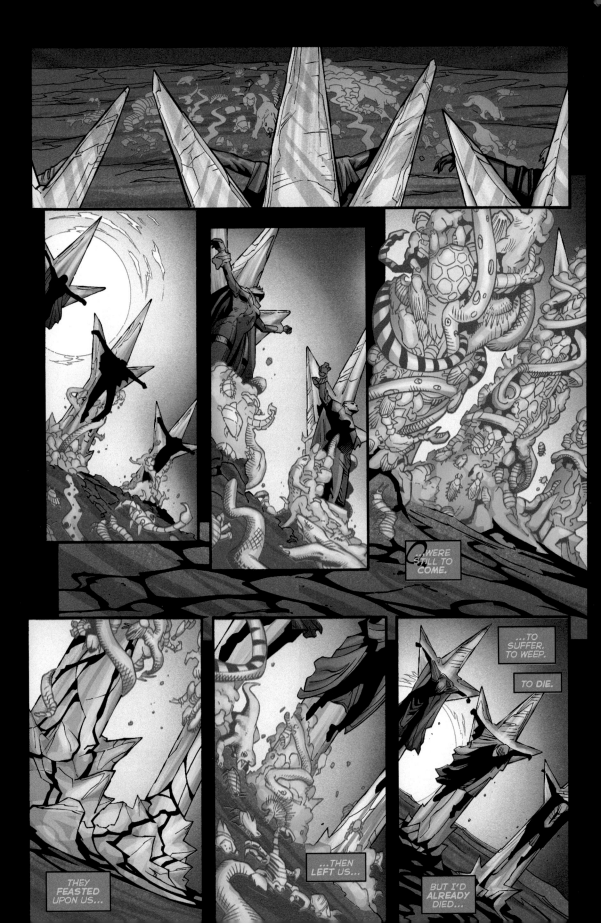

...WERE STILL TO COME.

...TO SUFFER. TO WEEP.

TO DIE.

THEY FEASTED UPON US...

...THEN LEFT US...

BUT I'D ALREADY DIED...

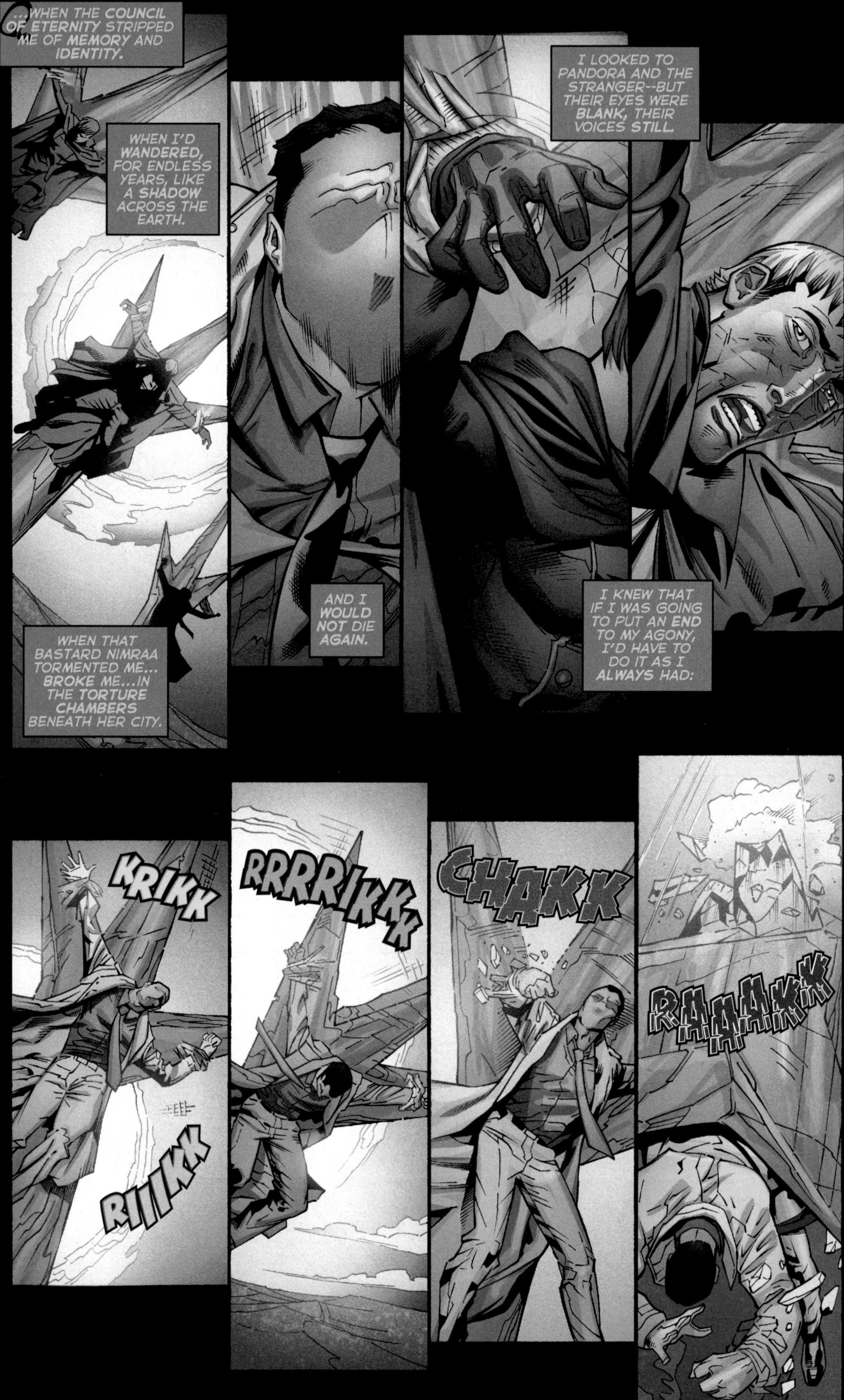
...WHEN THE COUNCIL OF ETERNITY STRIPPED ME OF MEMORY AND IDENTITY.
WHEN I'D WANDERED, FOR ENDLESS YEARS, LIKE A SHADOW ACROSS THE EARTH.
WHEN THAT BASTARD NIMRAA TORMENTED ME... BROKE ME...IN THE TORTURE CHAMBERS BENEATH HER CITY.
AND I WOULD NOT DIE AGAIN.
I LOOKED TO PANDORA AND THE STRANGER--BUT THEIR EYES WERE BLANK, THEIR VOICES STILL.
I KNEW THAT IF I WAS GOING TO PUT AN END TO MY AGONY, I'D HAVE TO DO IT AS I ALWAYS HAD:
KRIKK
RIIIKK
RRRRIKKK
CHAKK
RAAAKKK

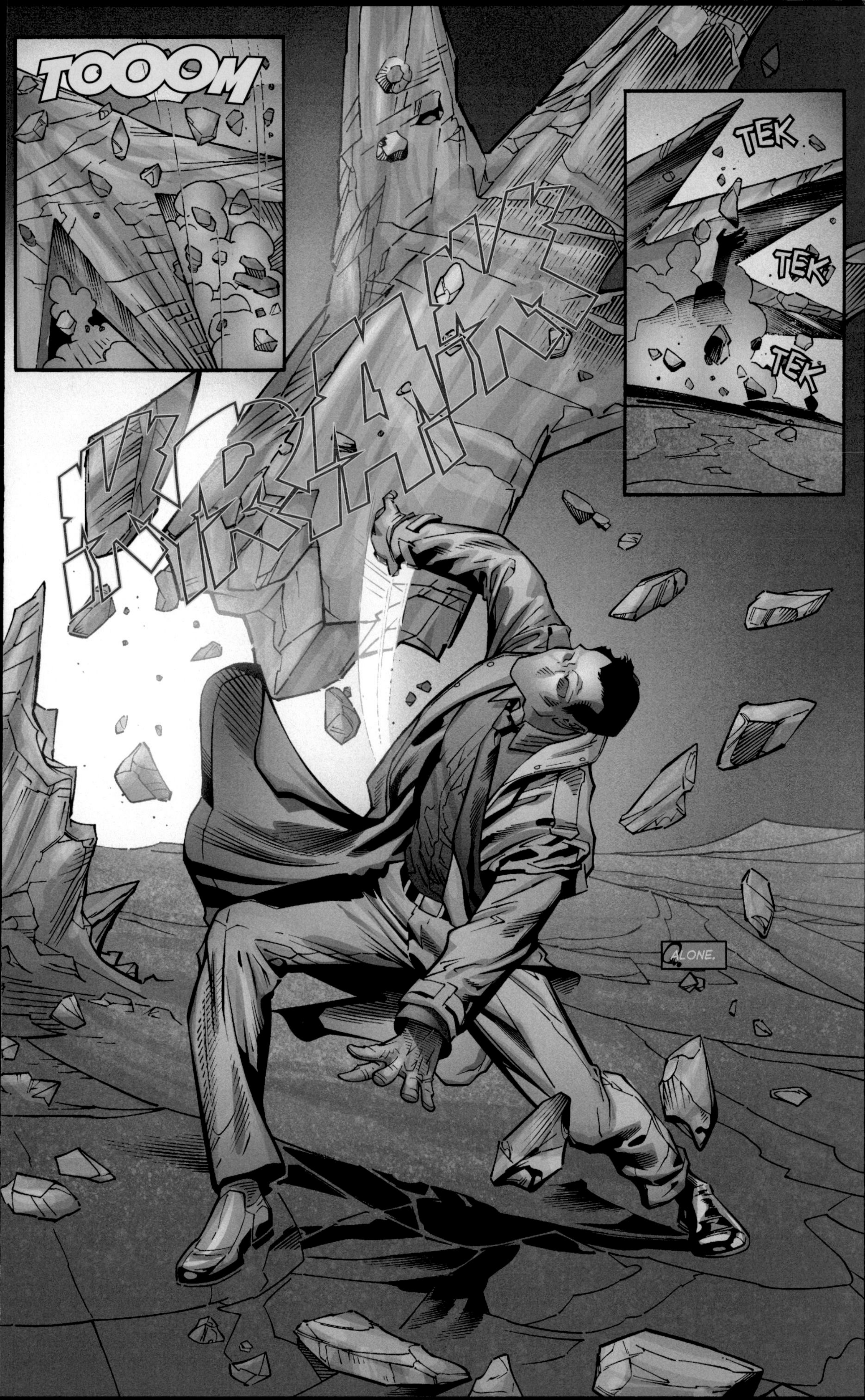
TOOOM
TEK
TEK
TEK
ALONE.

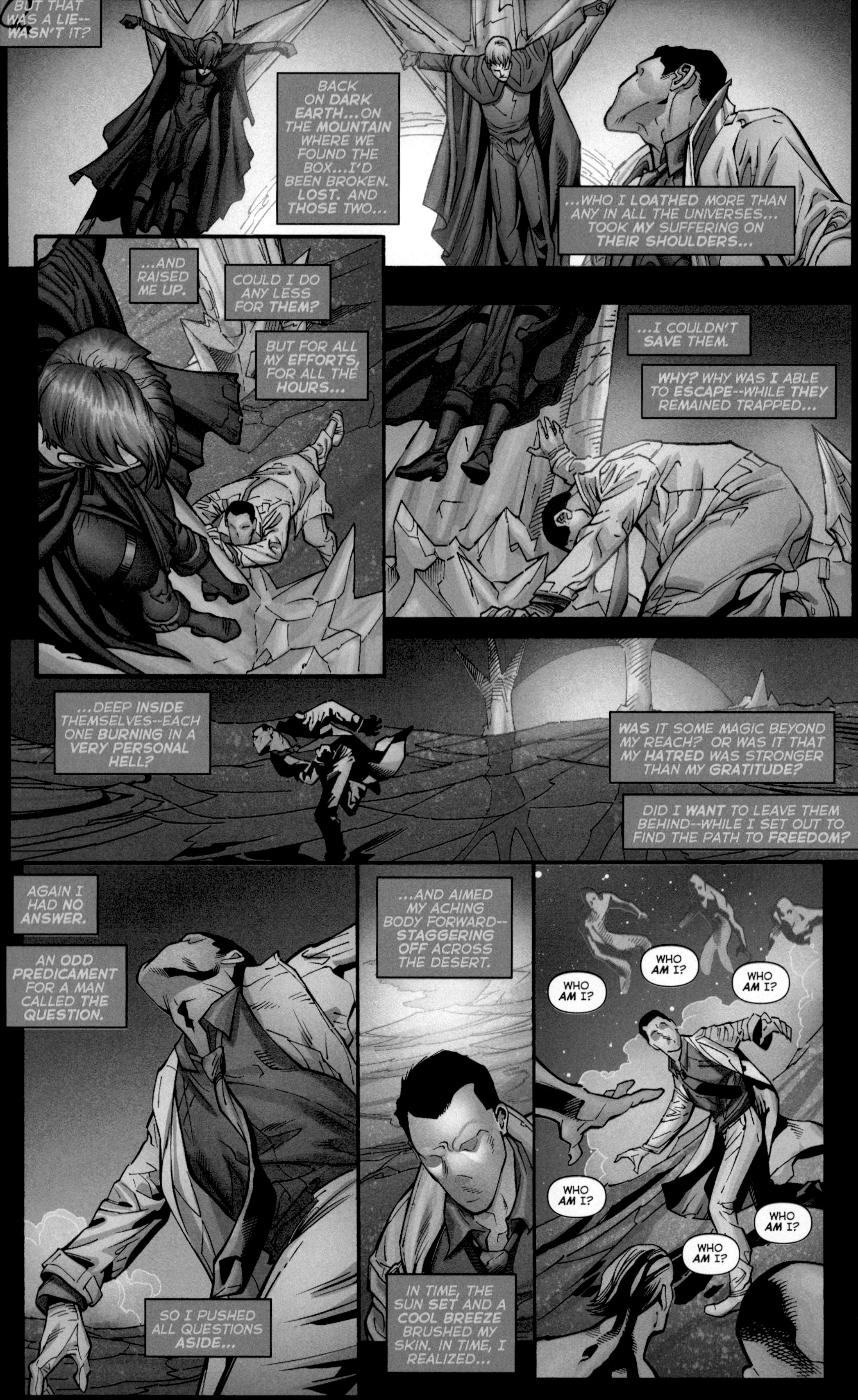
BUT THAT WAS A LIE--WASN'T IT?
BACK ON DARK EARTH...ON THE MOUNTAIN WHERE WE FOUND THE BOX...I'D BEEN BROKEN. LOST. AND THOSE TWO...
...WHO I LOATHED MORE THAN ANY IN ALL THE UNIVERSES... TOOK MY SUFFERING ON THEIR SHOULDERS...
...AND RAISED ME UP.
COULD I DO ANY LESS FOR THEM?
BUT FOR ALL MY EFFORTS, FOR ALL THE HOURS...
...I COULDN'T SAVE THEM.
WHY? WHY WAS I ABLE TO ESCAPE--WHILE THEY REMAINED TRAPPED...
...DEEP INSIDE THEMSELVES--EACH ONE BURNING IN A VERY PERSONAL HELL?
WAS IT SOME MAGIC BEYOND MY REACH? OR WAS IT THAT MY HATRED WAS STRONGER THAN MY GRATITUDE?
DID I WANT TO LEAVE THEM BEHIND--WHILE I SET OUT TO FIND THE PATH TO FREEDOM?
AGAIN I HAD NO ANSWER.
AN ODD PREDICAMENT FOR A MAN CALLED THE QUESTION.
SO I PUSHED ALL QUESTIONS ASIDE...
...AND AIMED MY ACHING BODY FORWARD--STAGGERING OFF ACROSS THE DESERT.
IN TIME, THE SUN SET AND A COOL BREEZE BRUSHED MY SKIN. IN TIME, I REALIZED...
WHO AM I?
WHO AM I?
WHO AM I?
WHO AM I?
WHO AM I?
WHO AM I?

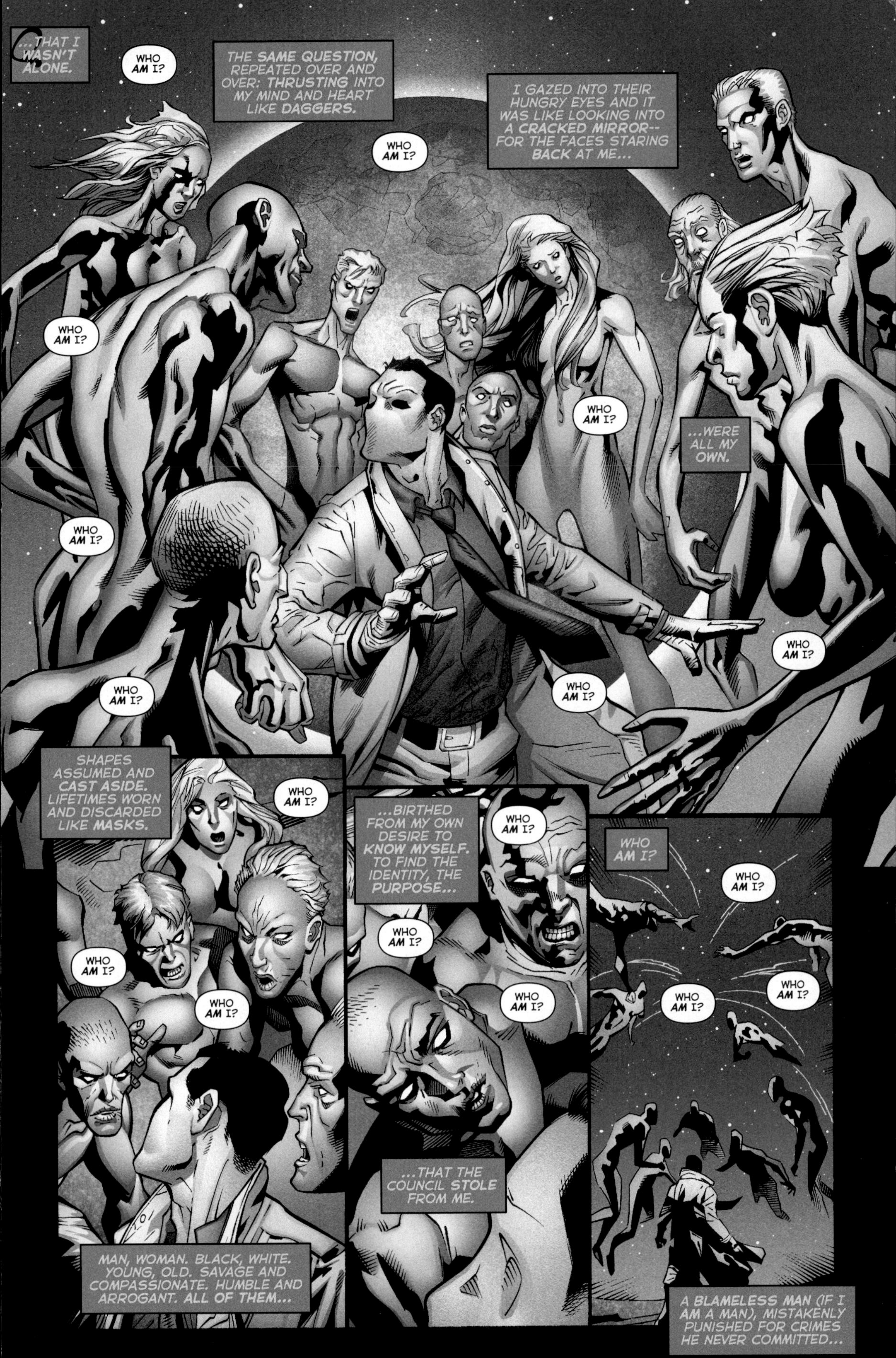
...THAT I WASN'T ALONE.
WHO AM I?
THE SAME QUESTION, REPEATED OVER AND OVER: THRUSTING INTO MY MIND AND HEART LIKE DAGGERS.
WHO AM I?
I GAZED INTO THEIR HUNGRY EYES AND IT WAS LIKE LOOKING INTO A CRACKED MIRROR-- FOR THE FACES STARING BACK AT ME...
WHO AM I?
WHO AM I?
WHO AM I?
...WERE ALL MY OWN.
WHO AM I?
WHO AM I?
WHO AM I?
SHAPES ASSUMED AND CAST ASIDE. LIFETIMES WORN AND DISCARDED LIKE MASKS.
WHO AM I?
WHO AM I?
WHO AM I?
MAN, WOMAN. BLACK, WHITE. YOUNG, OLD. SAVAGE AND COMPASSIONATE. HUMBLE AND ARROGANT. ALL OF THEM...
...BIRTHED FROM MY OWN DESIRE TO KNOW MYSELF. TO FIND THE IDENTITY, THE PURPOSE...
WHO AM I?
WHO AM I?
WHO AM I?
...THAT THE COUNCIL STOLE FROM ME.
WHO AM I?
WHO AM I?
WHO AM I?
WHO AM I?
A BLAMELESS MAN (IF I AM A MAN), MISTAKENLY PUNISHED FOR CRIMES HE NEVER COMMITTED...

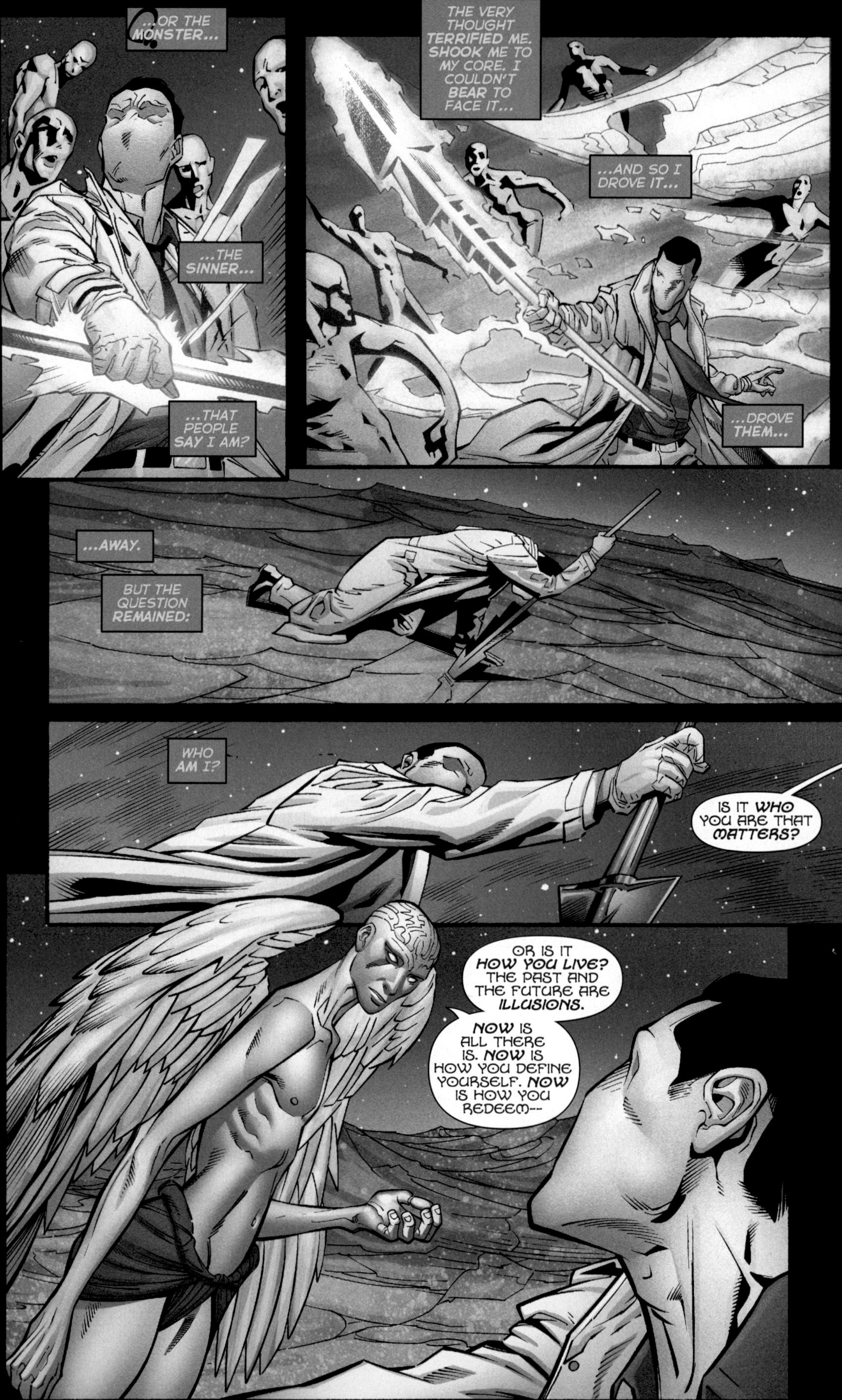

...OR THE MONSTER...
...THE SINNER...
...THAT PEOPLE SAY I AM?
THE VERY THOUGHT TERRIFIED ME. SHOOK ME TO MY CORE. I COULDN'T BEAR TO FACE IT...
...AND SO I DROVE IT...
...DROVE THEM...
...AWAY.
BUT THE QUESTION REMAINED:
WHO AM I?
IS IT WHO YOU ARE THAT MATTERS?
OR IS IT HOW YOU LIVE? THE PAST AND THE FUTURE ARE ILLUSIONS.
NOW IS ALL THERE IS. NOW IS HOW YOU DEFINE YOURSELF. NOW IS HOW YOU REDEEM--

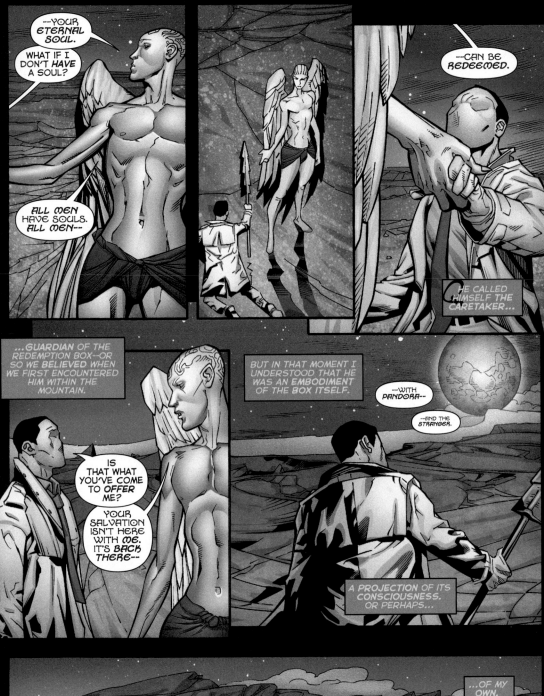

--YOUR ETERNAL SOUL.

WHAT IF I DON'T *HAVE* A SOUL?

ALL MEN HAVE SOULS. ALL MEN--

--CAN BE REDEEMED.

HE CALLED HIMSELF THE CARETAKER...

...GUARDIAN OF THE REDEMPTION BOX--OR SO WE BELIEVED WHEN WE FIRST ENCOUNTERED HIM WITHIN THE MOUNTAIN.

IS THAT WHAT YOU'VE COME TO *OFFER* ME?

YOUR SALVATION ISN'T HERE WITH *ME.* IT'S *BACK THERE*--

BUT IN THAT MOMENT I UNDERSTOOD THAT HE WAS AN EMBODIMENT OF THE BOX ITSELF.

--WITH PANDORA--

--AND THE STRANGER.

A PROJECTION OF ITS CONSCIOUSNESS. OR PERHAPS...

...OF MY OWN.

WHATEVER THE TRUTH, I KNEW HE WAS RIGHT. FOR NOW, AT LEAST, MY FATE, MY FUTURE...

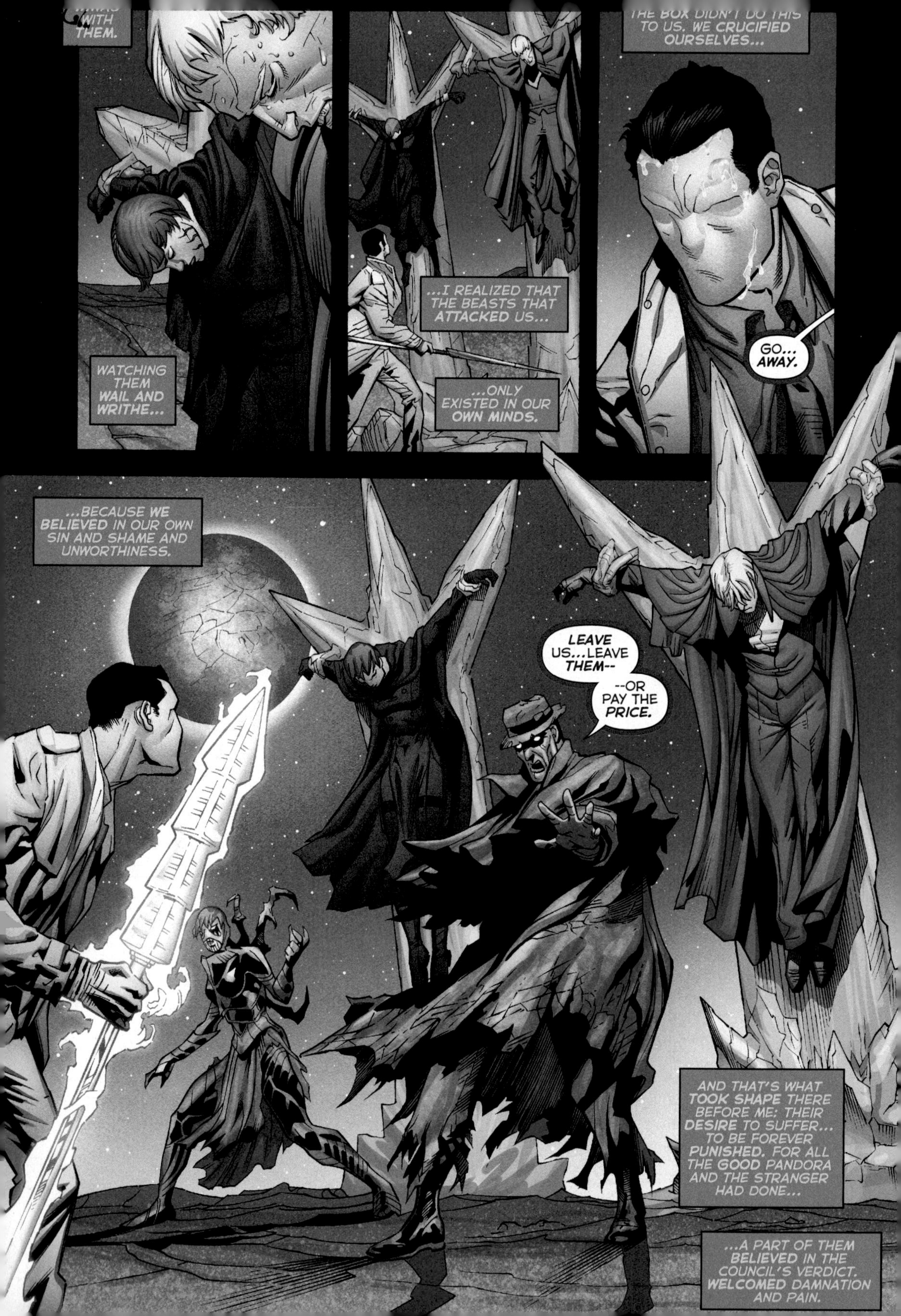
...I WAS WITH THEM.
WATCHING THEM WAIL AND WRITHE...
...I REALIZED THAT THE BEASTS THAT ATTACKED US...
...ONLY EXISTED IN OUR OWN MINDS.
THE BOX DIDN'T DO THIS TO US. WE CRUCIFIED OURSELVES...
GO... AWAY.
...BECAUSE WE BELIEVED IN OUR OWN SIN AND SHAME AND UNWORTHINESS.
LEAVE US...LEAVE THEM--
--OR PAY THE PRICE.
AND THAT'S WHAT TOOK SHAPE THERE BEFORE ME: THEIR DESIRE TO SUFFER... TO BE FOREVER PUNISHED. FOR ALL THE GOOD PANDORA AND THE STRANGER HAD DONE...
...A PART OF THEM BELIEVED IN THE COUNCIL'S VERDICT. WELCOMED DAMNATION AND PAIN.

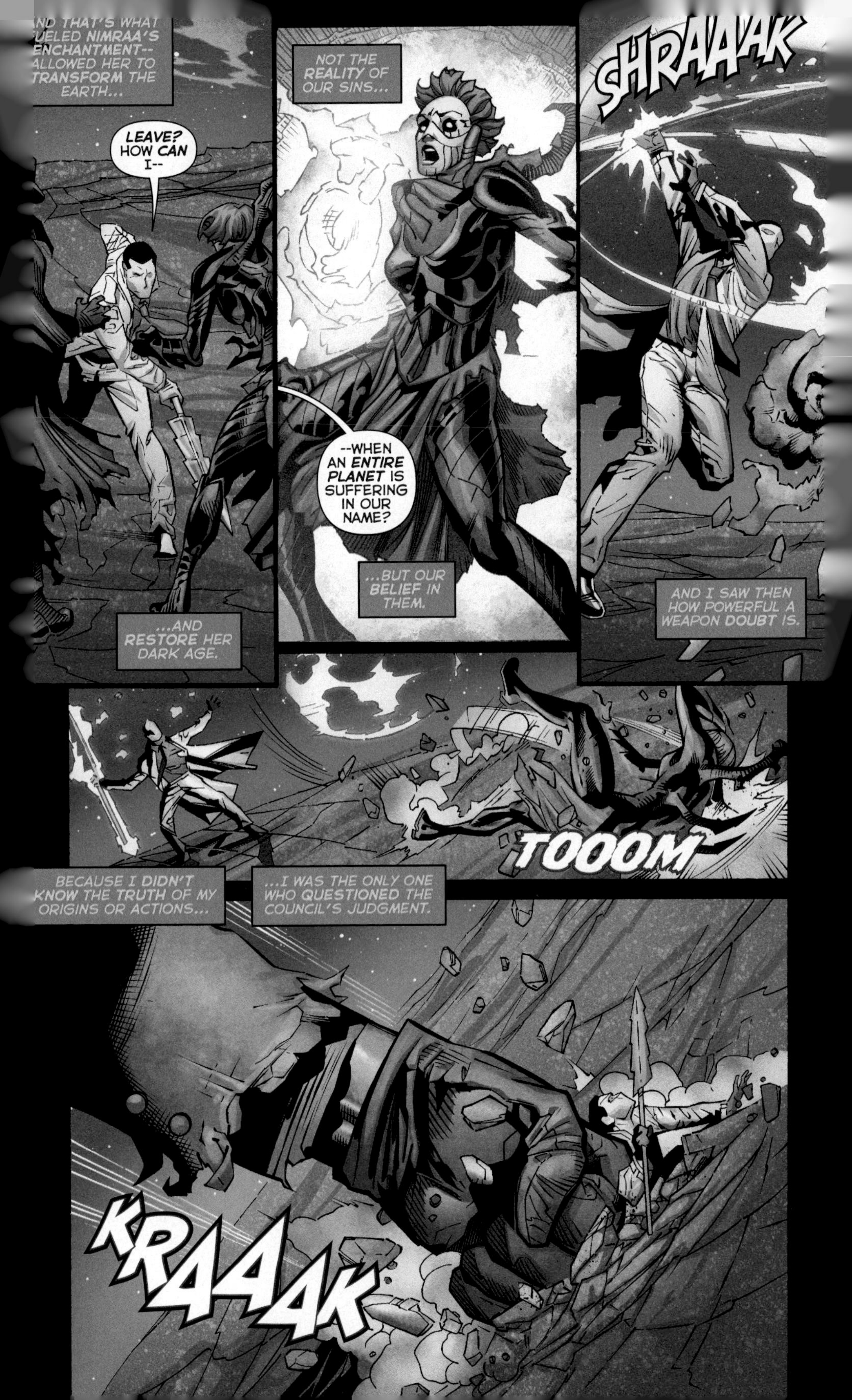

AND THAT'S WHAT FUELED NIMRAA'S ENCHANTMENT--ALLOWED HER TO TRANSFORM THE EARTH...
LEAVE? HOW CAN I--
...AND RESTORE HER DARK AGE.
NOT THE REALITY OF OUR SINS...
--WHEN AN ENTIRE PLANET IS SUFFERING IN OUR NAME?
...BUT OUR BELIEF IN THEM.
SHRAAAK
AND I SAW THEN HOW POWERFUL A WEAPON DOUBT IS.
TOOOM
BECAUSE I DIDN'T KNOW THE TRUTH OF MY ORIGINS OR ACTIONS...
...I WAS THE ONLY ONE WHO QUESTIONED THE COUNCIL'S JUDGMENT.
KRAAAK

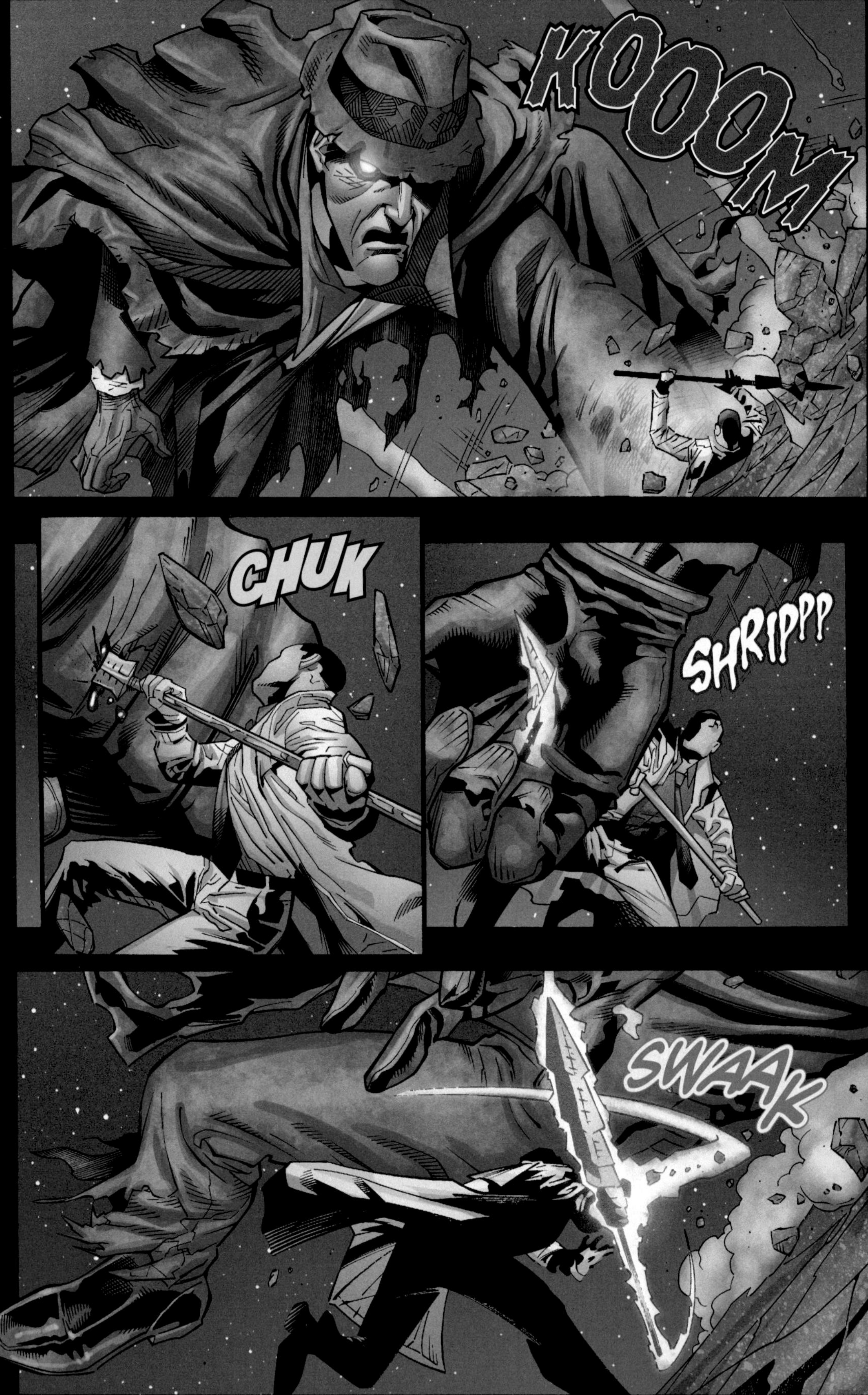
KOOOM
CHUK
SHRIPPP
SWAAK

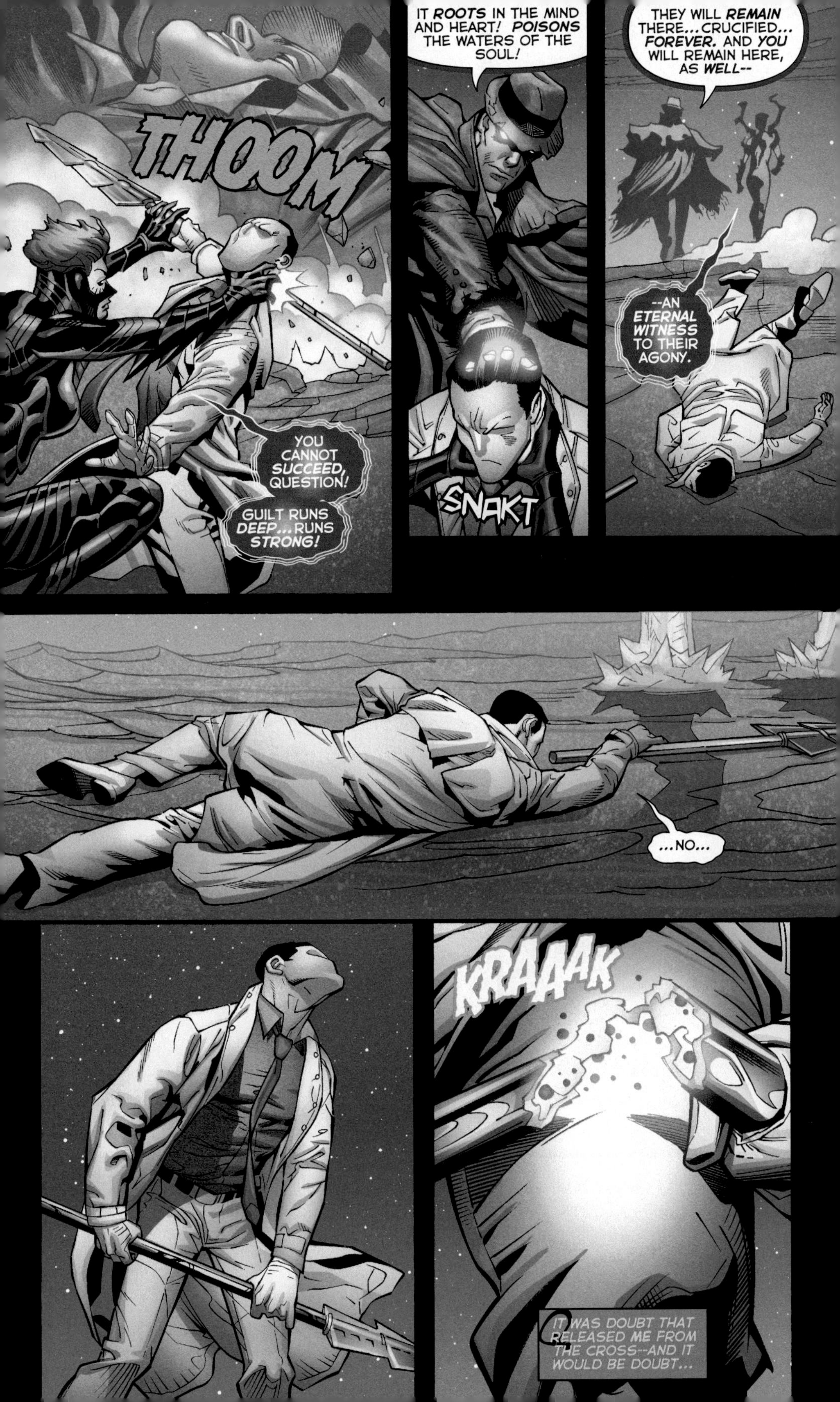

THOOM
YOU CANNOT SUCCEED, QUESTION!
GUILT RUNS DEEP...RUNS STRONG!
IT ROOTS IN THE MIND AND HEART! POISONS THE WATERS OF THE SOUL!
SNAKT
THEY WILL REMAIN THERE...CRUCIFIED... FOREVER. AND YOU WILL REMAIN HERE, AS WELL--
--AN ETERNAL WITNESS TO THEIR AGONY.
...NO...
KRAAAK
IT WAS DOUBT THAT RELEASED ME FROM THE CROSS--AND IT WOULD BE DOUBT...

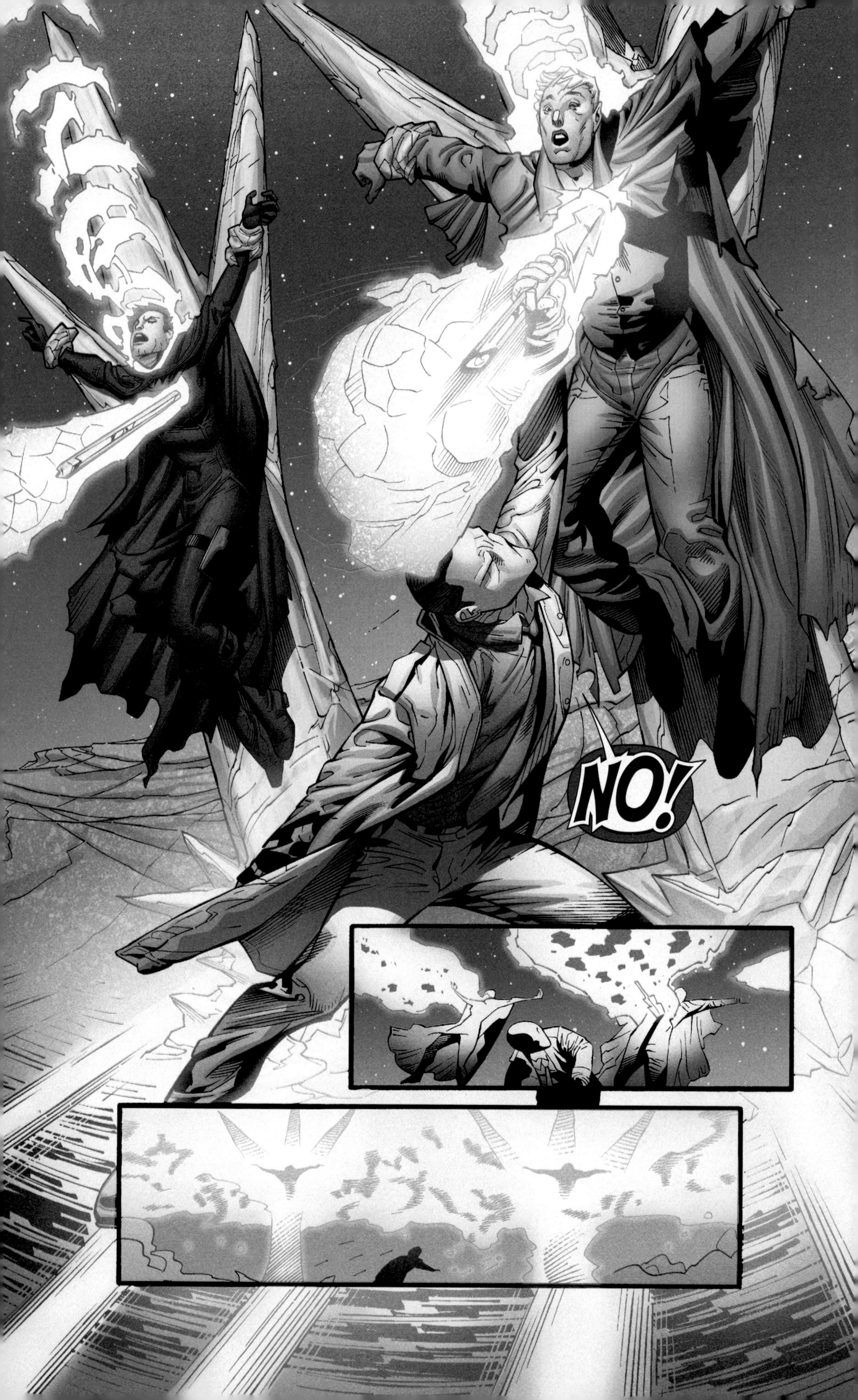
NO!

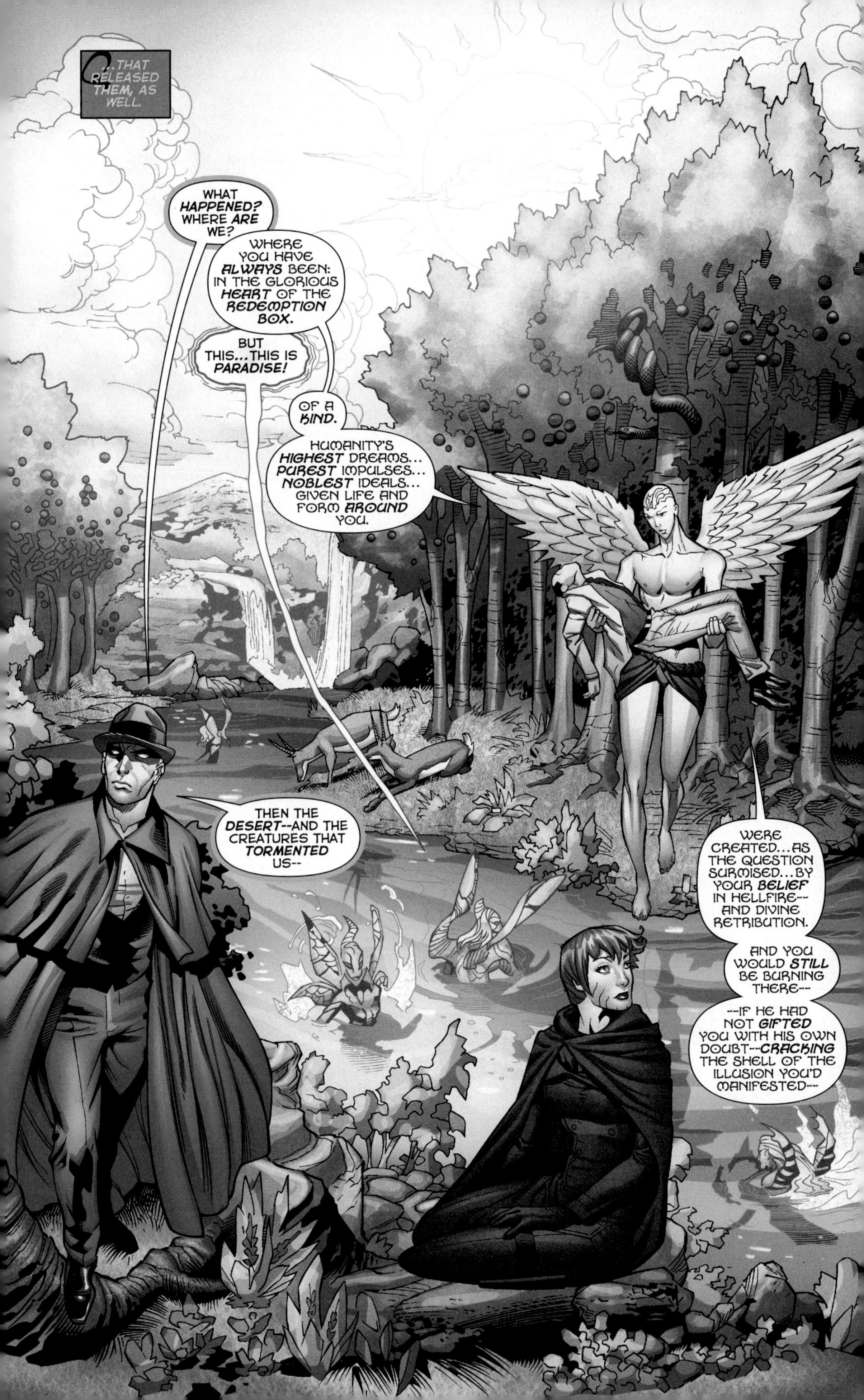
...THAT RELEASED THEM, AS WELL.
WHAT HAPPENED? WHERE ARE WE?
WHERE YOU HAVE ALWAYS BEEN: IN THE GLORIOUS HEART OF THE REDEMPTION BOX.
BUT THIS...THIS IS PARADISE!
OF A KIND.
HUMANITY'S HIGHEST DREAMS... PUREST IMPULSES... NOBLEST IDEALS... GIVEN LIFE AND FORM AROUND YOU.
THEN THE DESERT--AND THE CREATURES THAT TORMENTED US--
WERE CREATED...AS THE QUESTION SURMISED...BY YOUR BELIEF IN HELLFIRE--AND DIVINE RETRIBUTION.
AND YOU WOULD STILL BE BURNING THERE--
--IF HE HAD NOT GIFTED YOU WITH HIS OWN DOUBT--CRACKING THE SHELL OF THE ILLUSION YOU'D MANIFESTED--

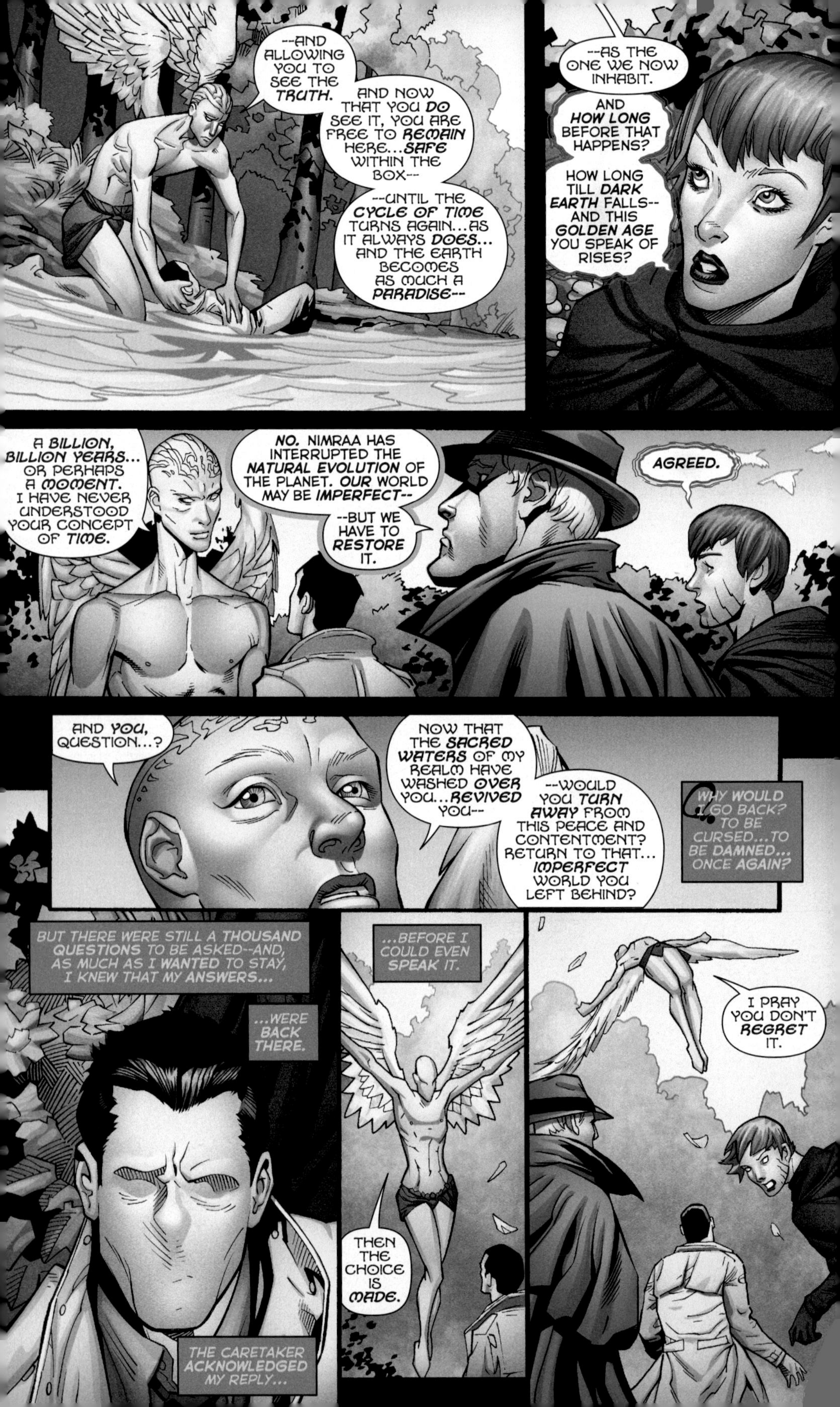

--AND ALLOWING YOU TO SEE THE TRUTH.
AND NOW THAT YOU DO SEE IT, YOU ARE FREE TO REMAIN HERE...SAFE WITHIN THE BOX---
--UNTIL THE CYCLE OF TIME TURNS AGAIN...AS IT ALWAYS DOES... AND THE EARTH BECOMES AS MUCH A PARADISE--
--AS THE ONE WE NOW INHABIT.
AND HOW LONG BEFORE THAT HAPPENS?
HOW LONG TILL DARK EARTH FALLS--AND THIS GOLDEN AGE YOU SPEAK OF RISES?
A BILLION, BILLION YEARS... OR PERHAPS A MOMENT. I HAVE NEVER UNDERSTOOD YOUR CONCEPT OF TIME.
NO. NIMRAA HAS INTERRUPTED THE NATURAL EVOLUTION OF THE PLANET. OUR WORLD MAY BE IMPERFECT--
--BUT WE HAVE TO RESTORE IT.
AGREED.
AND YOU, QUESTION...?
NOW THAT THE SACRED WATERS OF MY REALM HAVE WASHED OVER YOU...REVIVED YOU--
--WOULD YOU TURN AWAY FROM THIS PEACE AND CONTENTMENT? RETURN TO THAT... IMPERFECT WORLD YOU LEFT BEHIND?
WHY WOULD I GO BACK? TO BE CURSED...TO BE DAMNED... ONCE AGAIN?
BUT THERE WERE STILL A THOUSAND QUESTIONS TO BE ASKED--AND, AS MUCH AS I WANTED TO STAY, I KNEW THAT MY ANSWERS...
...WERE BACK THERE.
THE CARETAKER ACKNOWLEDGED MY REPLY...
...BEFORE I COULD EVEN SPEAK IT.
THEN THE CHOICE IS MADE.
I PRAY YOU DON'T REGRET IT.

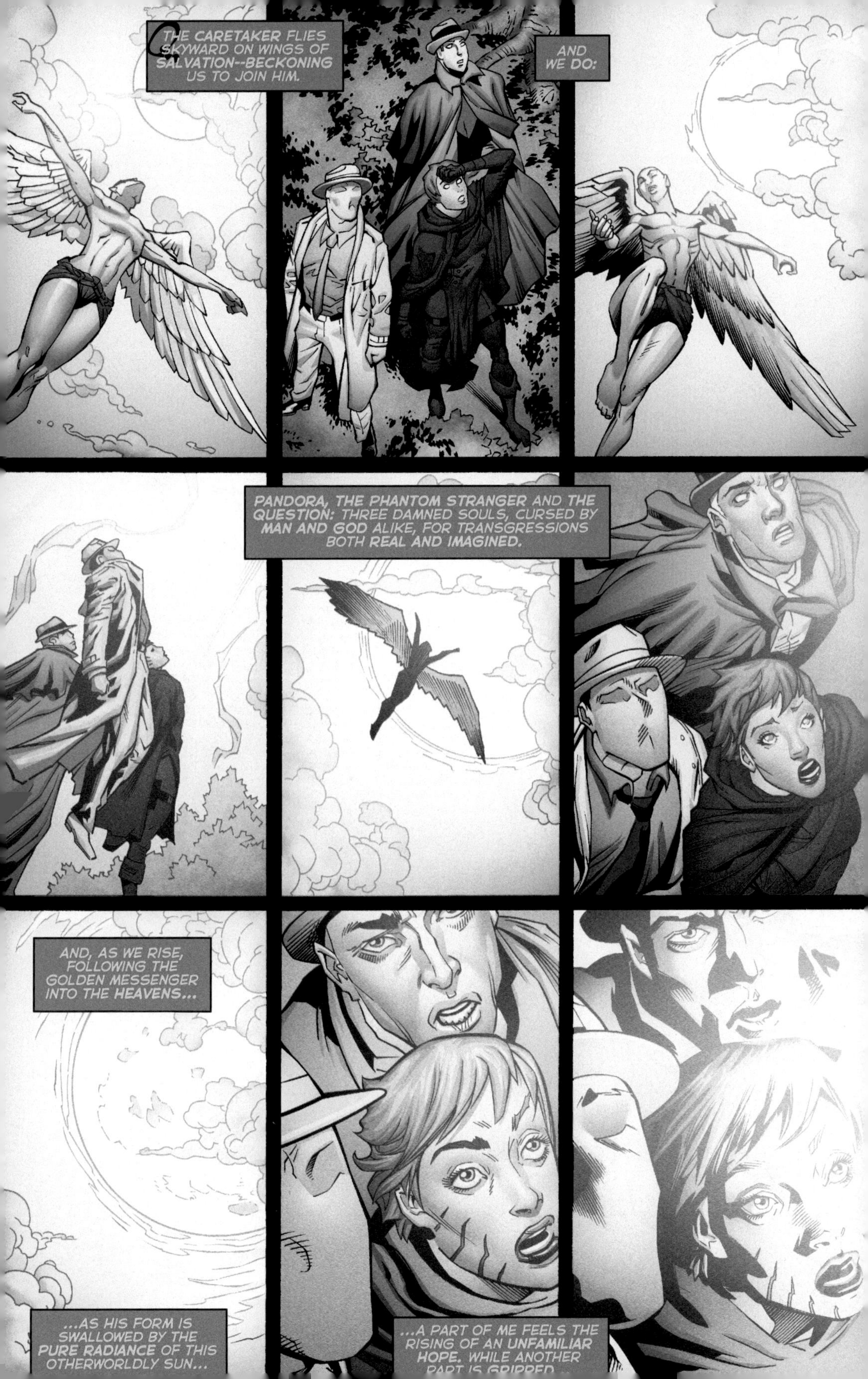
THE CARETAKER FLIES SKYWARD ON WINGS OF SALVATION--BECKONING US TO JOIN HIM.
AND WE DO:
PANDORA, THE PHANTOM STRANGER AND THE QUESTION: THREE DAMNED SOULS, CURSED BY MAN AND GOD ALIKE, FOR TRANSGRESSIONS BOTH REAL AND IMAGINED.
AND, AS WE RISE, FOLLOWING THE GOLDEN MESSENGER INTO THE HEAVENS...
...AS HIS FORM IS SWALLOWED BY THE PURE RADIANCE OF THIS OTHERWORLDLY SUN...
...A PART OF ME FEELS THE RISING OF AN UNFAMILIAR HOPE. WHILE ANOTHER

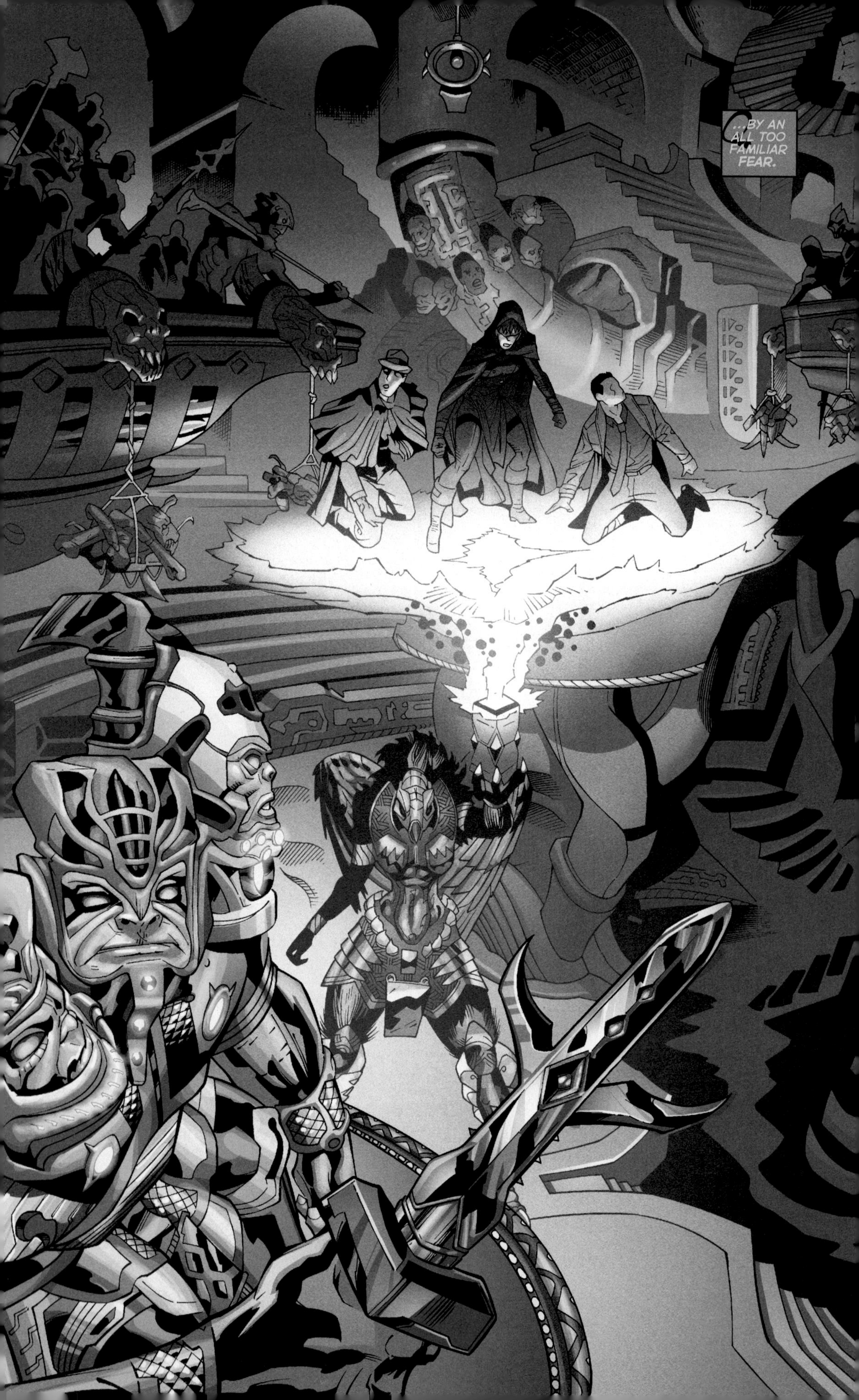
...BY AN ALL TOO FAMILIAR FEAR.

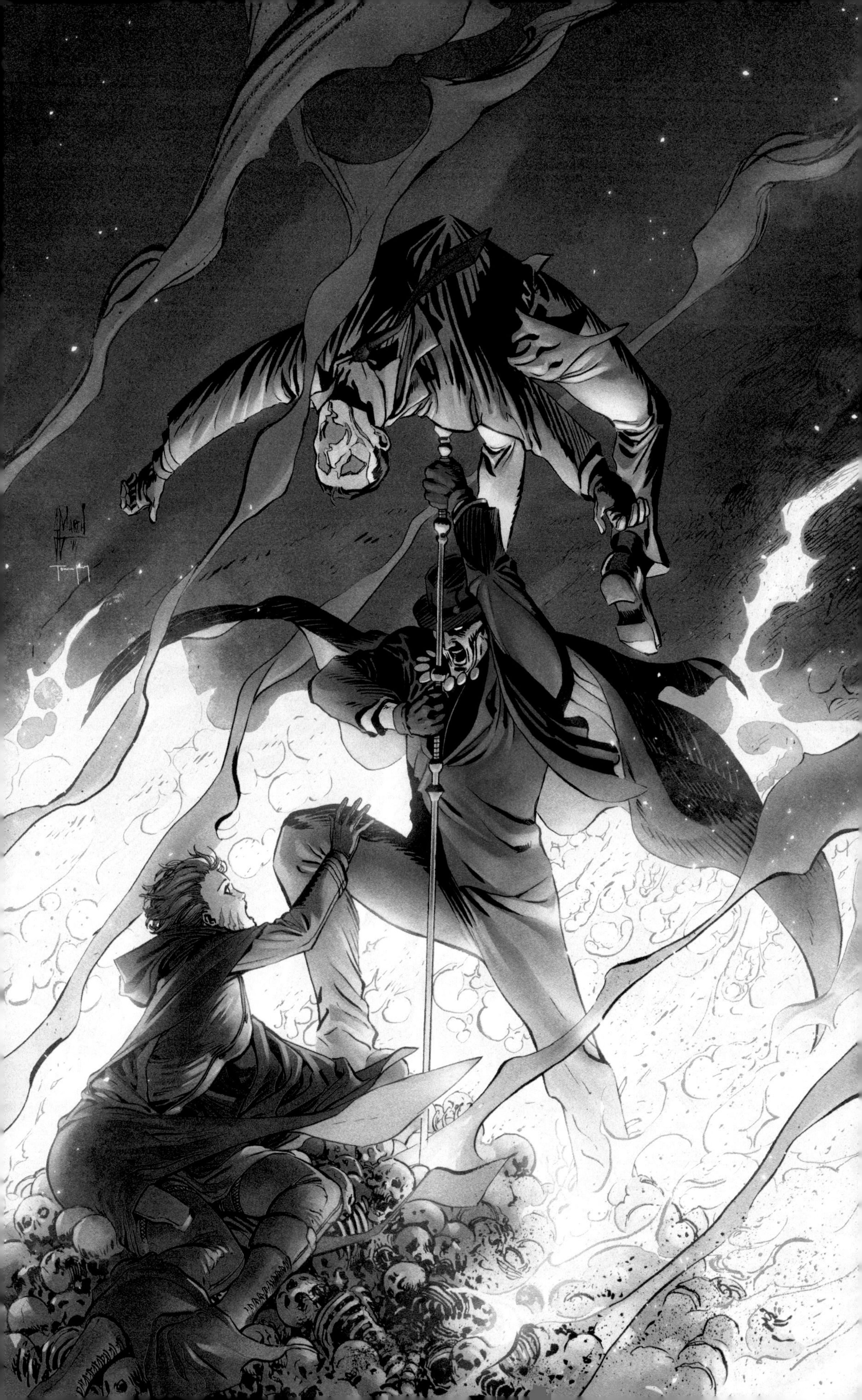

PART SIX: THE OFFERING

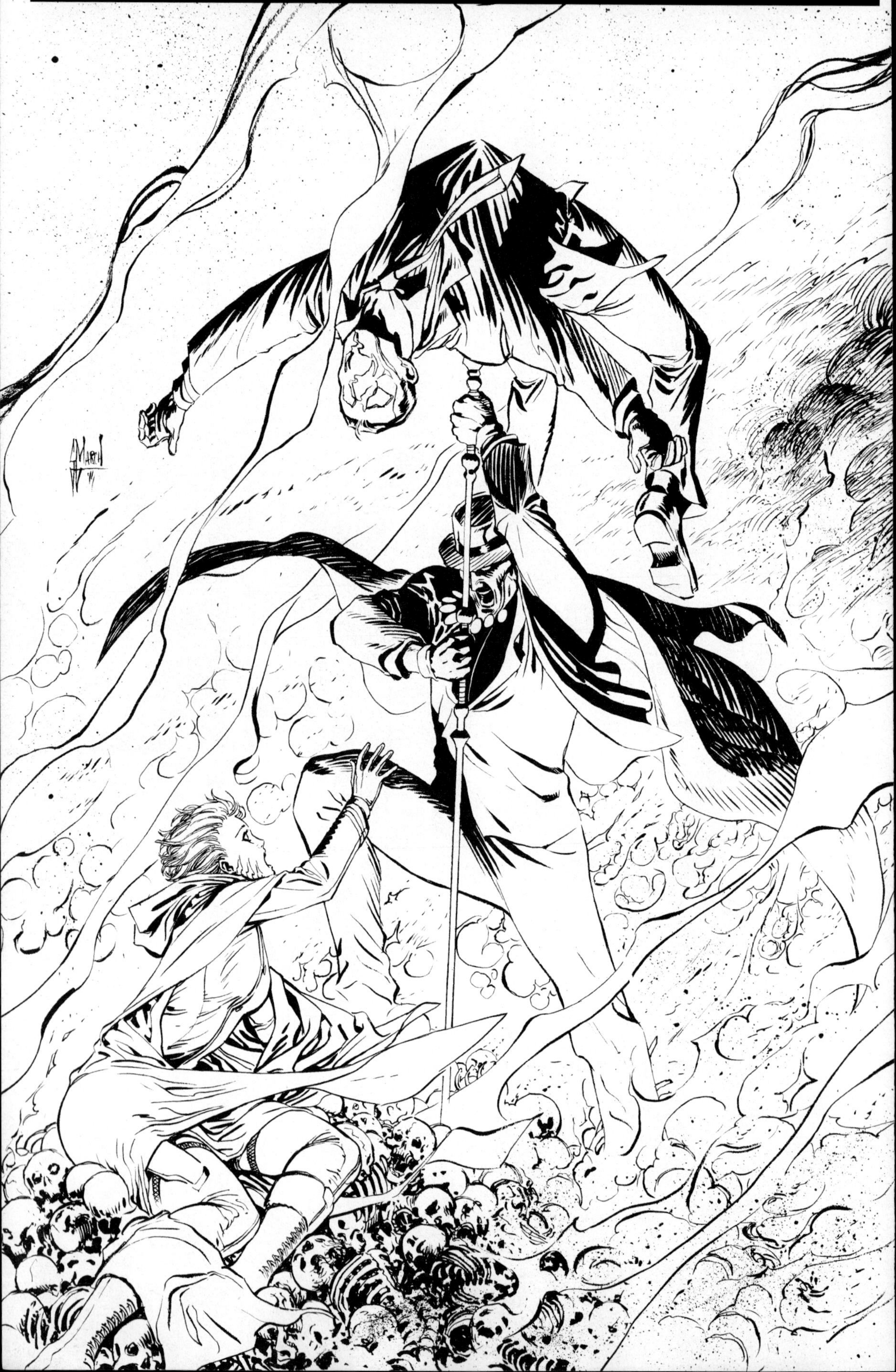

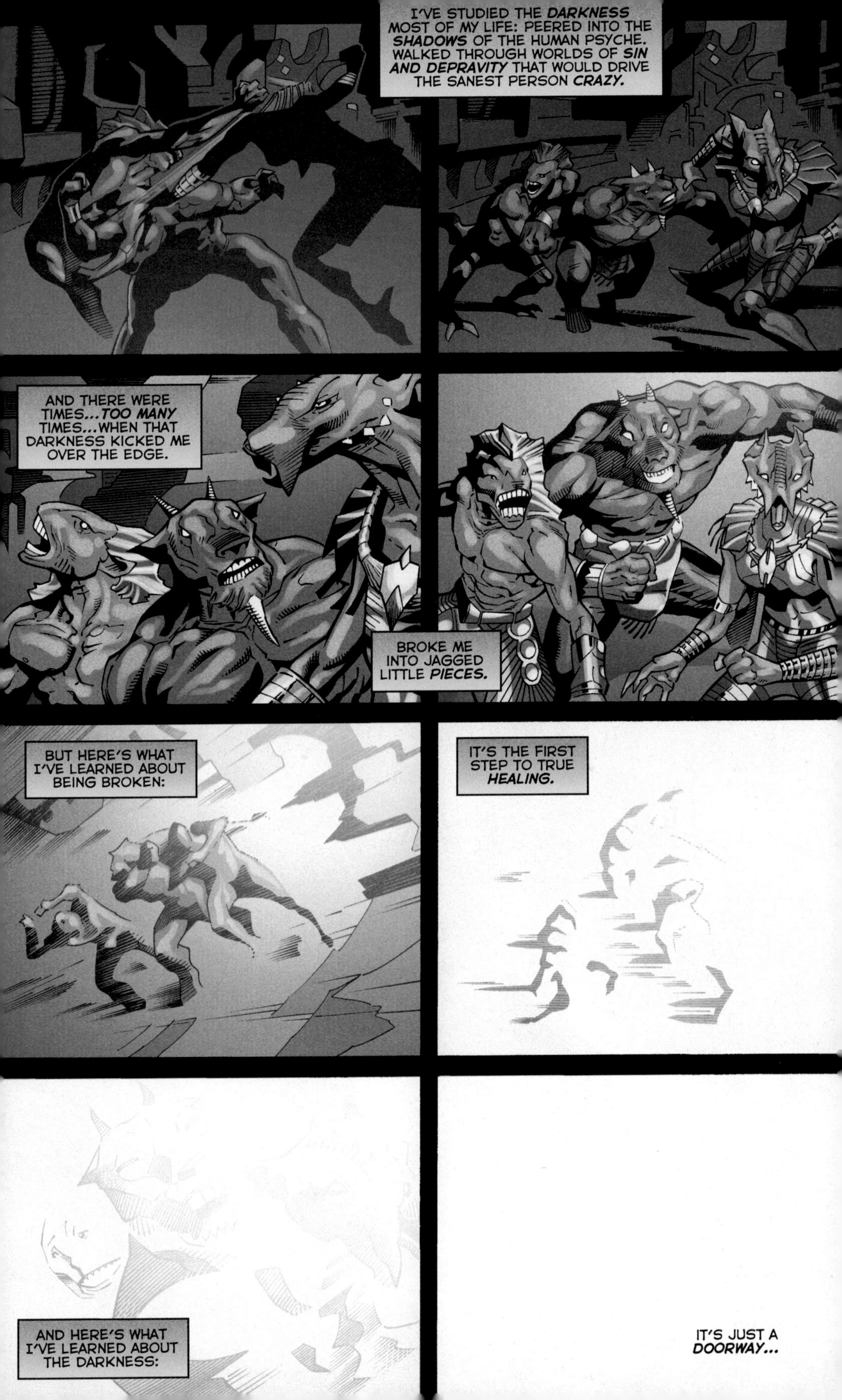
I'VE STUDIED THE *DARKNESS* MOST OF MY LIFE: PEERED INTO THE *SHADOWS* OF THE HUMAN PSYCHE. WALKED THROUGH WORLDS OF *SIN AND DEPRAVITY* THAT WOULD DRIVE THE SANEST PERSON *CRAZY.*
AND THERE WERE TIMES...*TOO MANY* TIMES...WHEN THAT DARKNESS KICKED ME OVER THE EDGE.
BROKE ME INTO JAGGED LITTLE *PIECES.*
BUT HERE'S WHAT I'VE LEARNED ABOUT BEING BROKEN:
IT'S THE FIRST STEP TO TRUE *HEALING.*
AND HERE'S WHAT I'VE LEARNED ABOUT THE DARKNESS:
IT'S JUST A *DOORWAY...*

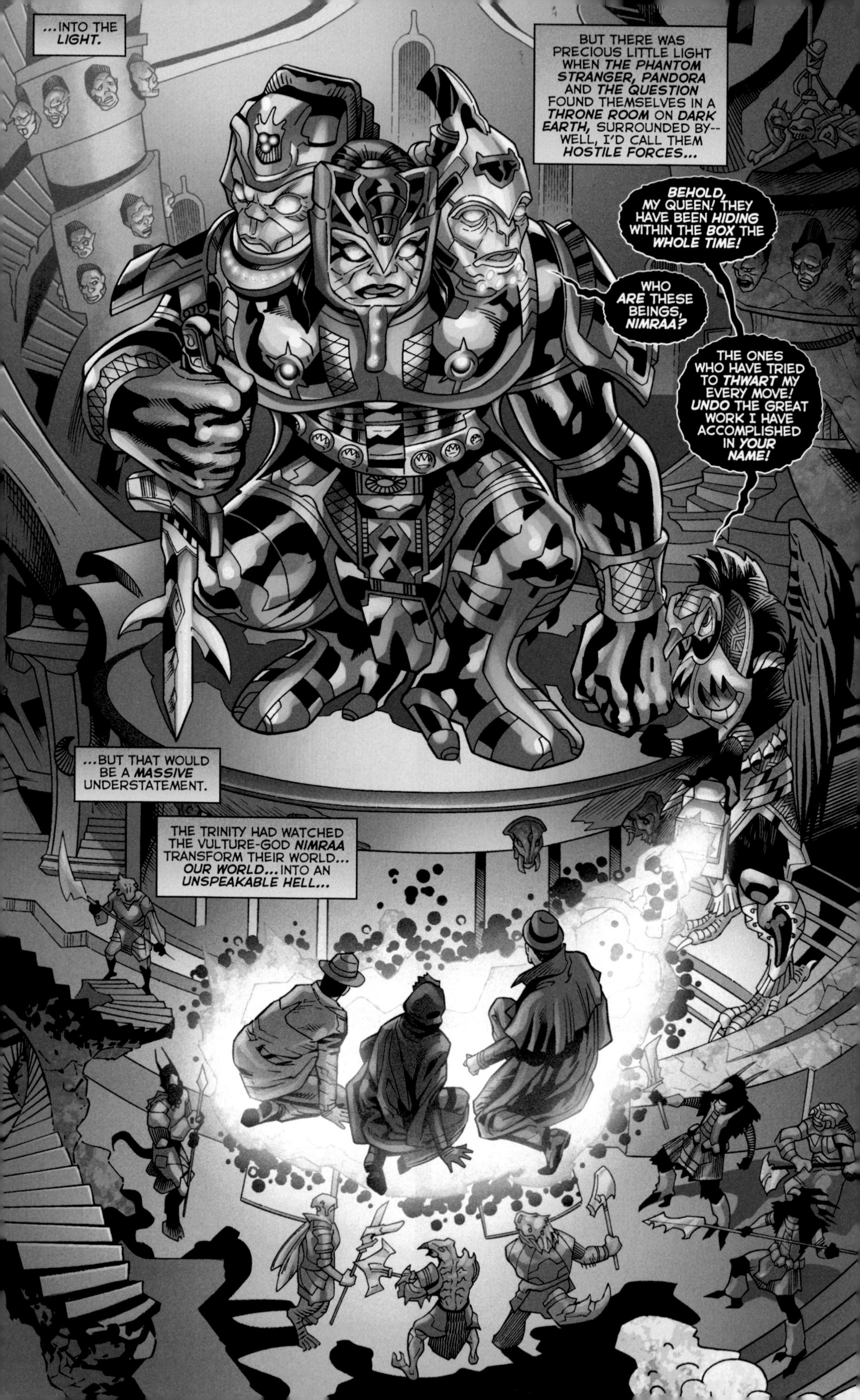
...INTO THE LIGHT.
BUT THERE WAS PRECIOUS LITTLE LIGHT WHEN THE PHANTOM STRANGER, PANDORA AND THE QUESTION FOUND THEMSELVES IN A THRONE ROOM ON DARK EARTH, SURROUNDED BY-- WELL, I'D CALL THEM HOSTILE FORCES...
BEHOLD, MY QUEEN! THEY HAVE BEEN HIDING WITHIN THE BOX THE WHOLE TIME!
WHO ARE THESE BEINGS, NIMRAA?
THE ONES WHO HAVE TRIED TO THWART MY EVERY MOVE! UNDO THE GREAT WORK I HAVE ACCOMPLISHED IN YOUR NAME!
...BUT THAT WOULD BE A MASSIVE UNDERSTATEMENT.
THE TRINITY HAD WATCHED THE VULTURE-GOD NIMRAA TRANSFORM THEIR WORLD... OUR WORLD... INTO AN UNSPEAKABLE HELL...

...AND THEY WERE DETERMINED TO CHANGE IT *BACK.*

BRING THEM TO US.

QUESTION... *PANDORA...* CAN YOU--?

OUR ORDEAL WITHIN THE *REDEMPTION BOX* HAS LEFT US *ALL* DRAINED, STRANGER.

PERHAPS WE WERE TOO QUICK TO LEAVE *THE CARETAKER'S* SIDE...?

OF COURSE IT WOULD'VE HELPED IF THEY'D HAD SOME KIND OF *PLAN...*

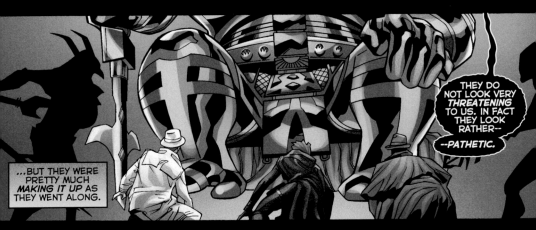

THEY DO NOT LOOK VERY *THREATENING* TO US. IN FACT THEY LOOK RATHER--

--PATHETIC.

...BUT THEY WERE PRETTY MUCH *MAKING IT UP* AS THEY WENT ALONG.

YET NIMRAA TELLS US THAT YOU THREE ARE *SORCERERS* OF GREAT CUNNING AND ABILITY--

--CAPABLE OF BRINGING OUR KINGDOM *CRASHING DOWN* AROUND US.

WHO *ARE* YOU?

WE ARE *VENNA*--QUEEN OF DARK EARTH. HASN'T OUR SERVANT *TOLD* YOU ABOUT US?

YOUR *SERVANT?* WE THOUGHT THIS WAS *NIMRAA'S* WORLD. THAT *SHE* WAS IN COMMAND.

IF YOU THOUGHT *THAT*--

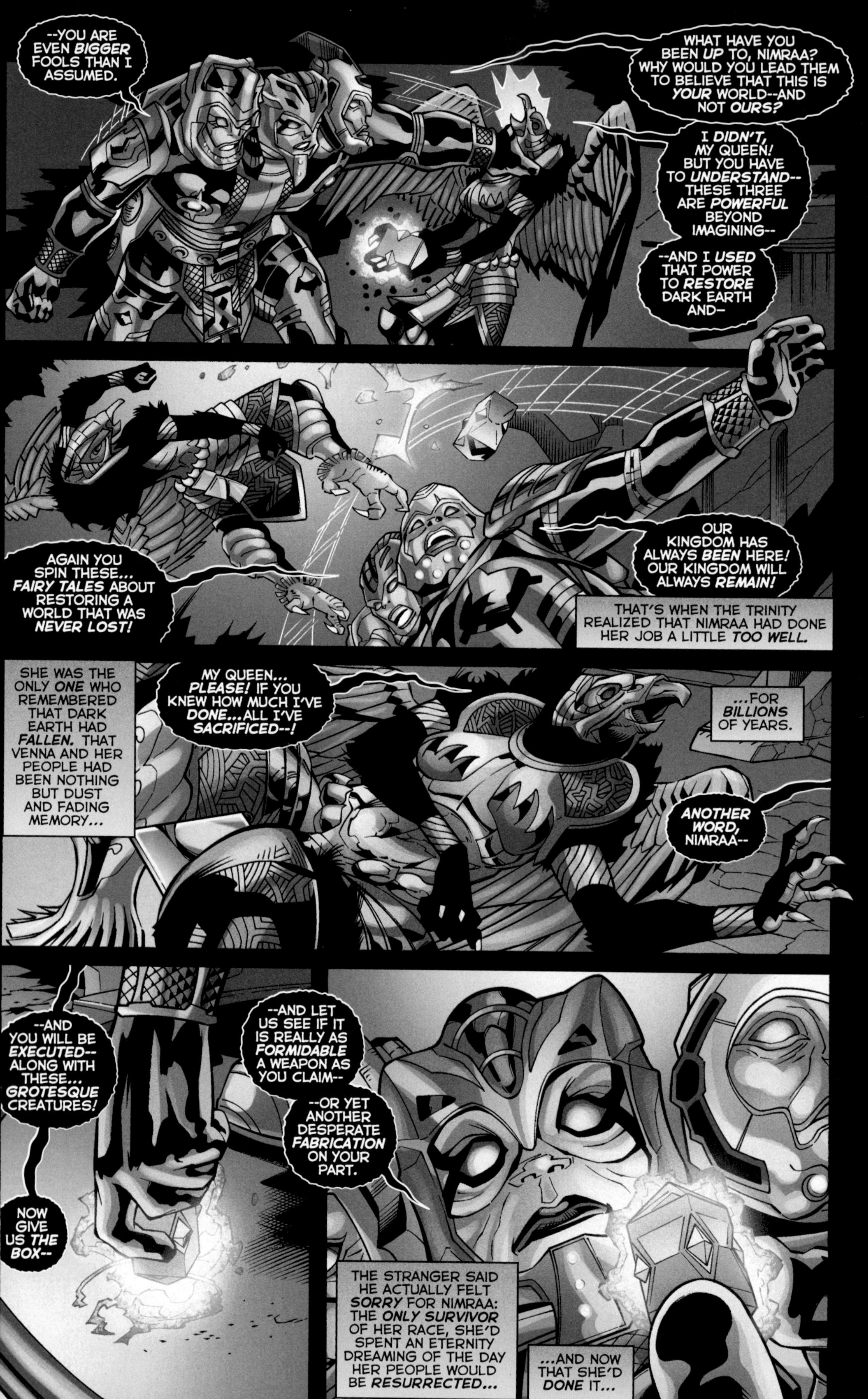
--YOU ARE EVEN BIGGER FOOLS THAN I ASSUMED.
WHAT HAVE YOU BEEN UP TO, NIMRAA? WHY WOULD YOU LEAD THEM TO BELIEVE THAT THIS IS YOUR WORLD--AND NOT OURS?
I DIDN'T, MY QUEEN! BUT YOU HAVE TO UNDERSTAND-- THESE THREE ARE POWERFUL BEYOND IMAGINING--
--AND I USED THAT POWER TO RESTORE DARK EARTH AND--
AGAIN YOU SPIN THESE... FAIRY TALES ABOUT RESTORING A WORLD THAT WAS NEVER LOST!
OUR KINGDOM HAS ALWAYS BEEN HERE! OUR KINGDOM WILL ALWAYS REMAIN!
THAT'S WHEN THE TRINITY REALIZED THAT NIMRAA HAD DONE HER JOB A LITTLE TOO WELL.
SHE WAS THE ONLY ONE WHO REMEMBERED THAT DARK EARTH HAD FALLEN. THAT VENNA AND HER PEOPLE HAD BEEN NOTHING BUT DUST AND FADING MEMORY...
MY QUEEN... PLEASE! IF YOU KNEW HOW MUCH I'VE DONE...ALL I'VE SACRIFICED--!
...FOR BILLIONS OF YEARS.
ANOTHER WORD, NIMRAA--
--AND YOU WILL BE EXECUTED-- ALONG WITH THESE... GROTESQUE CREATURES!
NOW GIVE US THE BOX--
--AND LET US SEE IF IT IS REALLY AS FORMIDABLE A WEAPON AS YOU CLAIM--
--OR YET ANOTHER DESPERATE FABRICATION ON YOUR PART.
THE STRANGER SAID HE ACTUALLY FELT SORRY FOR NIMRAA: THE ONLY SURVIVOR OF HER RACE, SHE'D SPENT AN ETERNITY DREAMING OF THE DAY HER PEOPLE WOULD BE RESURRECTED...
...AND NOW THAT SHE'D DONE IT...

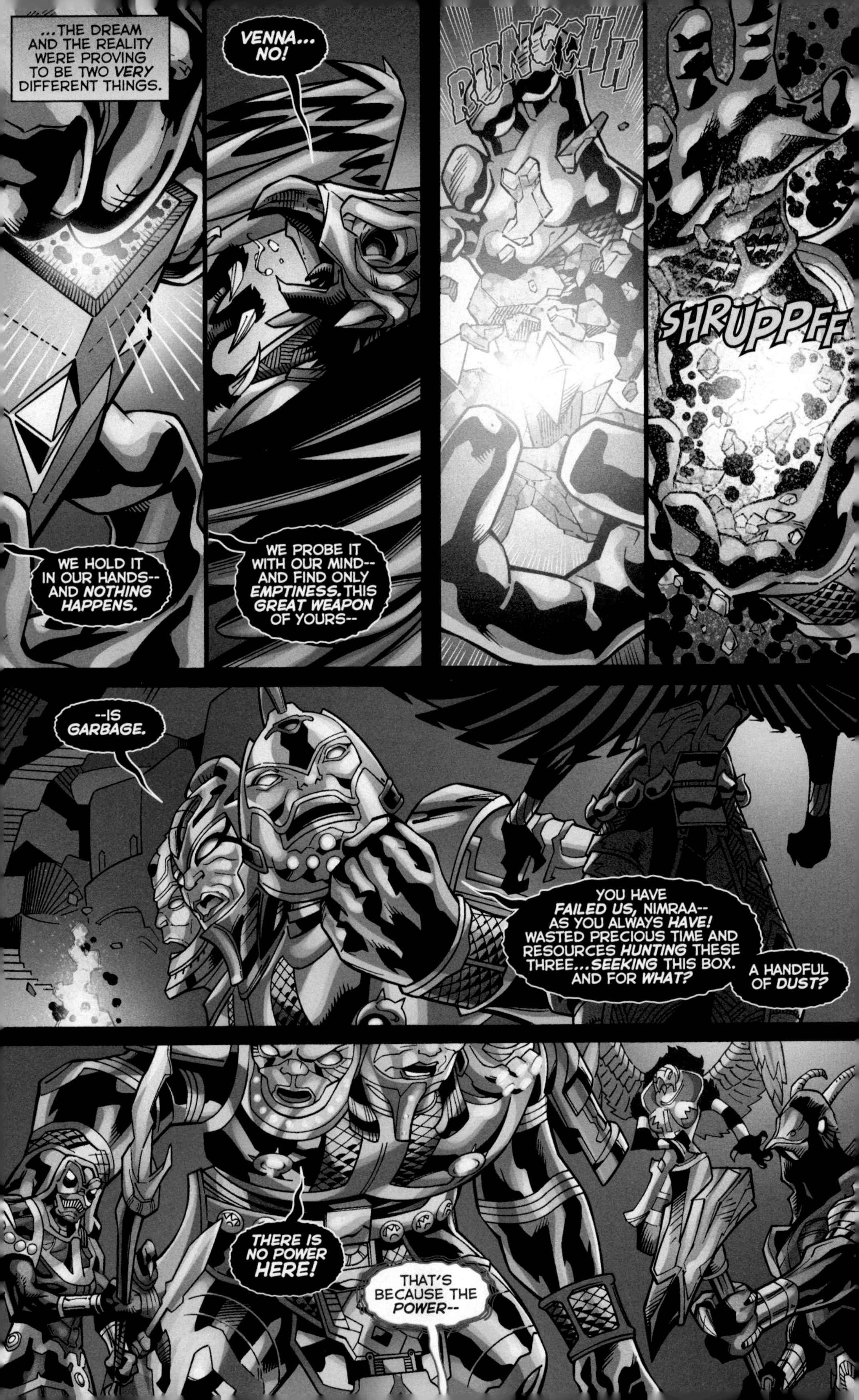
...THE DREAM AND THE REALITY WERE PROVING TO BE TWO VERY DIFFERENT THINGS.
WE HOLD IT IN OUR HANDS-- AND NOTHING HAPPENS.
VENNA... NO!
WE PROBE IT WITH OUR MIND-- AND FIND ONLY EMPTINESS. THIS GREAT WEAPON OF YOURS--
RUNCCHH
SHRUPPFF
--IS GARBAGE.
YOU HAVE FAILED US, NIMRAA-- AS YOU ALWAYS HAVE! WASTED PRECIOUS TIME AND RESOURCES HUNTING THESE THREE...SEEKING THIS BOX. AND FOR WHAT?
A HANDFUL OF DUST?
THERE IS NO POWER HERE!
THAT'S BECAUSE THE POWER--

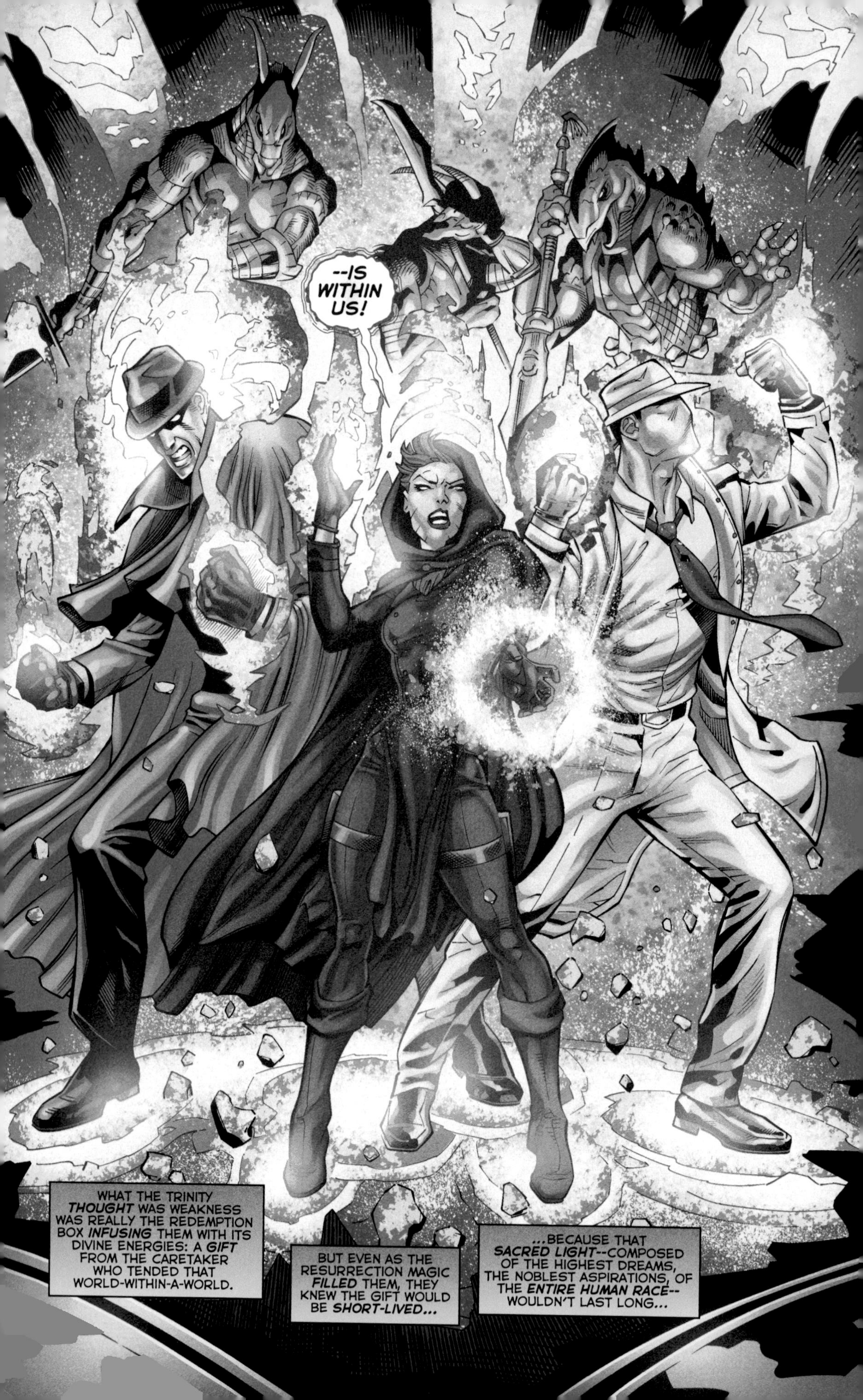
--IS WITHIN US!
WHAT THE TRINITY THOUGHT WAS WEAKNESS WAS REALLY THE REDEMPTION BOX INFUSING THEM WITH ITS DIVINE ENERGIES: A GIFT FROM THE CARETAKER WHO TENDED THAT WORLD-WITHIN-A-WORLD.
BUT EVEN AS THE RESURRECTION MAGIC FILLED THEM, THEY KNEW THE GIFT WOULD BE SHORT-LIVED...
...BECAUSE THAT SACRED LIGHT--COMPOSED OF THE HIGHEST DREAMS, THE NOBLEST ASPIRATIONS, OF THE ENTIRE HUMAN RACE--WOULDN'T LAST LONG...

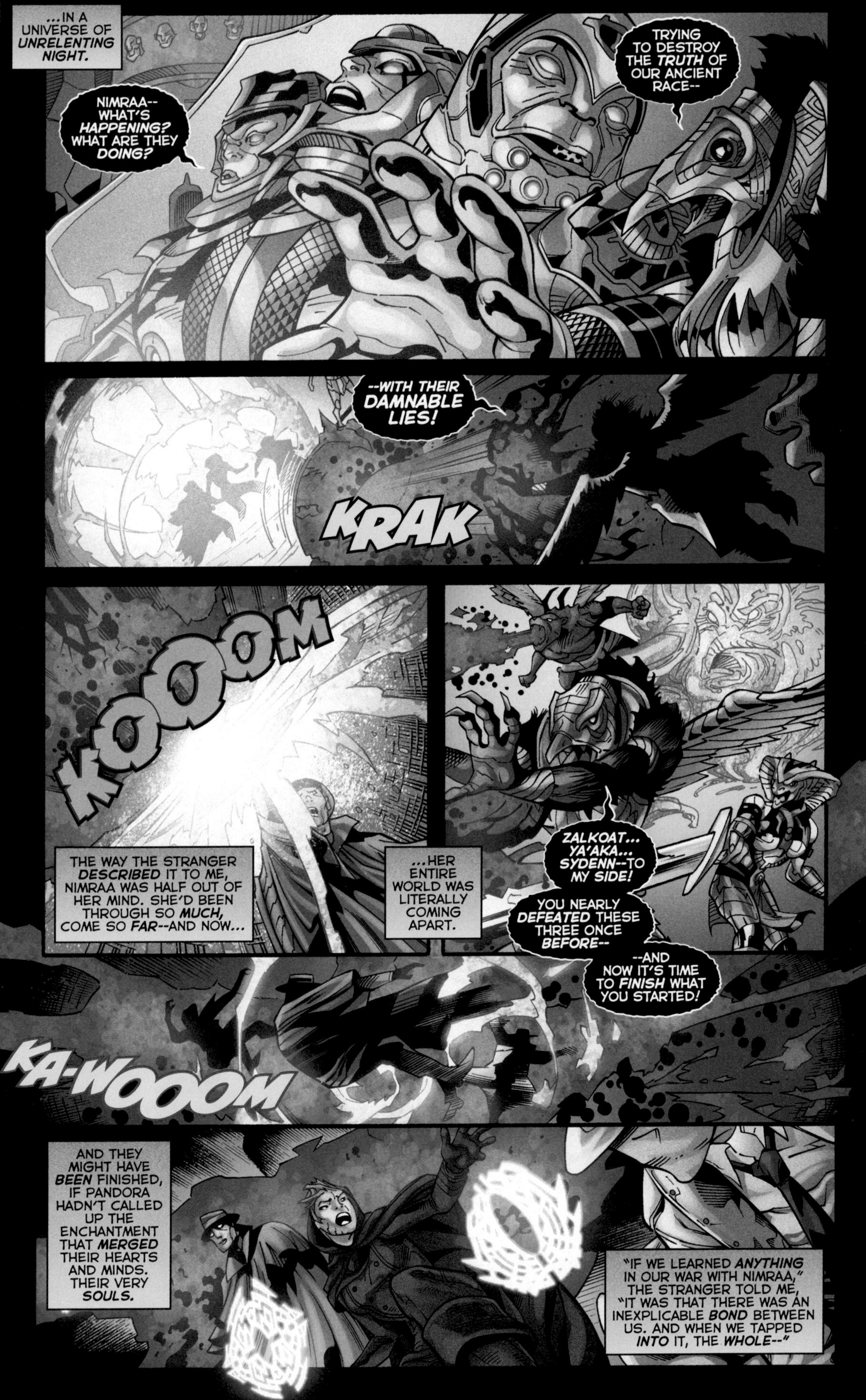
...IN A UNIVERSE OF UNRELENTING NIGHT.
NIMRAA-- WHAT'S HAPPENING? WHAT ARE THEY DOING?
TRYING TO DESTROY THE TRUTH OF OUR ANCIENT RACE--
--WITH THEIR DAMNABLE LIES!
KRAK
KOOOOM
THE WAY THE STRANGER DESCRIBED IT TO ME, NIMRAA WAS HALF OUT OF HER MIND. SHE'D BEEN THROUGH SO MUCH, COME SO FAR--AND NOW...
...HER ENTIRE WORLD WAS LITERALLY COMING APART.
ZALKOAT... YA'AKA... SYDENN--TO MY SIDE!
YOU NEARLY DEFEATED THESE THREE ONCE BEFORE--
--AND NOW IT'S TIME TO FINISH WHAT YOU STARTED!
KA-WOOOM
AND THEY MIGHT HAVE BEEN FINISHED, IF PANDORA HADN'T CALLED UP THE ENCHANTMENT THAT MERGED THEIR HEARTS AND MINDS. THEIR VERY SOULS.
"IF WE LEARNED ANYTHING IN OUR WAR WITH NIMRAA," THE STRANGER TOLD ME, "IT WAS THAT THERE WAS AN INEXPLICABLE BOND BETWEEN US. AND WHEN WE TAPPED INTO IT, THE WHOLE--"

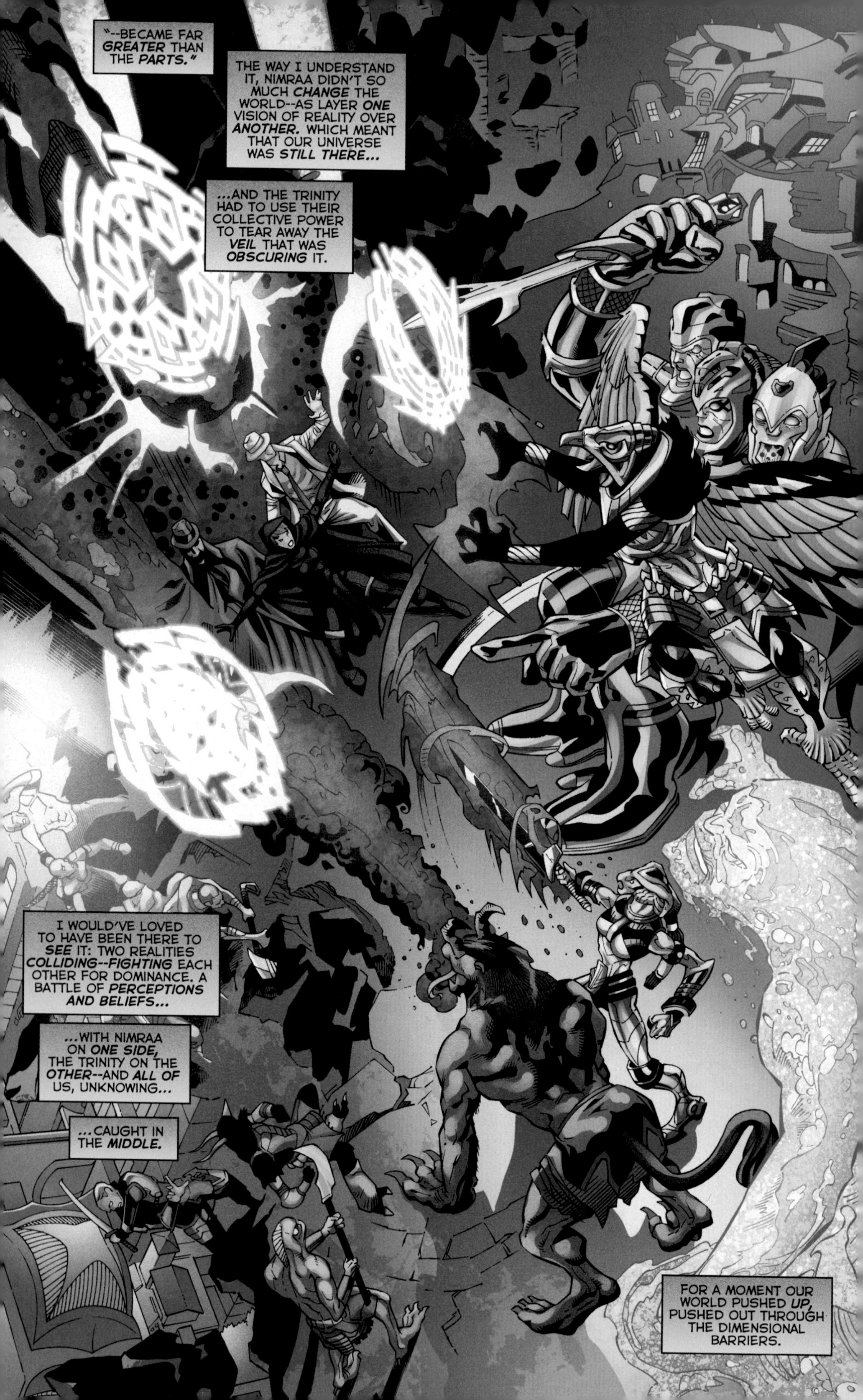
"--BECAME FAR GREATER THAN THE PARTS."
THE WAY I UNDERSTAND IT, NIMRAA DIDN'T SO MUCH CHANGE THE WORLD--AS LAYER ONE VISION OF REALITY OVER ANOTHER. WHICH MEANT THAT OUR UNIVERSE WAS STILL THERE...
...AND THE TRINITY HAD TO USE THEIR COLLECTIVE POWER TO TEAR AWAY THE VEIL THAT WAS OBSCURING IT.
I WOULD'VE LOVED TO HAVE BEEN THERE TO SEE IT: TWO REALITIES COLLIDING--FIGHTING EACH OTHER FOR DOMINANCE. A BATTLE OF PERCEPTIONS AND BELIEFS...
...WITH NIMRAA ON ONE SIDE, THE TRINITY ON THE OTHER--AND ALL OF US, UNKNOWING...
...CAUGHT IN THE MIDDLE.
FOR A MOMENT OUR WORLD PUSHED UP, PUSHED OUT THROUGH THE DIMENSIONAL BARRIERS.

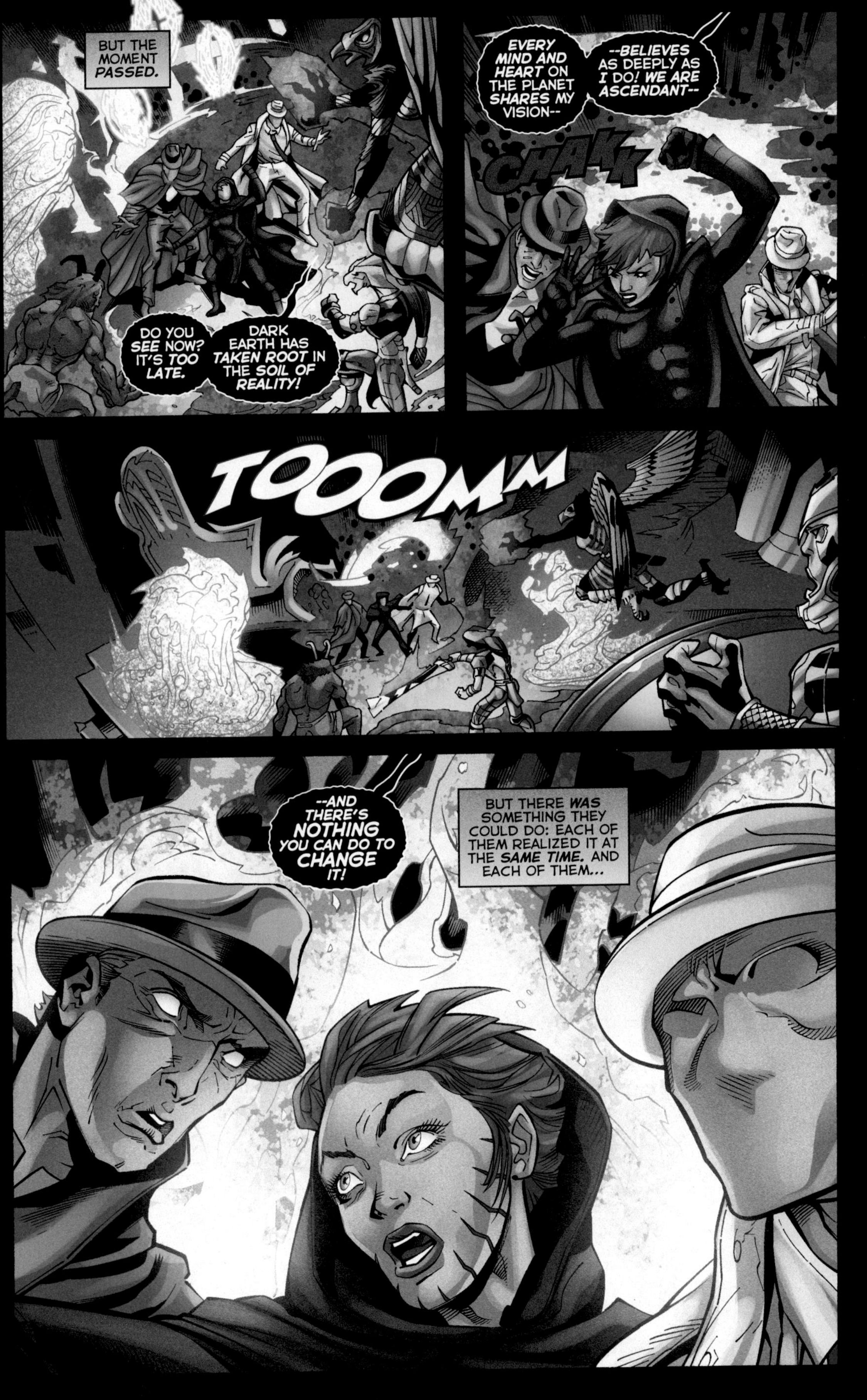
BUT THE MOMENT PASSED.
DO YOU SEE NOW? IT'S TOO LATE.
DARK EARTH HAS TAKEN ROOT IN THE SOIL OF REALITY!
EVERY MIND AND HEART ON THE PLANET SHARES MY VISION--
--BELIEVES AS DEEPLY AS I DO! WE ARE ASCENDANT--
CHAKK
TOOOMM
--AND THERE'S NOTHING YOU CAN DO TO CHANGE IT!
BUT THERE WAS SOMETHING THEY COULD DO: EACH OF THEM REALIZED IT AT THE SAME TIME. AND EACH OF THEM...

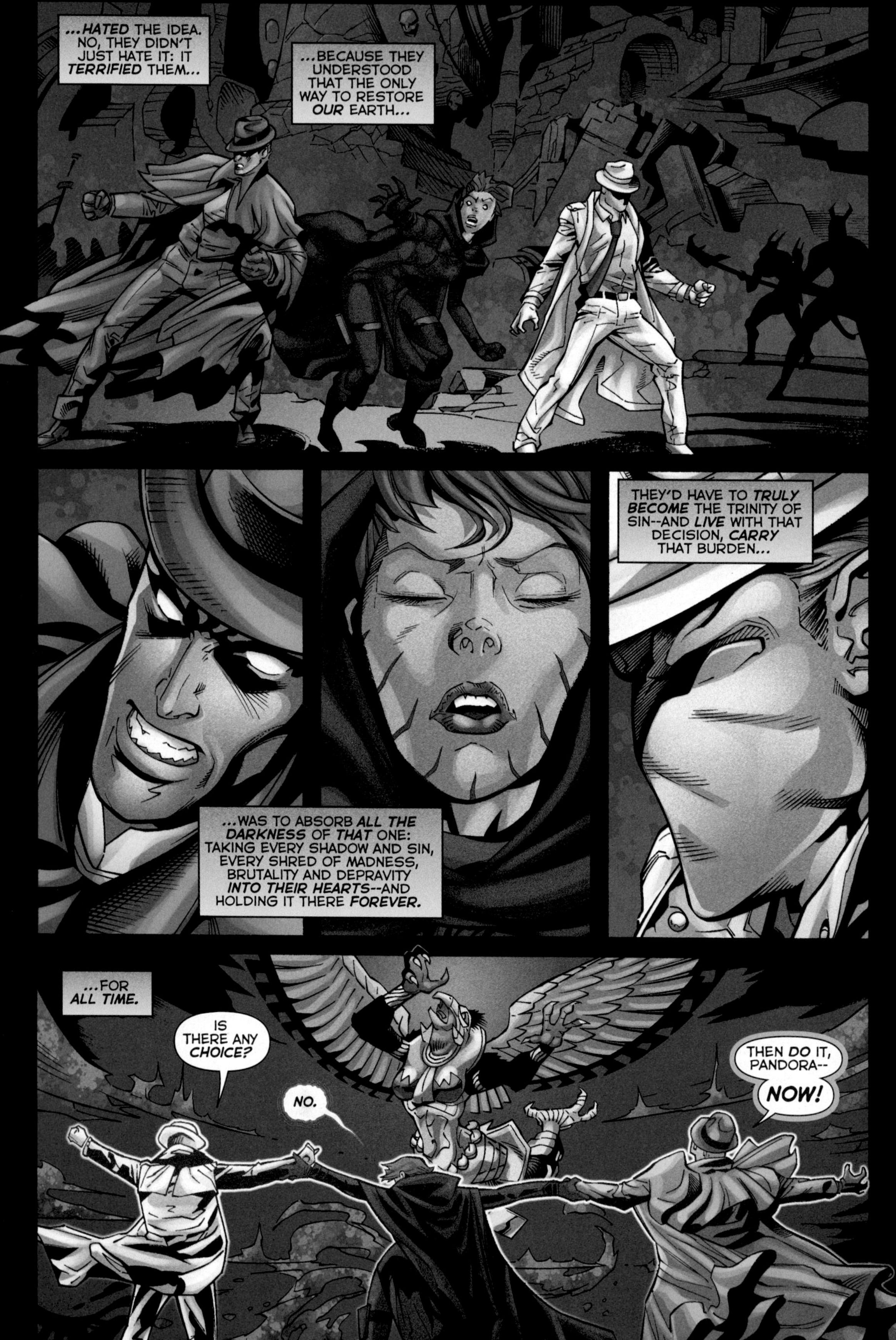
...HATED THE IDEA. NO, THEY DIDN'T JUST HATE IT: IT TERRIFIED THEM...
...BECAUSE THEY UNDERSTOOD THAT THE ONLY WAY TO RESTORE OUR EARTH...
THEY'D HAVE TO TRULY BECOME THE TRINITY OF SIN--AND LIVE WITH THAT DECISION, CARRY THAT BURDEN...
...WAS TO ABSORB ALL THE DARKNESS OF THAT ONE: TAKING EVERY SHADOW AND SIN, EVERY SHRED OF MADNESS, BRUTALITY AND DEPRAVITY INTO THEIR HEARTS--AND HOLDING IT THERE FOREVER.
...FOR ALL TIME.
IS THERE ANY CHOICE?
NO.
THEN DO IT, PANDORA-- NOW!

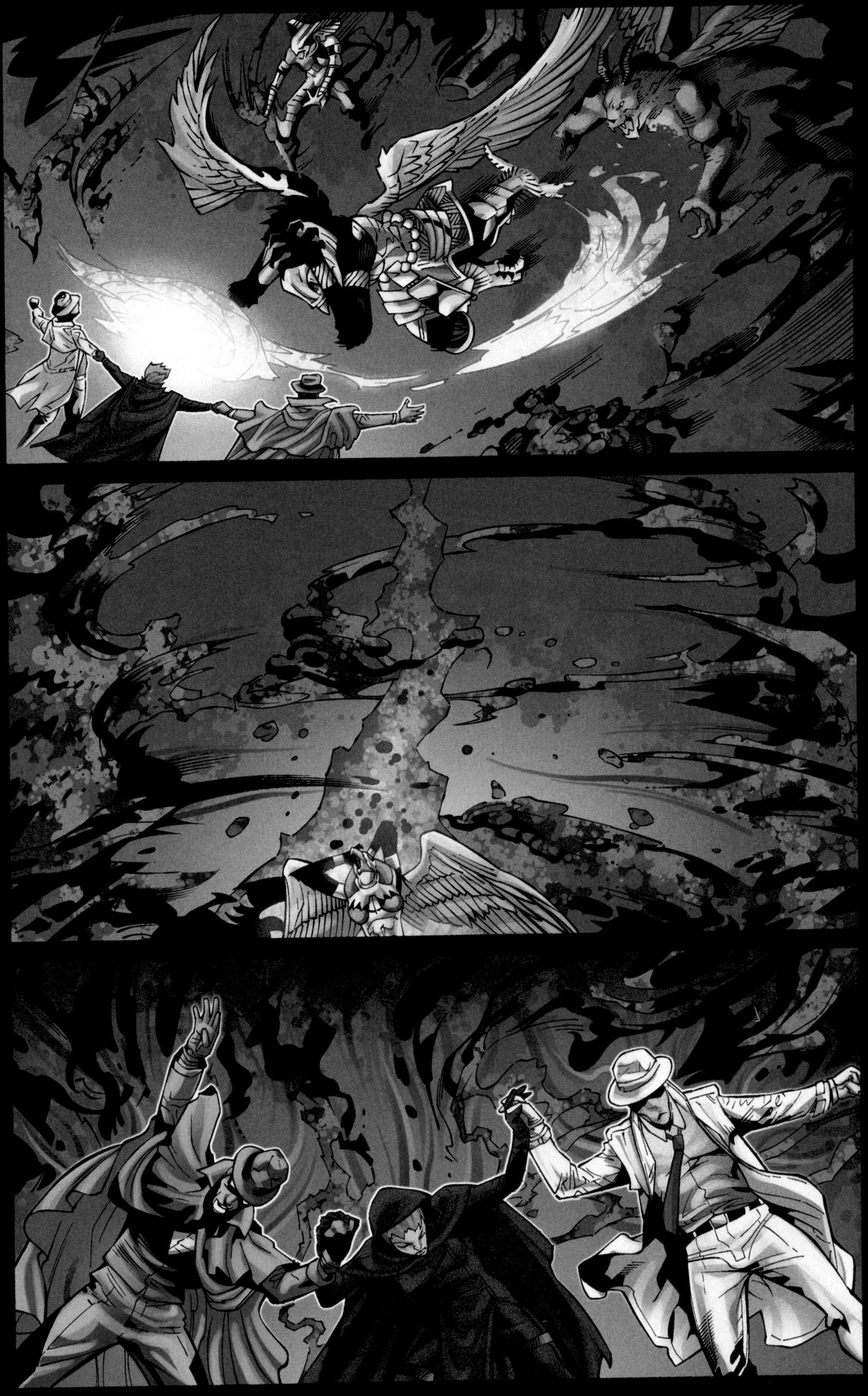

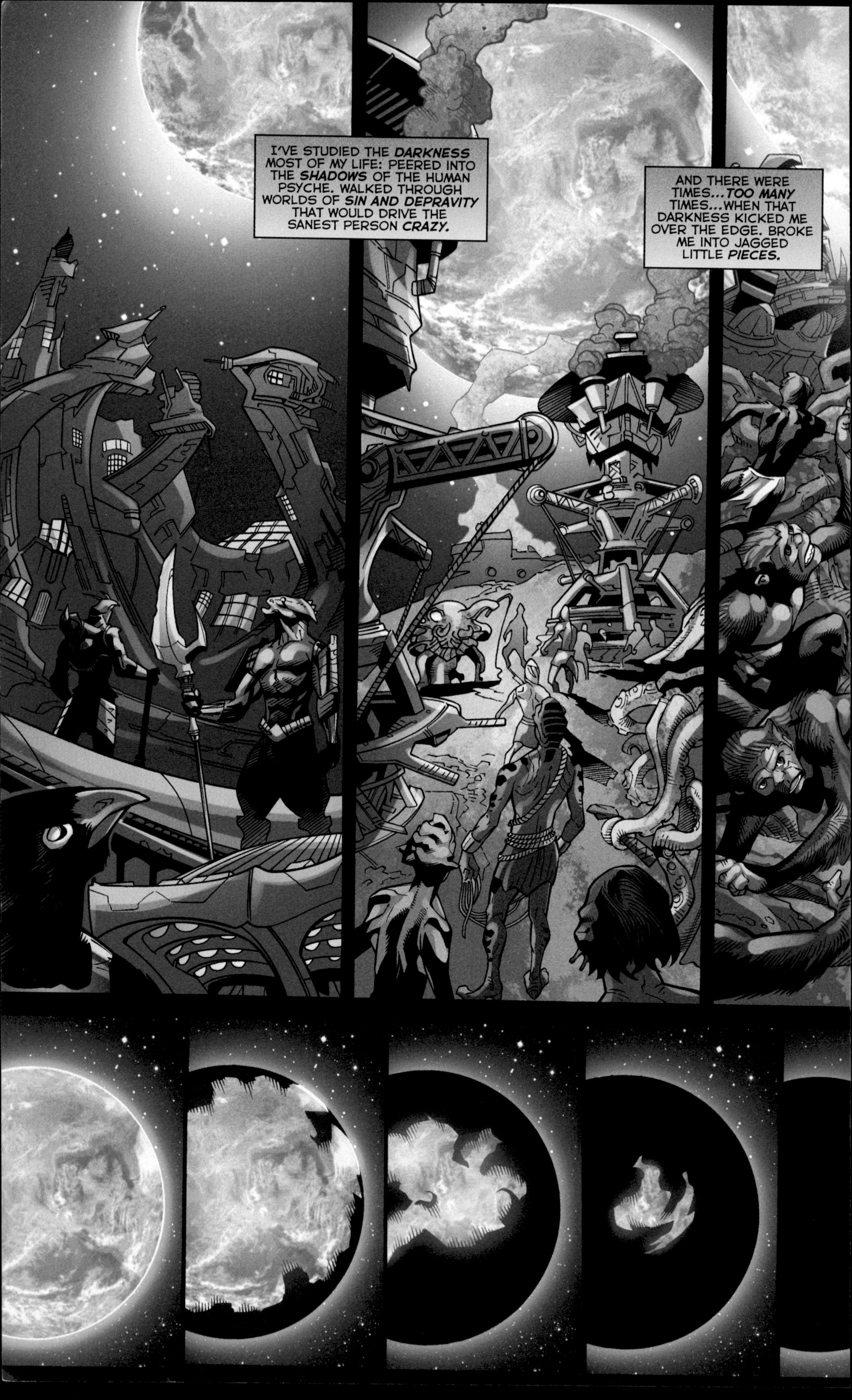
I'VE STUDIED THE DARKNESS MOST OF MY LIFE: PEERED INTO THE SHADOWS OF THE HUMAN PSYCHE. WALKED THROUGH WORLDS OF SIN AND DEPRAVITY THAT WOULD DRIVE THE SANEST PERSON CRAZY.
AND THERE WERE TIMES...TOO MANY TIMES...WHEN THAT DARKNESS KICKED ME OVER THE EDGE. BROKE ME INTO JAGGED LITTLE PIECES.

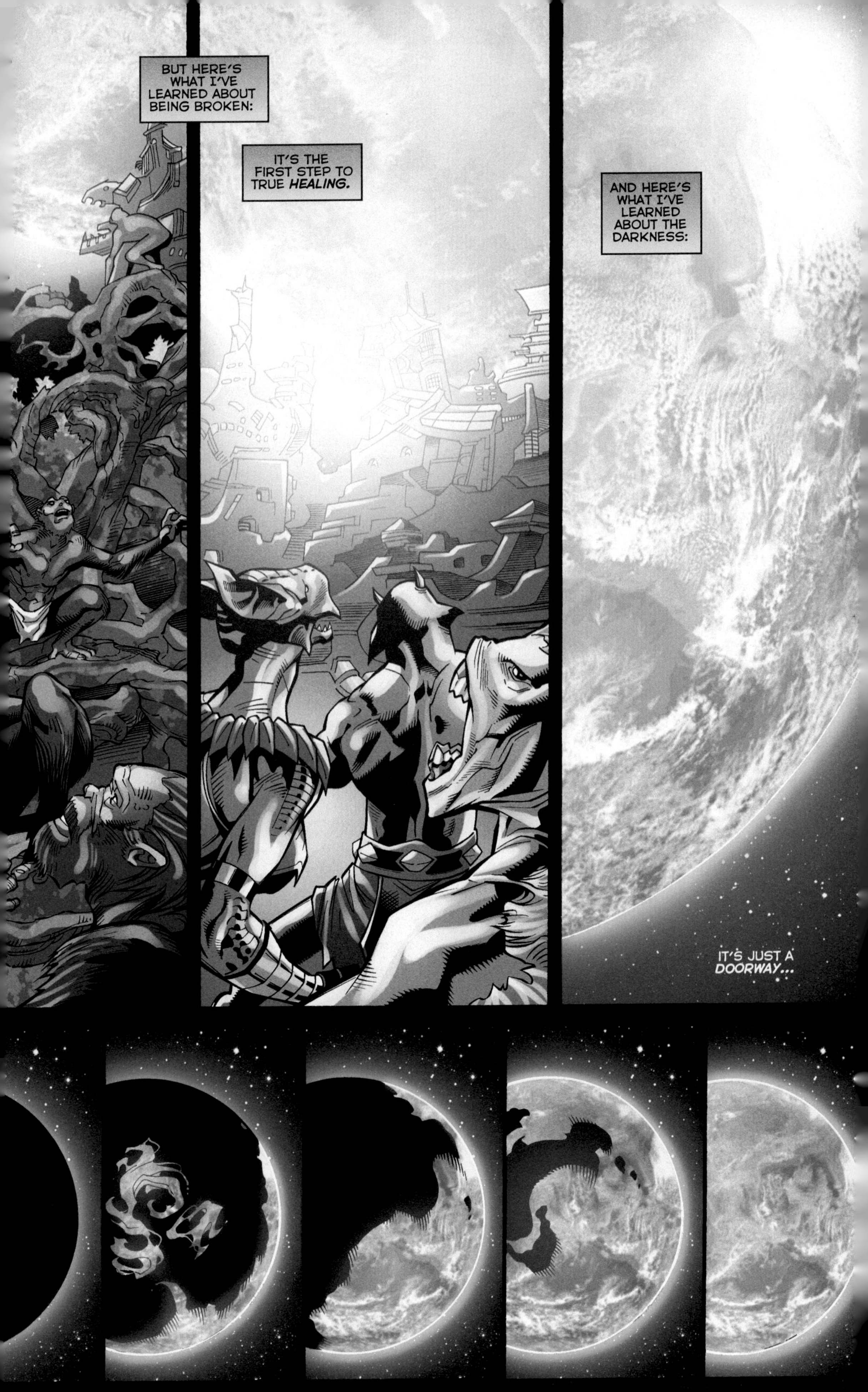

BUT HERE'S WHAT I'VE LEARNED ABOUT BEING BROKEN:
IT'S THE FIRST STEP TO TRUE *HEALING.*
AND HERE'S WHAT I'VE LEARNED ABOUT THE DARKNESS:
IT'S JUST A *DOORWAY...*

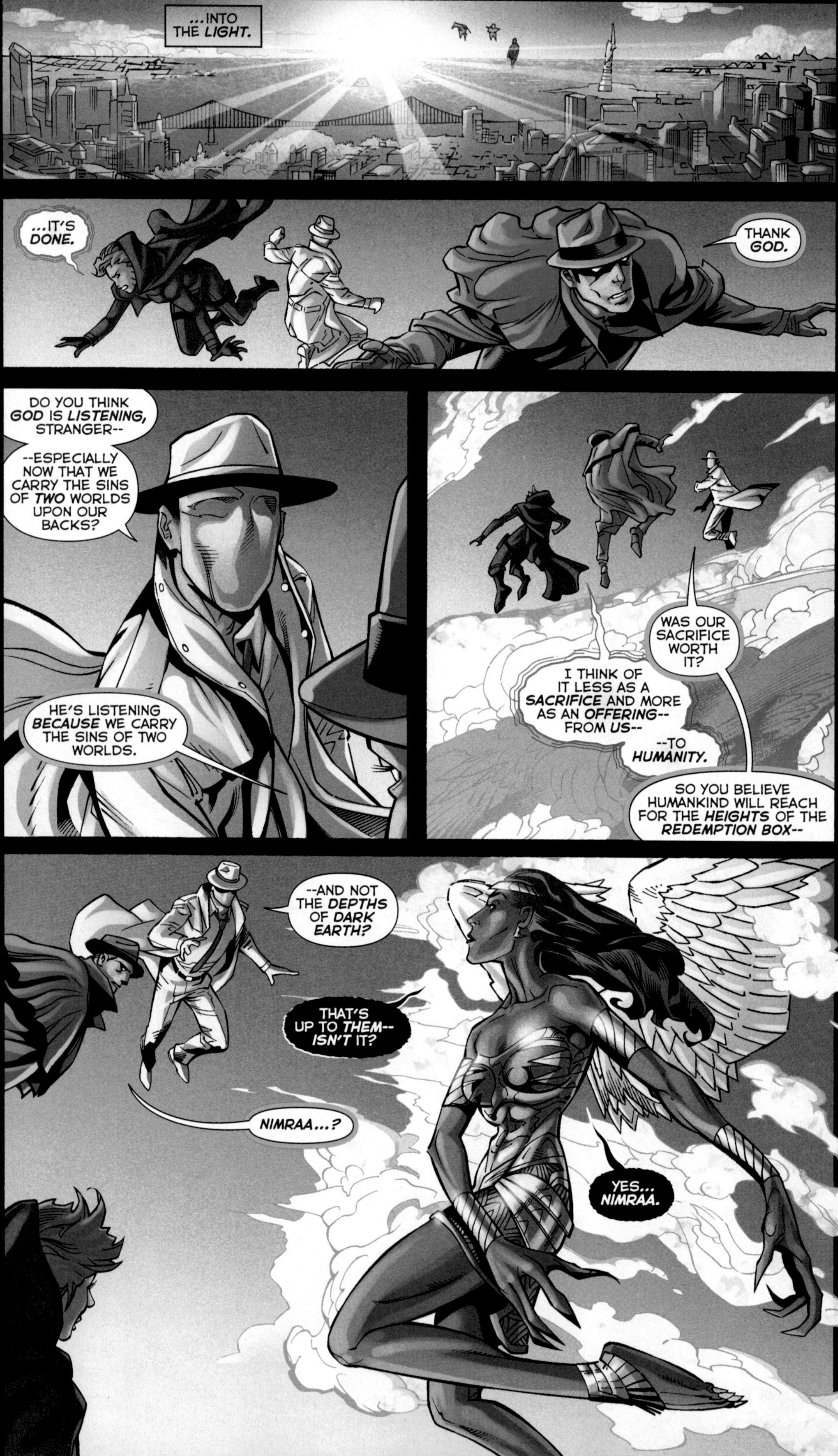
...INTO THE LIGHT.
...IT'S DONE.
THANK GOD.
DO YOU THINK GOD IS LISTENING, STRANGER--
--ESPECIALLY NOW THAT WE CARRY THE SINS OF TWO WORLDS UPON OUR BACKS?
HE'S LISTENING BECAUSE WE CARRY THE SINS OF TWO WORLDS.
WAS OUR SACRIFICE WORTH IT?
I THINK OF IT LESS AS A SACRIFICE AND MORE AS AN OFFERING-- FROM US--
--TO HUMANITY.
SO YOU BELIEVE HUMANKIND WILL REACH FOR THE HEIGHTS OF THE REDEMPTION BOX--
--AND NOT THE DEPTHS OF DARK EARTH?
THAT'S UP TO THEM-- ISN'T IT?
NIMRAA...?
YES... NIMRAA.

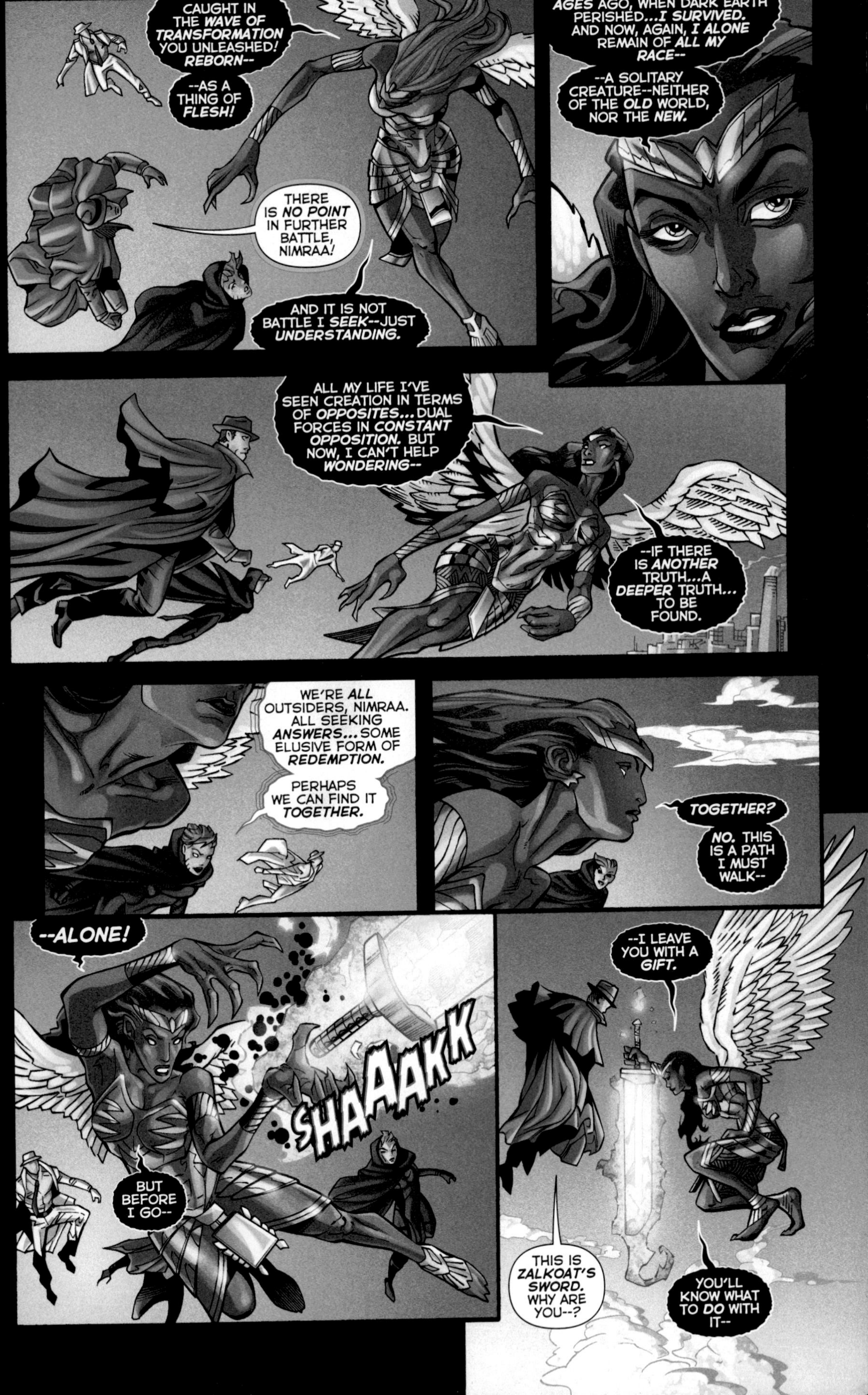
CAUGHT IN THE WAVE OF TRANSFORMATION YOU UNLEASHED! REBORN--
--AS A THING OF FLESH!
THERE IS NO POINT IN FURTHER BATTLE, NIMRAA!
AND IT IS NOT BATTLE I SEEK--JUST UNDERSTANDING.
AGES AGO, WHEN DARK EARTH PERISHED...I SURVIVED. AND NOW, AGAIN, I ALONE REMAIN OF ALL MY RACE--
--A SOLITARY CREATURE--NEITHER OF THE OLD WORLD, NOR THE NEW.
ALL MY LIFE I'VE SEEN CREATION IN TERMS OF OPPOSITES...DUAL FORCES IN CONSTANT OPPOSITION. BUT NOW, I CAN'T HELP WONDERING--
--IF THERE IS ANOTHER TRUTH...A DEEPER TRUTH...TO BE FOUND.
WE'RE ALL OUTSIDERS, NIMRAA. ALL SEEKING ANSWERS...SOME ELUSIVE FORM OF REDEMPTION.
PERHAPS WE CAN FIND IT TOGETHER.
TOGETHER?
NO. THIS IS A PATH I MUST WALK--
--ALONE!
SHAAAKK
BUT BEFORE I GO--
--I LEAVE YOU WITH A GIFT.
THIS IS ZALKOAT'S SWORD. WHY ARE YOU--?
YOU'LL KNOW WHAT TO DO WITH IT--

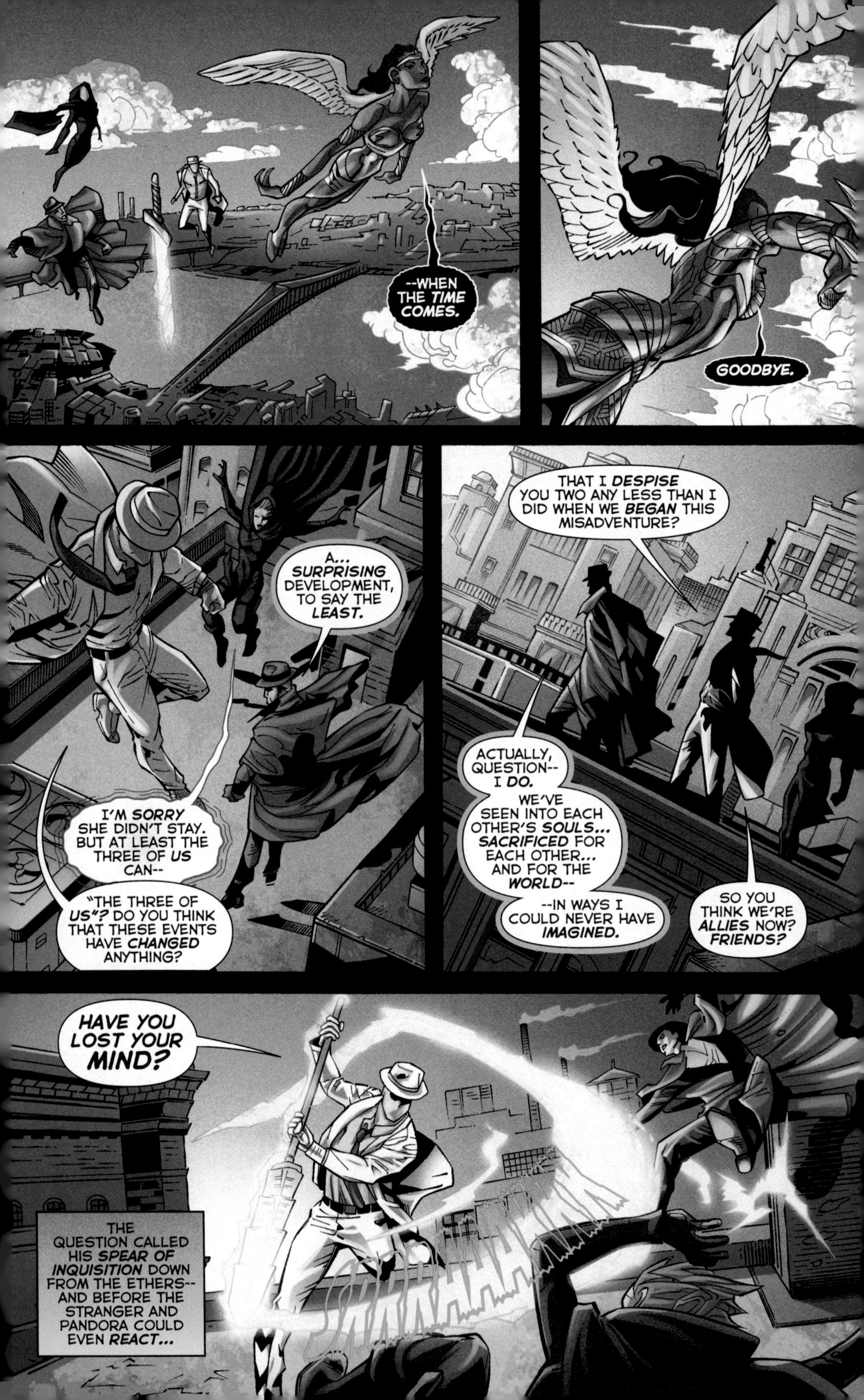
--WHEN THE TIME COMES.
GOODBYE.
A... SURPRISING DEVELOPMENT, TO SAY THE LEAST.
I'M SORRY SHE DIDN'T STAY. BUT AT LEAST THE THREE OF US CAN--
"THE THREE OF US"? DO YOU THINK THAT THESE EVENTS HAVE CHANGED ANYTHING?
THAT I DESPISE YOU TWO ANY LESS THAN I DID WHEN WE BEGAN THIS MISADVENTURE?
ACTUALLY, QUESTION-- I DO.
WE'VE SEEN INTO EACH OTHER'S SOULS... SACRIFICED FOR EACH OTHER... AND FOR THE WORLD--
--IN WAYS I COULD NEVER HAVE IMAGINED.
SO YOU THINK WE'RE ALLIES NOW? FRIENDS?
HAVE YOU LOST YOUR MIND?
THE QUESTION CALLED HIS SPEAR OF INQUISITION DOWN FROM THE ETHERS-- AND BEFORE THE STRANGER AND PANDORA COULD EVEN REACT...

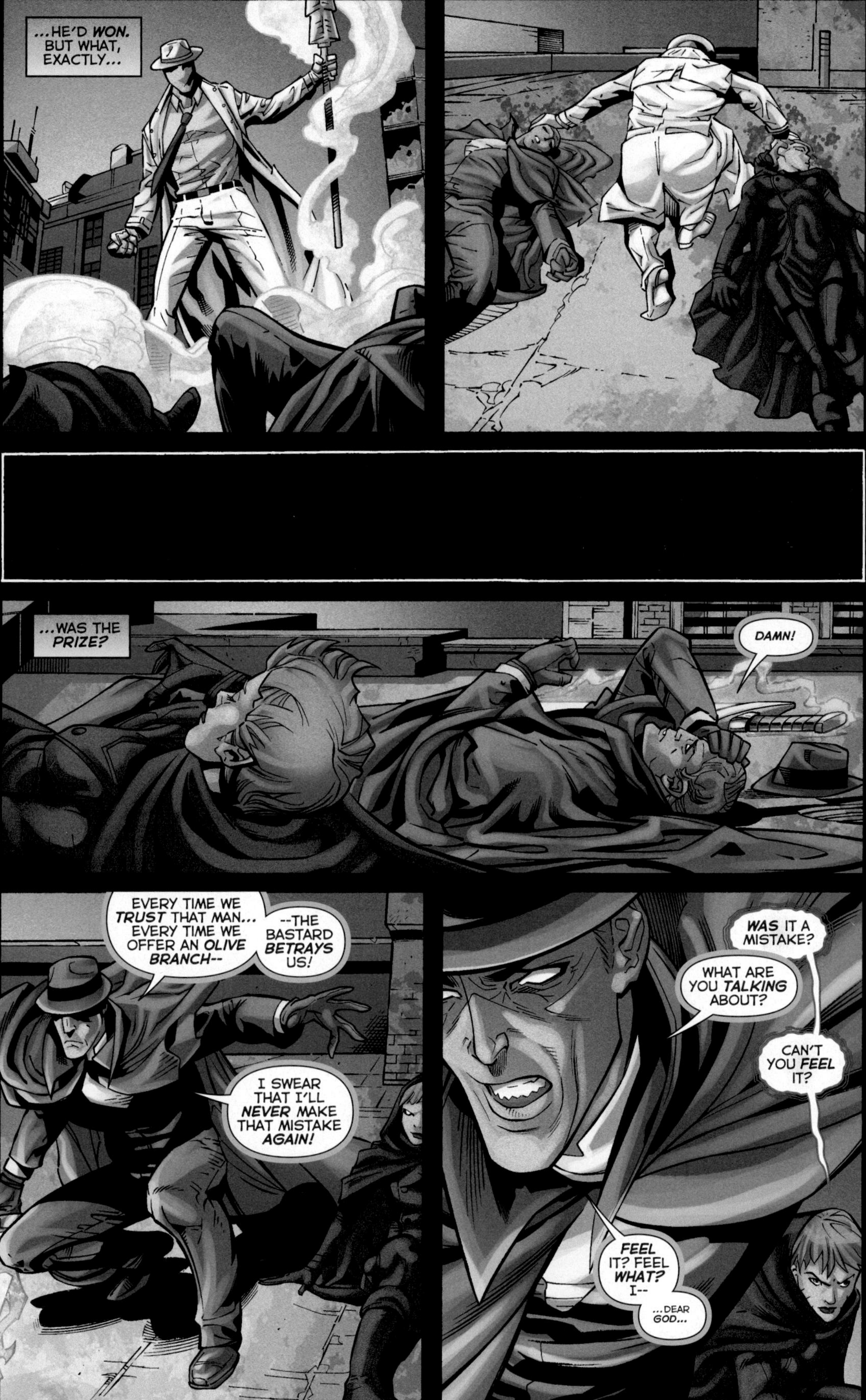
...HE'D WON. BUT WHAT, EXACTLY...
...WAS THE PRIZE?
DAMN!
EVERY TIME WE TRUST THAT MAN... EVERY TIME WE OFFER AN OLIVE BRANCH--
--THE BASTARD BETRAYS US!
I SWEAR THAT I'LL NEVER MAKE THAT MISTAKE AGAIN!
WAS IT A MISTAKE?
WHAT ARE YOU TALKING ABOUT?
CAN'T YOU FEEL IT?
FEEL IT? FEEL WHAT? I--
...DEAR GOD...

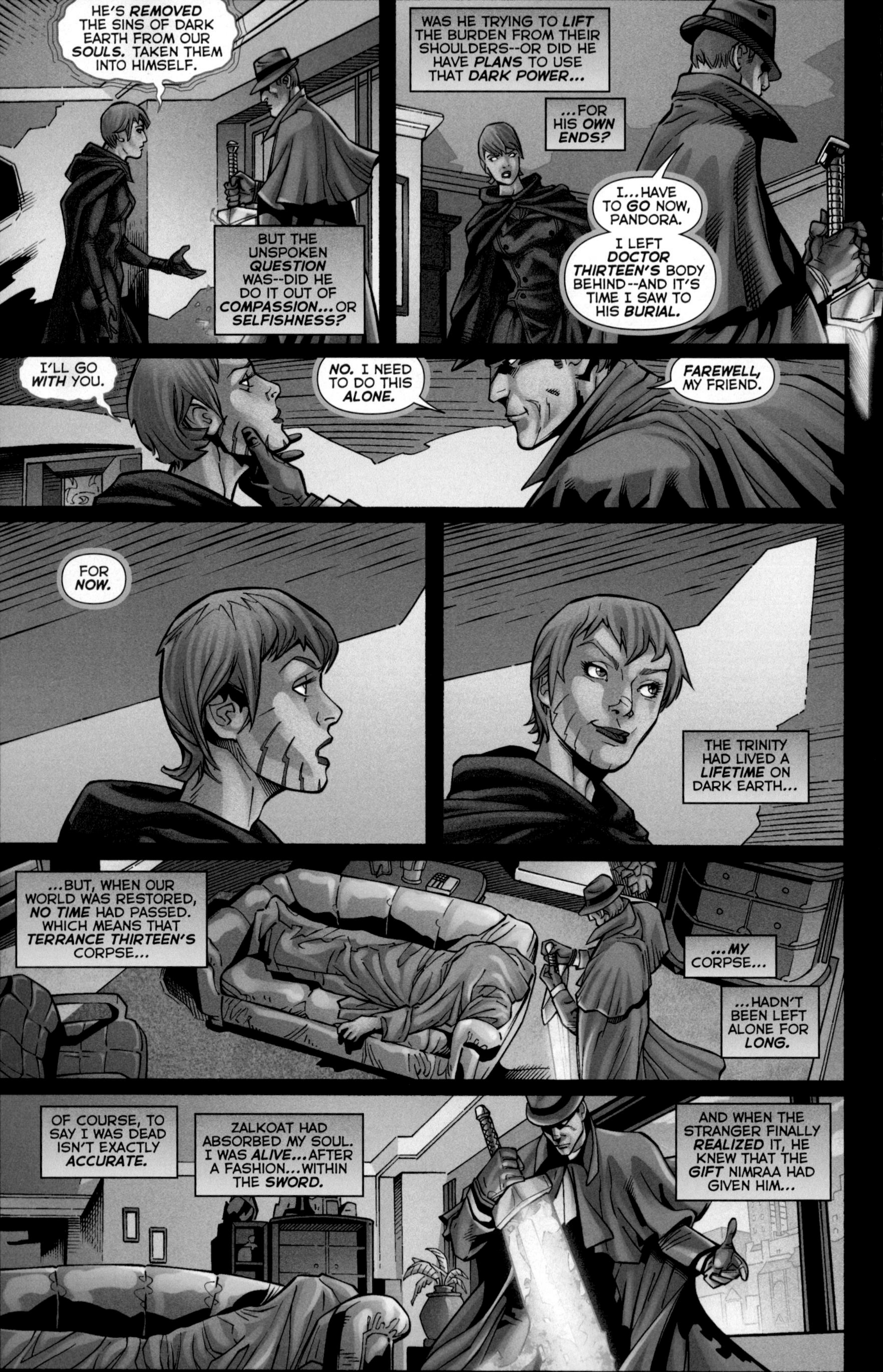
HE'S REMOVED THE SINS OF DARK EARTH FROM OUR SOULS. TAKEN THEM INTO HIMSELF.
BUT THE UNSPOKEN QUESTION WAS--DID HE DO IT OUT OF COMPASSION...OR SELFISHNESS?
WAS HE TRYING TO LIFT THE BURDEN FROM THEIR SHOULDERS--OR DID HE HAVE PLANS TO USE THAT DARK POWER...
...FOR HIS OWN ENDS?
I...HAVE TO GO NOW, PANDORA.
I LEFT DOCTOR THIRTEEN'S BODY BEHIND--AND IT'S TIME I SAW TO HIS BURIAL.
I'LL GO WITH YOU.
NO. I NEED TO DO THIS ALONE.
FAREWELL, MY FRIEND.
FOR NOW.
THE TRINITY HAD LIVED A LIFETIME ON DARK EARTH...
...BUT, WHEN OUR WORLD WAS RESTORED, NO TIME HAD PASSED. WHICH MEANS THAT TERRANCE THIRTEEN'S CORPSE...
...MY CORPSE...
...HADN'T BEEN LEFT ALONE FOR LONG.
OF COURSE, TO SAY I WAS DEAD ISN'T EXACTLY ACCURATE.
ZALKOAT HAD ABSORBED MY SOUL. I WAS ALIVE...AFTER A FASHION...WITHIN THE SWORD.
AND WHEN THE STRANGER FINALLY REALIZED IT, HE KNEW THAT THE GIFT NIMRAA HAD GIVEN HIM...

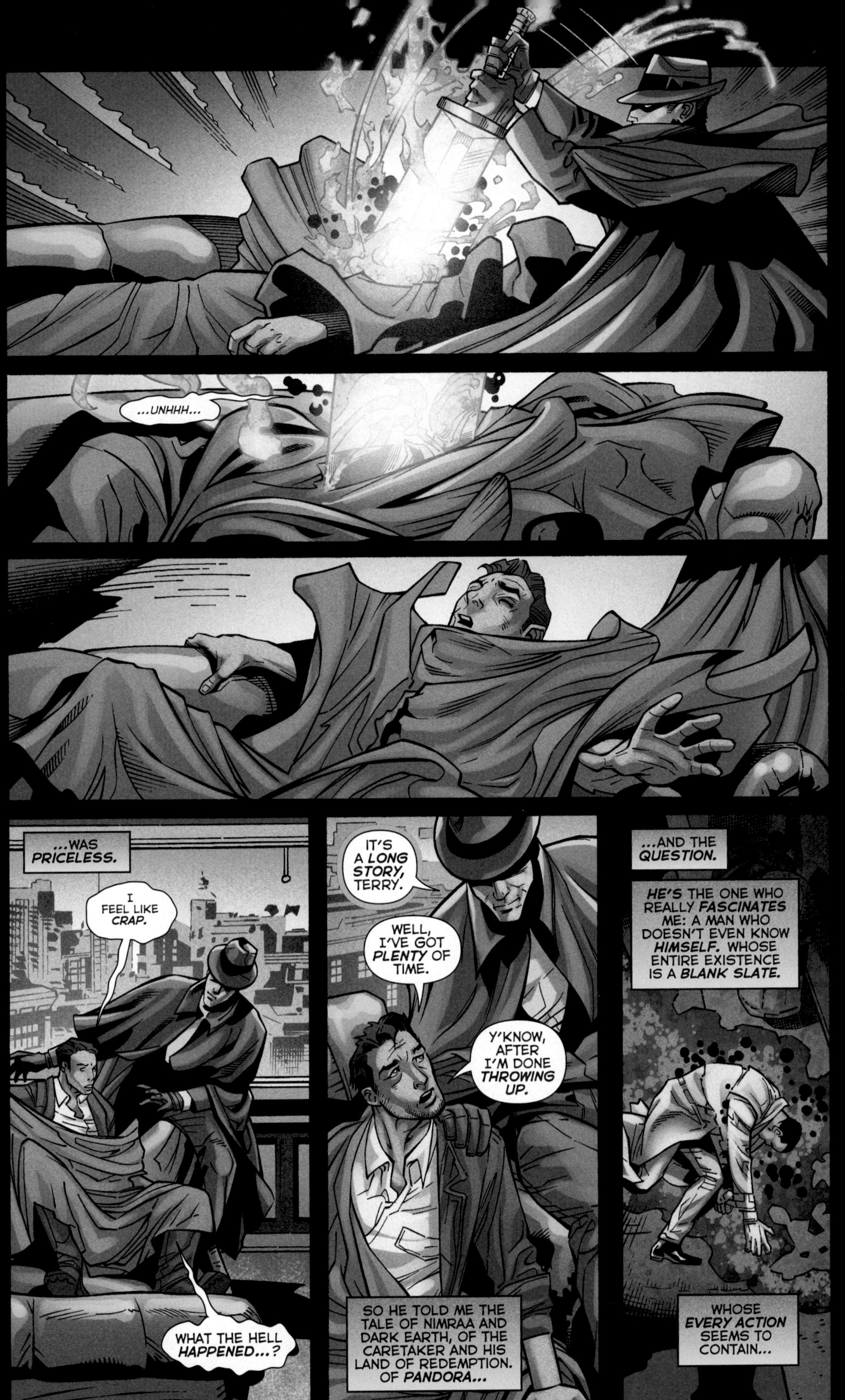
...UNHHH...
...WAS PRICELESS.
I FEEL LIKE CRAP.
WHAT THE HELL HAPPENED...?
IT'S A LONG STORY, TERRY.
WELL, I'VE GOT PLENTY OF TIME.
Y'KNOW, AFTER I'M DONE THROWING UP.
SO HE TOLD ME THE TALE OF NIMRAA AND DARK EARTH, OF THE CARETAKER AND HIS LAND OF REDEMPTION. OF PANDORA...
...AND THE QUESTION.
HE'S THE ONE WHO REALLY FASCINATES ME: A MAN WHO DOESN'T EVEN KNOW HIMSELF. WHOSE ENTIRE EXISTENCE IS A BLANK SLATE.
WHOSE EVERY ACTION SEEMS TO CONTAIN...

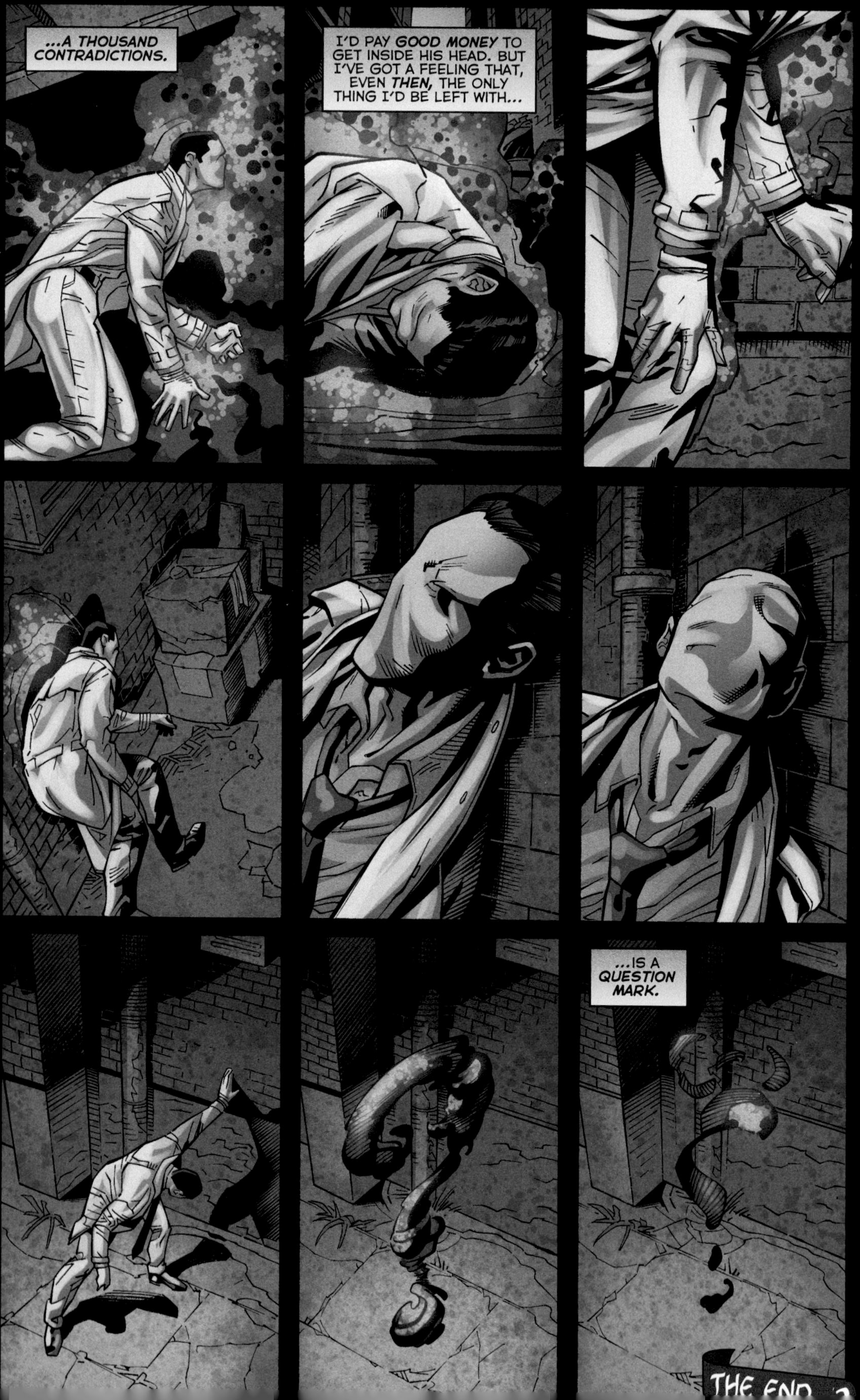
...A THOUSAND CONTRADICTIONS.
I'D PAY GOOD MONEY TO GET INSIDE HIS HEAD. BUT I'VE GOT A FEELING THAT, EVEN THEN, THE ONLY THING I'D BE LEFT WITH...
...IS A QUESTION MARK.
THE END

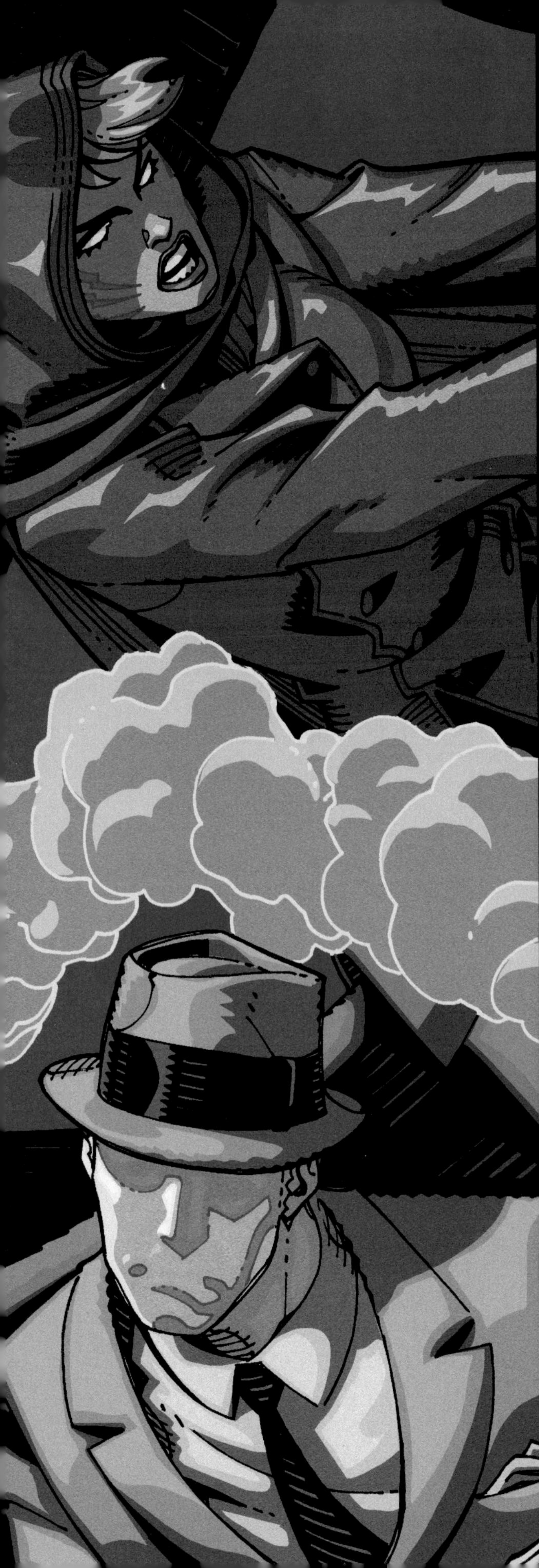

VARIANT COVER GALLERY

TRINITY OF SIN #1
VARIANT COVER BY
CULLY HAMNER

TRINITY OF SIN #2
VARIANT COVER BY
SCOTT HEPBURN

TRINITY OF SIN #3
VARIANT COVER BY
JUAN FERREYRA

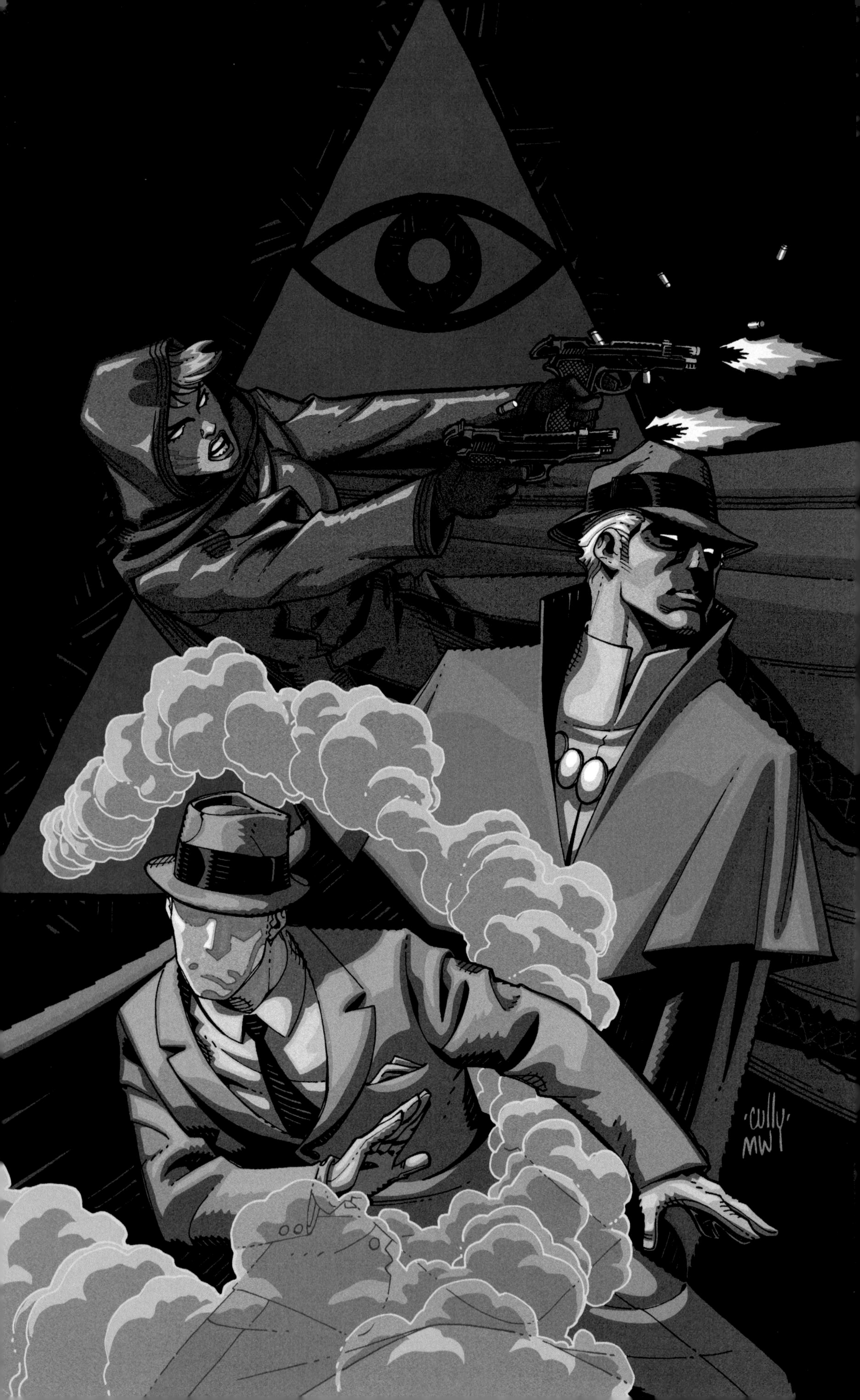
·cully·
MW

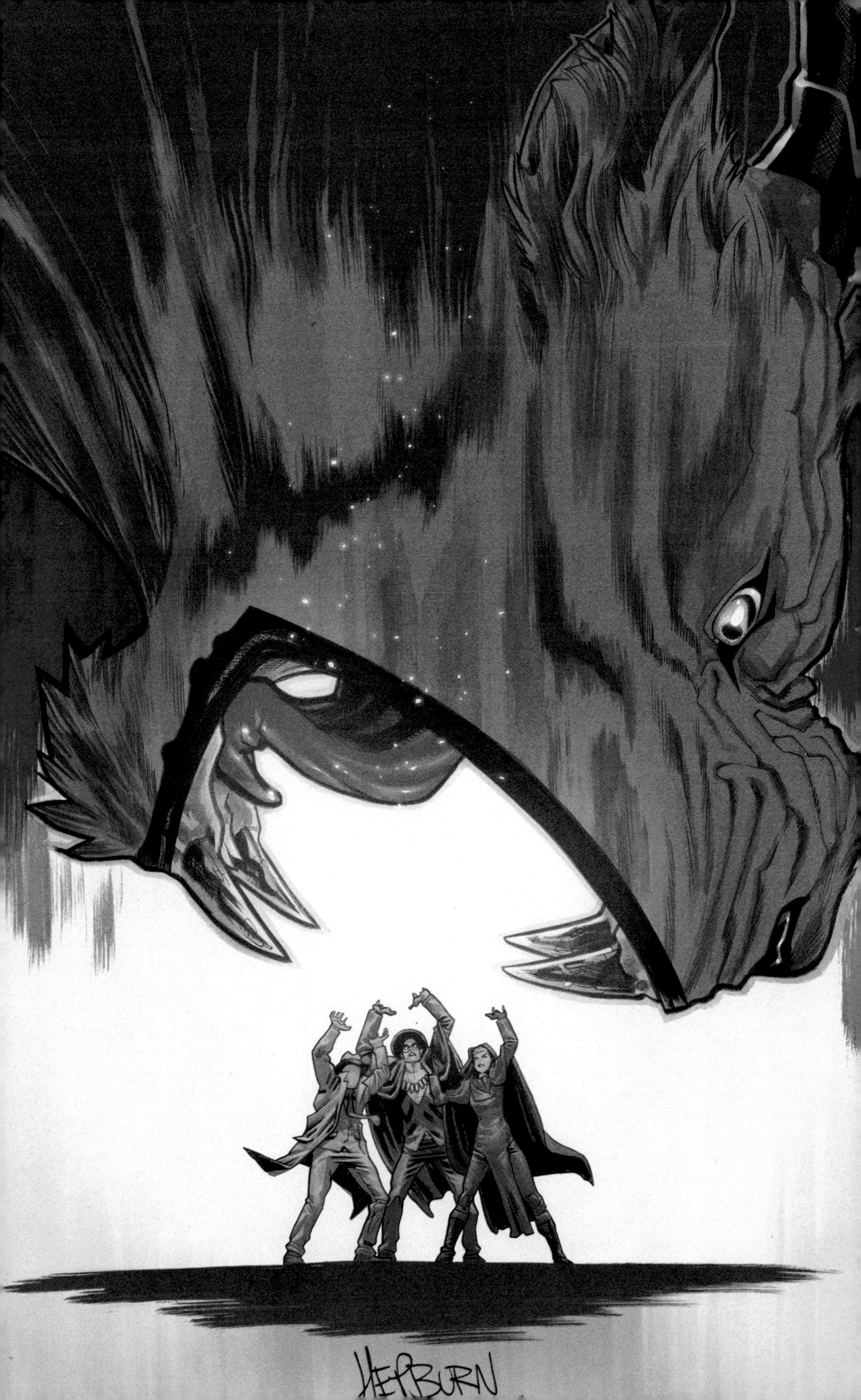
HEPBURN

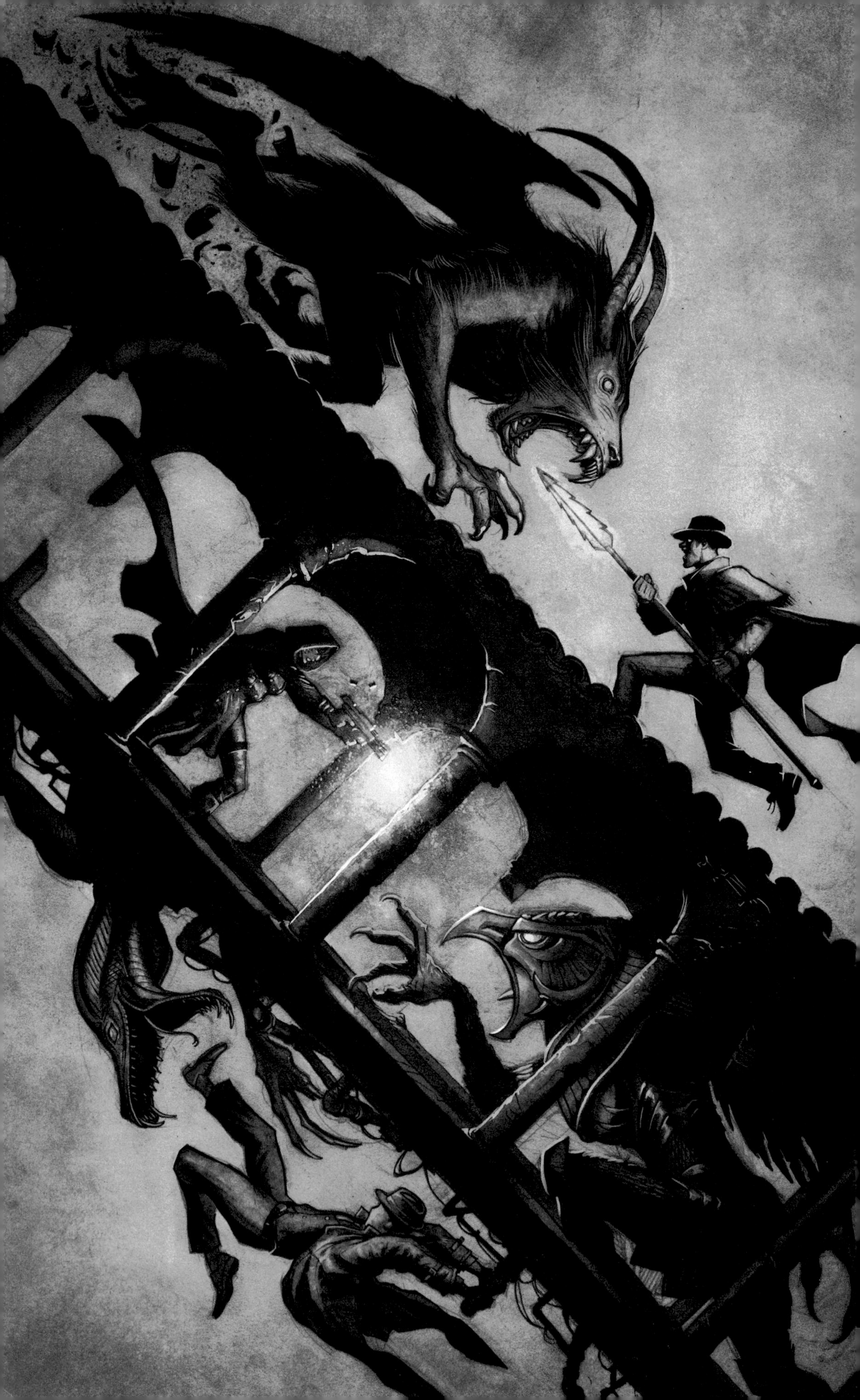

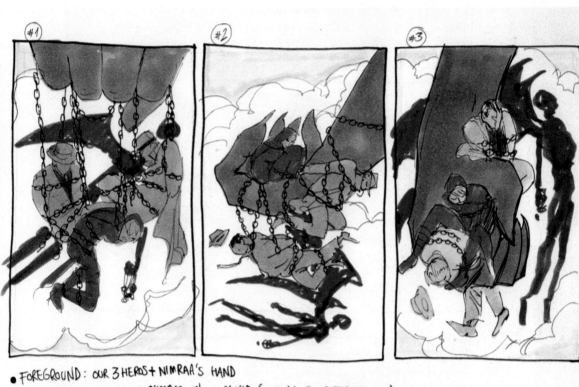

- FOREGROUND: OUR 3 HEROS + NIMRAA'S HAND
- BACKGROUND: SHADOW OF NIMRAA ON A CLOUD (+ SHADOW OF OUR TINY 3 HEROS)
  I CAN DO A RED SKY (LIKE HELL).   BIG QUESTION: NIMRAA <u>FLIGHTS</u>, RIGHT?
  (SHE'S GOT WINGS)

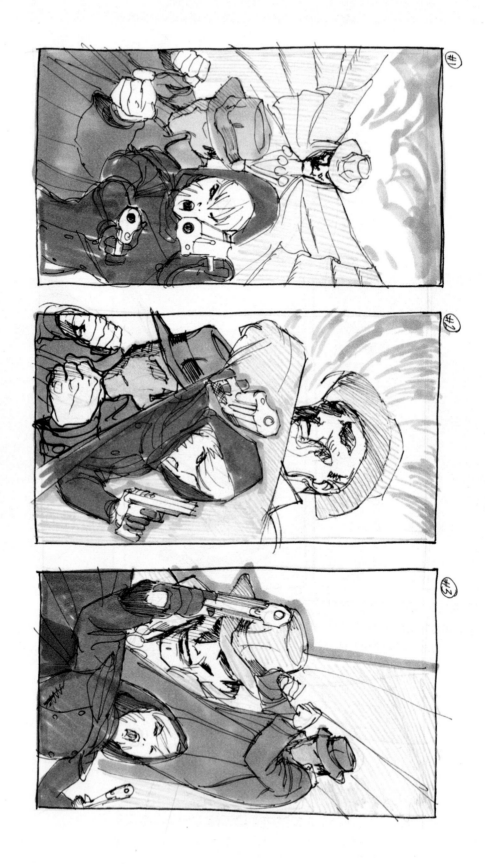

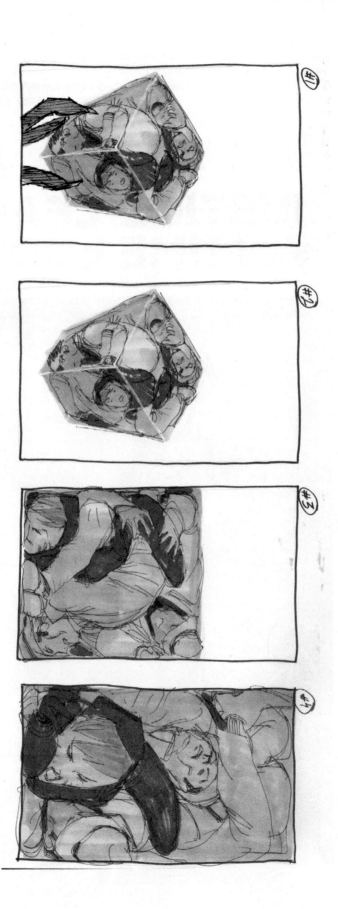

"Welcoming to new fans looking to get into superhero comics for the first time and old fans who gave up on the funny-books long ago."
—SCRIPPS HOWARD NEWS SERVICE

START AT THE BEGINNING!

JUSTICE LEAGUE VOLUME 1: ORIGIN

AQUAMAN VOLUME 1: THE TRENCH

THE SAVAGE HAWKMAN VOLUME 1: DARKNESS RISING

GREEN ARROW VOLUME 1: THE MIDAS TOUCH

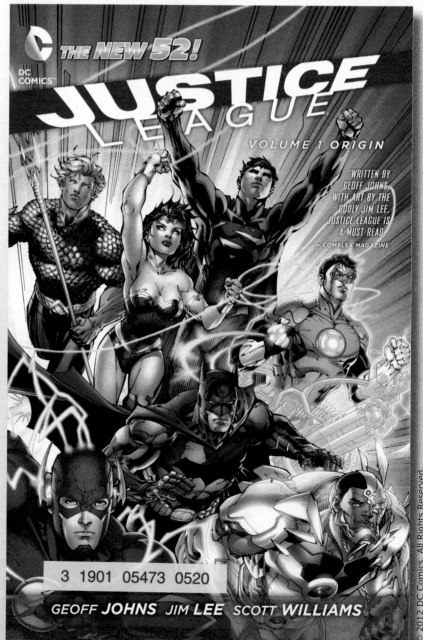

3 1901 05473 0520

GEOFF JOHNS JIM LEE SCOTT WILLIAMS